BETWEEN BELIEF AND UNBELIEF

BETWEEN BELIEF
AND UNBELIEF

PAUL W. PRUYSER

HARPER & ROW, PUBLISHERS

NEW YORK, EVANSTON, SAN FRANCISCO, LONDON

ACKNOWLEDGMENTS

Grateful acknowledgment is made to the following:

Harcourt Brace Jovanovich, Inc. for permission to quote from "Choruses from 'The Rock,' " by T. S. Eliot in his *Collected Poems 1909–1962,* copyright © 1963 by Harcourt Brace & Co.

John Wiley & Sons, Inc. for permission to reuse material in Chapter III, *Provisional Conceptualizations of Unbelief.* This material stems from a paper first presented by me to the Society for the Scientific Study of Religion in 1971. It was published under the title "Problems of Definition and Conception in the Psychological Study of Religious Unbelief" as a chapter in *Changing Perspectives in the Scientific Study of Religion,* edited by Allen W. Eister, copyright © 1974 by John Wiley & Sons, Inc. and reprinted by permission.

FIRST EDITION

Designed by Sidney Feinberg

Library of Congress Cataloging in Publication Data

Pruyser, Paul W
  Between belief and unbelief.
  Bibliography: p.
  1. Belief and doubt. I. Title.
BF773.P78 1974   121   73–18686
ISBN 0–06–066700–1

Contents

Preface   xi

Foreword   xv

I. Sacred and Secular Contexts of Beliefs   1

    Introduction   1
    From Sacred Cosmos to Pluralism   3
    Secularization: A Pluralistic Process   12

II. Religious Beliefs and Alienation   21

    Political Alienation of the Oppressed from Religion   25
    Religious Alienation   26
    Classical Forms of Religious Alienation Updated   29
    Features of Modern Alienation   38

III. A Psychological Perspective on Unbelief   44

    Object Relations and the Search for Satisfaction (A Theoretical Interlude)   45
    Provisional Conceptualizations of Unbelief   52

IV. Dealing with Dependency and Autonomy   66

    Coming to Terms with Dependency   67

What Is Humility?   73
Coming to Terms with Autonomy   80
Obedience, Then and Now   90

V. Coming to Terms with Mystery   95

The Rediscovery of Mystery   97
The Mystery of Evil Reappreciated   101
Mysterium Tremendum et Fascinosum   103
Is There a Talent for the Experience of Mystery,
    Numinosity, and the Transcendent?   107
Belief and Disbelief in Mystery   114
Mystery and De-Alienation   120

VI. Coming to Terms with Options   123

Willing to Believe or Disbelieve   124
The Divided Self   132
Making Easy and Felicitous What in Any Case
    Is Necessary   148
More   153

VII. Coming to Terms with Providence   157

Disbelief in Providence   164
Coping with Malevolence   173
Care and Hope as Aspects of Providence   177

VIII. Coming to Terms with Fantasy   188

Functions of Fantasy   191
Living with Illusions   196
Appeal and Affront of Ritual   205
Enjoyment of Myth   213
Belief in Myths   220

IX. Coming to Terms with Reality   221

Dealing with Ontological Options   223
The Outer and the Inner Tremendum   230
Commonsense Reality: How Plain Is it?   234
The Integrative Power of the Transitional Sphere   240

X. Between Belief and Unbelief   245

   Beliefs as Love Objects   248
   Beliefs as Hate Objects   256
   Toleration of Beliefs, and Belief in Tolerance 262

   Bibliographical Notes   271

   Index   287

Preface

Among the many reasons and conscious motives for writing this work are some that should be shared with the reader, to allow him to place the book in perspective.

First, a scholarly work on such a "hot" theme as belief and unbelief requires considerable personal involvement and existential engagement on the part of the writer. My ambition to do an honest, scientific job on the topic required objectivity and faithfulness to the observations that form the starting point of conceptual inquiry and systematization. My ambition to be at the same time a clinician (which I am by profession) imposed a special selectivity: a penchant for reasoning within a useful, pragmatic theoretical framework which lacks tightness and elegance but is clinically fascinating because of its hospitality to the messy details of life, and a proneness to seeing the conflictual origins and elements in many situations which may appear pure and simple to a layman. In addition, there is something in the very nature of belief, disbelief, and unbelief that is likely to make the student a participant, at some level, in the material with which he deals.

Rather than being afraid lest some of my own beliefs slip through the mazes of scholarly constraints, I have considered it more honest to myself and my readers to show that I am a participant-observer in the issues with which I deal. This will become obvious in the selectivity of my focus of inquiry, in what I have left out, in what I have played up and played down, in the implicit or explicit evaluative comments of the text, and in what I consciously advocate. In other words, I do assume in this book a posture toward my topic. The keen reader will quickly discern it, and he is free to judge it from the angle of his own posture.

Second, when my *A Dynamic Psychology of Religion* was published in 1968 it received positive reviews and was quickly adopted as a textbook in universities. For this I am grateful, but I am even more grateful for a critical review by André Godin, of *Lumen Vitae,* who pointed out that a modern book on the psychology of religion must deal with the contemporary phenomena of secularization, disaffiliation from religion and religious institutions, disbelief, and unbelief. My book had not dealt with these topics. At about the time of Godin's review, the Society for the Scientific Study of Religion adopted "Unbelief" for the theme of one of its annual meetings and asked me to plan that portion of the program. Various scholars who read papers on this subject gave me further stimulation to try my own hand at it.

Third, the current cultural scene seems to produce a bewildering panoply of attitudes toward, and experimentations with, religious beliefs and practices. One sees strong enchantments with religious ideas and forms as well as strong aversions to established religious traditions and yesterday's theologies. Beliefs and forms that had seemed for some time to be dying are suddenly experiencing an upsurge of interest. Religion is again a fashionable topic among students in higher education and even at cocktail parties, and so are disputes about any kind of belief and disbelief, religious or irreligious.

This book, then, is a contribution to the psychology of religion, as my previous book was. I have been encouraged to write it by many friends, colleagues, and students. Stimulating events, such as speeches and panel presentations, have contrived to keep me engaged in the topic and give my thoughts about it a definitive form. Upon my appointment to the Henry March

Pfeiffer Professorship in the Menninger Foundation I began to present the larger part of this book as the "Pfeiffer Lectures" of 1972–73. The interdisciplinary audience included colleagues and students in the allied mental health professions—psychiatrists, psychologists, social workers, nurses, clergymen, adjunctive therapists, and administrators—as well as many laymen. The theme and the issues were fascinating, and speaking about them fulfilled a definite need.

The book also aims at being of use to members of the helping professions, especially in the psychiatric field, and their patients. Time and again we hear that psychiatric personnel feel uncomfortable in assessing the religious beliefs of their patients. We also hear that many patients feel uncomfortable in discussing their religious beliefs, their disbeliefs, or their aversions to beliefs and religious practices. Risking overstatement, one might say that there is in clinical practice a conspiracy of silence or a kind of self-imposed taboo on thorough discussions of religious ideas, convictions, and practices. Elsewhere I have reviewed the many reasons for this taboo.* But if my general thesis is correct—namely, that beliefs, disbeliefs, and unbelief reflect something about the nature of psychodynamic object relations and interpersonal experiences—this taboo must be relinquished, if only to promote better psychiatric assessment and therapy. My hope is that the present work will give psychiatrists as well as their patients greater comfort in exploring those reaches of the mind in which beliefs have their origin and function.

I owe a very special debt to three colleagues and friends who were willing to read the manuscript critically and let me benefit from their remarks and suggestions, each using a special professional vantage point. They are: J. Cotter Hirschberg, M.D., senior child psychiatrist in the Menninger Foundation and training analyst in the Topeka Institute for Psychoanalysis; Sydney Smith, Ph.D., clinical psychologist, director of the Menninger Foundation's postdoctoral training program in clinical psychol-

_____
*"Assessment of the Patient's Religious Attitudes in the Psychiatric Case Study" *Bulletin of the Menninger Clinic*, 35 (1971), 272–291.

ogy and editor of the *Bulletin of the Menninger Clinic;* and Kenneth R. Mitchell, B.D., Ph.D., director of the Menninger Foundation's Division of Religion and Psychiatry, whose doctorate is in the field of religion and personality. I thank them now publicly for their labors of love and ask that the reader will exonerate them from blame for anything he might not find to his liking in the text.

As before, Mrs. Kathleen Bryan, my secretary for years, has gone many extra miles in working on every phase and aspect of the manuscript, with keen eye and competent hand and above all with enthusiasm. I thank her warmly.

Finally, the dedication page hints at feelings of pleasure and gratitude so abundant that only the writing of a name can encompass them.

PAUL W. PRUYSER

Foreword

Beliefs and unbeliefs (and at times the pointed rejection of a specific tenet captured in the word "disbelief") beleaguer each individual's stream of consciousness and create tensions throughout the span of his life. Moreover, beliefs and unbeliefs are likely to present themselves to each individual fragmentarily rather than as holistic, grandly synthesized systems. Individuals are stormed at, from the outside as well as the inside, by random cultural snippets of belief, disbelief, and unbelief. Their own consciousness thus becomes a battleground on which beliefs and unbeliefs shiftingly contend. While *all* beliefs and their counterparts present dilemmas of choice, religious beliefs and their alternatives are an even more acute problem.

The exploration of religious beliefs and their alternatives should begin in today's world. My first chapter sketches the conspicuous features of this world, in which it is difficult to distinguish the sacred from the secular. In the next chapter we continue this situational exploration by taking a closer look at the massive estrangement from religion that characterizes modern life, as well as the considerable alienation *within* religion, suffered by people whose ardent religious beliefs run counter to the dominant trends in the various religious establishments.

With this much awareness of the social context, we adopt a distinctly psychological viewpoint which is maintained throughout the rest of the book. The viewpoint, which is clinical, tries to conceptualize unbelief and disbelief with the utmost intellectual integrity and the least possible bias. Inner conflicts, agonizing struggles, unresolved ambivalences, and the ways in which people cope with their problems are discussed, thus incorporating subtleties of viewing and reasoning which require a rather complex theory to do justice to life's untidy details.

The following chapters present a series of themes which have gained stature in the psychology of religion as critical issues of belief and unbelief. Unlike Erik Erikson's well-known themes of identity formation, these issues are not presented as a developmental progression; they are taken as perennial problems relevant at any point along the arc of life, for they haunt man from the cradle to the grave. Developmental features are relevant, but they are dealt with as aspects of the themes rather than as functions of a fixed time sequence. In fact, the developmental view espoused in this book puts much stock in early childhood experiences in which *all* themes have some emotional roots which load the dice toward postures of belief or disbelief in any theme, conditioning personal acceptance or rejection, or, as the case may be, keeping a person caught in ambivalence.

Finally, in the last chapter, the psychological object relations theory that has undergirded this study leads to the view that beliefs are approached as love objects and hate objects in their own right, implying that coming to grips with any proposition of belief is a double process: loving some beliefs and hating other beliefs. The negative part is as important as the positive part, for identifying oneself as a believer, disbeliever, or unbeliever in any tenet entails sorting out one's love and hates. And that leads in turn to the book's coda: if the sorting out of beliefs and unbeliefs is indeed as laborious, complex, demanding, and continuous a task as this book indicates, it might be a sign of maturity when one's belief system contains an explicit belief in tolerance also, as a positive value in its own right. All of us, at any point in our lives, have so much reason to assess and reassess our own beliefs and unbeliefs that we should also believe in the value of "letting be with respect for the nature of divergent states of belief, if not states of being."

The keynote to this book, then, is that the life worth living and examining is a life lived in tension, and that tensions are a perennial feature of the human condition, though specific tension points and intensities fluctuate over time. Most chapters present a set of such tensions, chosen to illustrate some crucial question that is bound to come man's way and about which he is challenged to make up his mind so as to appease or embolden his heart. Hence, many chapter titles entail a challenge or task: the reader is asked to give thought to "dealing with" or "coming to terms with" some classical conundrum of belief or unbelief that is to be solved sooner or later in decisions valid *for* him, *by* him, and in terms of *his* feelings.

CHAPTER I

Sacred and Secular Contexts of Beliefs

Introduction

The concern of this study is capsuled in highly condensed form in Albert Einstein's statement: "I am a deeply religious unbeliever."[1]Einstein is not quoted here for the sake of marshaling a famous man's authority for my topic. Einstein was no theologian, nor did he claim to be an expert in mysticism. He was not in his own opinion a faithful Jew. He was not even versatile with words. What authority he had was vested in his brilliant reformulation of the principles of physics. I quote Einstein's statement because it is vivid, immediate, and pristine, and most of us, whether believers or unbelievers, can reverberate with it.

Another reason for quoting Einstein's words is that they were uttered by a man we can regard intellectually and culturally as our contemporary. He spoke for many of us, perhaps for a generation yet unborn, because he was in many respects ahead of his time. His very simple life style, his aversion to the tokens of the leisure class, and his cherishing of privacy are just now beginning to be rediscovered and adopted as values by thousands of young people who find that the psychic price one has to pay for conformity to the culture is at times too high. I do not imply that these young people will form the bulk of the new generation—maybe they will merely constitute a significant undercurrent of it. Nor would I dare to suggest that Einstein has any responsibility for their coming into being, as their spiritual father, for it seems unlikely that they would adopt Einstein as their hero, model themselves after him, or borrow his stature as authority for the stance they are taking. In fact, they will probably not seek any external or extrinsic authority for their choices at all. "Authority" in the singular has become a distasteful word to them, and "the authorities" have become positively repulsive. The modern concern, particularly among the young, has shifted from authority to authenticity, an idea whose virtues are being discovered through some serious altercations with the traditional notion of authority. And whether we are young or middle-aged, nearly all of us today have got our fingers burned by authority, either by trying to wield it or by trying to respond to it.

But who are these "young people," "modern people," and "contemporaries" whom I have conjured up so quickly? What is their situation in matters of belief and unbelief, religion and irreligion, which lie buried in Einstein's statement? Is it fair at all to speak of "them, out there" when I essay to deal with such a weighty topic as religion with its cognates and contrasts, which tend to lie precisely at the junction of the public and the private world? Would it not be better to speak frankly of ourselves, of "we" who occupy that anxiety-laden, ominous stretch of time at the end of the twentieth century which changes with such vehemence and rapidity that it sometimes taxes our capacity to cope with novelty and threatens to exceed the limit of our adaptation? For most of us over thirty, Toffler's *Future Shock*[2] is already a Present Shock, and our immediate past has already jarred us out of a number of ideas and attitudes which seemed at one time so normative or adaptive that they were, for a while at least, habitual.

How do we find ourselves described and understood, in regard to belief and unbelief or religion and irreligion, by those who have studied the human situation?

From Sacred Cosmos to Pluralism

If there is any common view in and among the social sciences, it is the developmental principle. We find ourselves most often described as products of a sequence of historical stages, or as participants in a phase that supplants antecedent phases and prepares new ones. In fact, the dominance of the developmental point of view is splendidly recognized in the differentiation that has taken place within social science itself since Comte: anthropology and archaeology are pointedly concerned with anything that is old, archaic, primitive, or close to roots and origins; sociology is generally concerned with the here and now or fairly recent, sometimes sharply focused on formulating and solving contemporary problems. Development is the keynote to most psychological theories. And even the theologians (not only Teilhard de Chardin) have learned to think not merely in historical terms but along the lines of developmental progression. All disciplines that deal with man and human affairs contain an abundance of terms coined with the prefixes "pre" and "post" and "trans," indicative of an incessant game of locating things and events on a time axis and comparing the past with the present, with the conviction that the past is somehow a preparation for today and that we are all "on the move" on a long, long journey. And anyone who has read Loren Eiseley's books[3], [4], [5] knows how compelling and moving and rich the developmental idea is.

This is not the place to give a formal account of the sum and substance of the developmental images which the social sciences have offered about man. A few bold sketchy strokes will be sufficient orientation to pursuing the questions about belief and unbelief which I intend to articulate.[6]

Anthropological literature is not only replete with references to religion and belief systems, but it often meets religion in the focal plane. In its study of peoples and ethnic groups (particularly those seemingly less complex than the ones from which its practitioners emerged), anthropology found, like the missionaries before them, that some societies abound in rituals, ceremonies, sacred objects, myths of origin, taboos, and above all a type of thinking that endows man, beast, man-made things, and the social order with a peculiar, spiritual energy. Often, the tribal head is held to have been descended from the gods, and sometimes the social leader is also worship leader, so that the roles of "king" and "priest" coalesce. Everything in such societies is sacred. Everything, including food gathering, fishing, hunting, sexual intercourse, and preparing children for adult responsibilities, is imbued with surplus values which give these acts spiritual significance. All reasoning about almost anything proceeds from an animistic belief in which anthropomorphic and theomorphic motifs freely shade into each other.

In such societies, the differentiation which gives rise to distinctions between the sacred and the secular has not (yet) taken place. The word "yet" is parenthetically inserted to indicate that the observers of such societies already take differentiation as the norm; looking back from that modern vantage point, they find the undifferentiated society primitive, lagging behind in the assumed normal push toward specialization and differentiation. They find such a society stuck to an early phase, and are fascinated by its retarded growth.

Many constructs have been used in efforts at understanding and "explaining" such societies devoted to the sacred. The Polynesian idea of "mana" has been conceptualized as a principle of energy and force and order. The assumed thought patterns of primitives have been analyzed as being on the hither side of the logical principle of noncontradiction. Their thinking has been described as "dreamlike," more or less autistic or omnipotent, and suffused by "mystical participation" of one person or thing in another, of the individual in the group, and of gods in man. Many scholars in comparative religion have endorsed and reinforced these explanations.

This picture of primitive man in an arrested society has not been received without criticism. There is the obvious question about capacity for and chances of survival, when whole peoples are romantically described as so dreamy that their poor fitness in the struggle for life would already have made them extinct. Lately, there has come a new appreciation of the capacity of so-called primitives for rational thought and adequate reality testing, an appreciation which is almost epitomized in the transition from the work of Lévy-Brühl[7] to the studies of Lévi-Strauss[8], Frenchmen both. But despite these long-overdue refinements and additions, the basic picture persists in our minds that before the dawn of civilization religion was so all-pervasive that irreligion and unbelief could simply not have existed. The lesson for one interested in unbelief, secularization, irreligion, or alternatives to the religious world view is that these are modern phenomena which require for their mere thinkability or possibility a developed state of man and society. Implicit in this lesson is that Einstein's distinction between belief and religion would not hold in the primitive, sacred culture in which creed and cult are one. In the old times, religion was identical with belief, perception of the world, action upon the world, and the order of society. Indeed, in such a setting there may have been no need for calling anything religious, no need even for the word "religion."

Another sketch must be drawn of a few basic sociological observations and concepts relevant to our topic. At a very high level of abstraction we find the concepts of differentiation and specialization, derived from historical reflections on our own, living societies and comparative studies of known and well-documented societies such as Periclean Greece, the ancient polis or city-state, imperial Rome, or dynastic Egypt. In such studies, attention can be variously drawn to class phenomena such as the existence of a courtly, priestly, or warrior class and its relation to power over the populace. Or it can focus on the gradual and sometimes very sharp separation between the sacred and the secular domains, indeed on the way in which domains as such come into being in the course of time. One can study the forms of religion in any such society, its institutionalization, its relation to the state, the pluralization of religion into competing religious systems, with the problems this imposes on a nation or an ethnic group. One learns that some rulers imposed their own tradition and beliefs upon those they ruled, that some religions merged into syncretistic cults and creeds, and that other religions were vigorously suppressed for fear that they might undermine the existing political order.

The basic lesson from such studies is that religion, once the be-all and end-all of primitive societies, becomes something special and distinct in complex societies. It becomes an institution next to other institutions, a power next to other powers, a belief next to other beliefs. Along with these overt distinctions may come covert distinctions. For instance, a citizen may find it prudent to participate in public religious ceremonies (cult) without endorsing the underlying belief system (creed), or to subscribe verbally to a belief without having much personal faith in its truth.

In the long run, differentiation and specialization will also produce the rudiments of religious pluralism, particularly when reading and writing become widely shared, when mobility across national boundaries increases, and when education becomes a value. The essence of pluralism, even when it is only nascent, is that people get a chance to see options between one religion and another, or between any religion and no religion. The particular religion of any group, even if dominant or imposed by armed might, is no longer held unquestioningly by every single group member. One can at least make an inner, private choice between options, even when the wisdom of the serpent would impel one to conform outwardly to the dominant system. With boldness added, an individual may attain a conversion, from one religion or belief to another; or a ruler may impose his own conversion on a whole population which is forced en masse to convert to a new belief and new religious practices. It has even been possible for some rulers to impose such mass conversions out of political opportunism and power plays. The very word "conversion" becomes needed only when people are presented with options.

The next step, which has been taken in most Western societies with greater or lesser heel dragging, is to declare religious pluralism the basis of the state and to make it a political principle. At this point, pluralism is an overt and prized fact of life for everybody. The social fabric now abounds in opportunities for everyone to compare and try out other creeds and cults, to read books about religions new and old and here and elsewhere, to see in the streets the peculiarities in dress, architecture, feast days, and manners which characterize each religious group. One has a chance to see some religions come and go, some established ones priding themselves on their ancient lineage, some new sects proud of their explosive break with the past.

The lesson in studying pluralism, the covert as well as the overt kind, is that religion gets involved in competition and becomes associated with defense and attack. New terms begin to be coined, such as "apologetics," which defends a particular faith against attacks; "catechetics," which provides systematic instruction in the propositions of belief, so worded that the difference of this belief from other belief systems stands out; "holy wars," which defend the integrity and territoriality of Islam against Christian encroachments; "evangelism" and "outreach" for the "conversion" of more and more people to a faith group. Cognitive emphasis comes to be placed on beliefs, "credos," "articles of faith," and "confessions." One gets not only various empirical forms of worship, but books which fix liturgies in particular ways, from the *Book of Common Worship* (common only to Anglicans, that is to say) to Luther's *Deutsche Messe.* One begins to hear of "Reformation" and "Counter Reformation"; of synods and councils and papal bulls. Indeed one becomes caught in a network of names describing distinct religious groups, from the simple word "Anabaptist" to the rather unwieldy designation "Church of Jesus Christ of Latter-day Saints," not to mention such emotive or ridiculing labels as "Holy Rollers" and "Quakers." After empires and princedoms have fallen or crumbled under the impact of religious movements, the state finds peace and stability in publicly admitting all religions and giving them equal protection under the law.

It is tempting to compare religious pluralism with the situation of a modern shopper who wants to supply his needs, whether for basic staples or for luxury items. He finds the market stratified and thinks he has ample choice. Religion too has its Brooks Brothers and Tiffanys and other exclusive establishments with prestigious merchandise. It has its Macys and Sears and Wanamakers for mainline needs, and its Woolworths and discount houses for low-cost goods. It has here and there a few small boutiques in which the client receives much personal attention. It has its mail-order houses requiring no personal visits at all. And it has plenty of advertising, from the somber gold-edged signboards in front of churches to the noisiest radio broadcasts. But, as in the marketplace, the individual is under constant pressure to conform, nevertheless, to certain canons of taste and style, and he will soon discover that there is not as much choice as he had thought: the manufacturers and the shopkeepers are always shrinking their wares to popular standards and mediocre tastes, amid the short flurries of fads and fashions.

The shopper's metaphor brings us close to another sociological observation about religion, known in the literature as "civil religion."[9] Just as the free market demands that everyone be at least a buyer, there is popular pressure in some pluralistic societies that everyone be at least religious. Religiosity per se becomes the hallmark of good citizenship, and conversely, many civic acts are adorned with religious trimmings, such as invocations, prayers, and coins with the inscription "In God We Trust." While the state displays no favoritism toward any particular religion, the citizenry (and sometimes the state) displays great favoritism toward religiousness. Faced with this observation, theologians have formulated a sharp distinction between religion and faith, going at times so far as to declare that religion is unbelief. In that vein, Kierkegaard[10] opposed Christendom to Christianity and Karl Barth[11] saw religiosity as a kind of popular naturalistic pastime which needed to be sharply confronted by the Word of God. That theme as such is not new: the Hebrew prophets played it out against the priests and the people of their time. But today the magnitude and strength of civil religion seem great, and it is deeply entrenched, much to the chagrin of the prophetic elements in various churches.

Articulate reflection on both religion and civil religion has come from an extremely interesting and scholarly branch of sociology known as the sociology of knowledge. It has roots in Marx and Feuerbach, both of whom pointed to the role of religion, any religion, as an instrument of social control. While Feuerbach[12] described how gods are made in man's image, and thus divine mysteries are gigantic projections of human affairs, Marx[13] saw religion as the sigh of the heart in a heartless world, turned by the powers that be as well as the oppressed themselves into an opium to soften the pain. Both propositions imply, though differently, that the way a man thinks about anything is embedded in his circumstances and that the contents of his consciousness, particularly his values and metaphysical speculations, are a functional adaptation to his class status and economic station in life. It thus becomes plausible—nay, likely—that thinking about cherished and sacred values, thinking with conviction and zeal, reflects the captivity in which persons and groups are held by their circumstances. Much of this proceeds unawares and stems from unconscious assumptions. Knowledge emerges from a social matrix, particularly the kind of knowledge traditionally described as beliefs. Beliefs can now be analyzed by criteria extrinsic to themselves: one can describe a social history or an economic history of beliefs and belief systems, to find that many of them are ideologies.

From the sociology of knowledge to the sociology of religion is only a short step. In fact, these two points of emphasis have been thoroughly intertwined since the brilliant work of Max Weber. In his celebrated essay *The Protestant Ethic and the Spirit of Capitalism*,[14] and the larger work, *Wirtschaft und Gesellschaft*,[15] he showed that religious beliefs are closely related to the social institutions of their time. The details of the belief system—some of the creedal assumptions—and the behavior to which they give rise are selectively reinforced by the dominant social conditions, and vice versa. In Weber's work there is no reductionism of religion to the social conditions, but rather a deepening of understanding of both terms in the correlation.

Within the broad concern of the sociology of knowledge special attention has been paid, of course, to people who are thinkers *par excellence*, namely, intellectuals. Though every age and culture has had its intellectuals, from Confucius and Socrates to Pico della Mirandola, Erasmus, and Voltaire, the emergence of a *class* or *community* of intellectuals is a relatively recent phenomenon of great significance to the history of ideas. It is significant also to the integrity of religion and belief. Edward Shills,[16] who has traced the history of the intellectual community, asserts that intellectual work arose originally from religious preoccupations, inasmuch as thinkers have always been deeply preoccupied with the ultimate ground of thought and experience. Contact with symbols is shared by intellectuals and religionists. Both groups are attuned to the sacred, though they would come to define the sacred in very different ways in the centuries following the decline of the monopoly which the great monastic orders once held on intellectual pursuits. Indeed, when that monopoly was effectively broken by the invention of movable type, cheap book production, and the gradual secularization of the European universities, intellectuals began to find themselves increasingly in tension with the religious authorities. They developed a profound distrust of ecclesiastical power as well as religious thought or theological reasoning.

Intellectuals tend to reject all extrinsic authority. Though they have traditions of their own, with considerable intrinsic authority—for example, admiration of originality, creativity, parsimony of expression, purism, and standards of competence and excellence—they claim the freedom to question or investigate everything, including those things held dear or sacred as values by many other people. Small wonder, then, that critiques of religion have been for some time a characteristic pastime of intellectuals, who may be motivated by fascination with the subject or by an attempt to speak to acutely felt tensions. Shills makes the even broader assertion that intellectuals, because of their orientation, almost inevitably live in tension with the value orientations which are inherent in the actual institutions of any society. He speaks not only of an alienation of intellectuals from the custodians of the institutional system, but also of an intra-intellectual alienation: ". . . it is the rejection by intellectuals of the inherited and prevailing values of those intellectuals who are already incorporated in ongoing social institutions."[16] (This speaks to the disregard which scientists of any kind may have for theologians, even when the latter may have superior minds.)

At any rate, Shills's work and similar studies would warn us that in any sociological or psychological assessment of belief or unbelief one must reckon with the existence of special values and special motives in intellectuals. Since this book is likely to be read by intellectuals who regard themselves as members of a special community, inheritors of a special tradition, and claimants to a special kind of freedom, it may not be amiss for me to avow at the beginning of this study that I consider myself a part of the intellectuals' community and share their great tradition of freedom to consider and choose.

The question has been raised: What or who supplies belief systems? What or who generates them? The answer most frequently given is that belief systems are generated and supplied by the culture. In fact, the production, maintenance, and transmission of belief systems and values are functions which define the word "culture." Durkheim[17] saw beliefs as collective representations which give stability to the social order. Marx saw beliefs largely as ideologies which develop as tools of the social order to maintain its stratification—in other words, to maintain the privileges of the few over the masses. We have already seen that intellectuals have developed belief systems of their own in an ongoing dialectic with all the other institutions of society and the vested authorities. A large body of studies devoted to the development of religious sects links the development of new belief systems, or novel rearrangements of old belief systems, to social oppression experienced by certain groups of people, or to cataclysmic periods in the history of mankind.

The tenor of most of these studies is that belief, once thought to have been a natural fact of creation or instilled by divine action, shows a bewildering diversity of origins and correlations with social and cultural processes. Belief and unbelief are by-products of the institutional specialization of religion and what Luckmann calls the "segregation of religious representations in the world view."[18] Beliefs and unbeliefs are functions of institutional domains and can be defined only in terms of how a specific institution interacts with other institutions. For this reason the previous sentence has suddenly introduced the plural form "unbeliefs." For if these sociological analyses are correct, the phenomena of unbelief are just as heterogeneous as those of belief.

To sum up, from a great variety of sociological studies, old and new, we find ourselves described as people whose ancestors have long been on the move. From the original sacred-cosmos patterns in which everything was unquestionably religious, a differentiation of the sacred into various religions ensued, which in turn led to the institutionalization of religion. Once religion is institutionalized, reflections by intellectual elites lead to the further pluralization of religious tenets, forms, and beliefs. In the long run, the pluralization of religion becomes legitimized by the political principle of pluralism, which helps diversify beliefs as well as unbeliefs.

As literacy increases among the masses of people, reflections about the social order lead to selective disavowals of religious beliefs in favor of secular beliefs, such as belief in progress, in the coming of a classless society, in humanitarian values, the realization of which may take an intense and enduring faith. We have indeed come a long, long way, and the journey has not been smooth. Some of our ancestors have been sent to the stake or had their tongues cut out for the beliefs they professed or the beliefs they refused to profess. We think we have left behind the mythical world views; that is, if we are willing to overlook the new myths that hold millions of modern minds in bondage, if not in physical captivity. We think we have left behind the autos-da-fé—that is, if we are willing to overlook the gas chambers of Buchenwald and Dachau. We think we have left behind the authoritarian impositions of belief by powers and principalities of state or church—if we are willing to overlook the enormous, insidious pressure which civil religion in all its forms brings to bear upon us. Every comfort gained by release from some frustration of the past seems to be counteracted by discomforts from new frustrations. We do not seem to have become less anxious or less bewildered. Though we may have come a long way, we are very much at sea.

Secularization: A Pluralistic Process

A crucial aspect of our cultural situation that has been described by social scientists and theologians alike is *secularization*. The word comes from the Latin *saeculum*, originally meaning the time of one human generation, and then broadened into "an age," "the spirit of the age," and finally "the world" Platonized as the scene on which things come and go as against the presumed eternity of ideas or the spirit. The Greek and Christian heritage of the word is so strong that we still, almost automatically, think of the secular as something opposed to the sacred, or as the worldly quotidian life as opposed to the lofty life of the spirit. State and Church are respectively the secular and the sacred domain. Caesar represents the secular or temporal order, in which taxes are levied and coins change hands; temple, priesthood, monastery, or church represent the divine order which lasts.

But that is a very partial view, derived from Greek thought. An earlier, Hebrew, conviction holds that the divine acts in and through human history, and that it is always concretely involved in "the present age." No distinction is made between a temporal and an eternal order, for in Hebrew experience time is always concrete as present and past and, to a lesser degree, future. To the extent that Christianity preserved this unique Hebrew time sense, and brought it into the Hellenistic world view, there has been a still, small voice of positive regard for the secular which, though it had a hard time being heard, served to correct the spiritual disapprobation with which the word has been tainted. And since the end of the nineteenth century, when critical scholarship began to rediscover that Hebrew element with admiration for its cogency, secularization has come to mean many different things to different people, particularly among theologians. Fundamentalists and supernaturalists damn it; Tillich, [19], [20] Bonhoeffer,[21] and Cox[22] praise it, and many others have mixed feelings about it or are bewildered by it.

Daniélou[23] has recently specified at least three major meanings of secularization. It may mean the disappearance of mythical conceptions from the traditional world view with a concomitant spread of scientific conceptions. It may also mean the special desacralization of life advocated originally by the Biblical prophets who fulminated against all idolatries, carried on into the present time by all those who consciously locate themselves within that Biblical tradition. And it may mean all those changes in self-awareness of modern man summed up in the idea that "man has come of age"—that the end of a long period of infantile dependency on divine arrangements and magical interventions has arrived.

As a scholarly concern or as a worry to the religious establishment, secularization has stimulated, and is attracting now, considerable interest from sociologists and religionists. Indeed it is one of those topics that seems to lead quite a few sociologists to a deep concern with religion and quite a few theologians and church historians to a profound involvement in sociology. This interpenetration of the two disciplines is not new. In the classic period of sociology from Comte to Weber and Durkheim the scientific study of religion çame close to being a religion, or at least a religious preoccupation, of the intellectual elite. Comte himself developed priestly views toward the end of his life. And Marx and his followers opposed the religious establishment out of a profound belief in the value and the realizability of a better life for mankind. Says Bellah, a contemporary sociologist: ". . . social science not only has implications for religion, but . . . it has religious implications or aspects within itself. I start with the assumption that the relation between religion and social science is complex and in some ways organic."[24]

Sociologists have had a relatively easy time studying secularization. They could describe it rather simply as the gradual detachment, already at work during the Enlightenment but recently sharply accelerated, of society from the influence of religious institutions. They could assemble statistics of waning church attendance or decline in formal religious affiliation. Or they could describe the seemingly diminishing role that feelings for the sacred play in modern technological society. If Durkheim, Simmel, and Weber could hold that religion acts as an integrative force which knits the social fabric together and confers stability upon its institutions, contemporary students simply do not observe this force on the same scale or with the same integrative thrust. Urbanization and industrialization have so enhanced mobility that families have lost their geographical continuity with previous generations, and with the dissolution of tribal patterns and local color has come a weakening of the authority formerly associated with religious teaching and the transmission of specific religious beliefs.

But along with secularization as a marked perceptible decline of religious authority and of the power of religious institutions over man's minds and affairs, secularization can also be described from the other angle in terms of a widening of the public domain and as a qualitative change in a person's sense of embeddedness. For instance, many social services formerly rendered by religious institutions have been taken over by the government. State and nondenominational universities have greatly increased in proportion to denominational institutions of higher learning. The scientific world view, the amount of scientific data and knowledge, and the prestige of scientific method have greatly gained ground at the expense of mythological thought and scriptural authority. Psychiatric therapy and psychological guidance have taken over a sizable part of what was formerly a pastoral care of souls. Money formerly spent on church tithes is now increasingly preempted by taxes.

Similarly, one can approach secularization as a qualitative change in human consciousness, particularly in regard to man's self-concept, the nature of his relations with others, and the locus of authority. The whole existentialist movement may be seen as an attempt to shift authority and responsibility from external locations to individuals themselves and to enthrone them within self-awareness. Democratization of political, economic, and religious institutions makes the individual a participant in power, or at least in the management of power. If ethical precepts and moral rules have begun to lose their divine origins or metaphysical halos, the individual becomes to a greater extent his own moral arbiter—with greater freedom as well as greater perplexity, both of which are likely to enhance his self-consciousness. It is of interest, however, that several of these features of secularization have been not only welcomed but activated by institutional religion from the moment that theology sought an existential mode of thought. Within the United States, existential ideas were imported from Europe by noted theologians well before they became known in literary and artistic circles and in psychiatry. The existential theologies of Barth and Tillich,* different as they are, forcefully opposed faith to religious belief and demanded an exquisitely personal appropriation of Christian tenets by the heart as well as the mind, within a church that was to be devalued as a religious or social institution and revalued as *koinonia* or mystical body, not by catechetical memorization but by listening to the *kerygma*.

Some secularization, then, is a deliberate result of systematic concentration by a highly particular religious faith group within Christianity upon itself, its origins, and its mission. Deliberate secularization has also been the hallmark of some very thoughtful elements in Judaism, for a much longer period. This may come as a surprise to some readers, but further observations may bring another surprise in the other direction. Some modern sociologists, particularly Parsons, feel that the secular order as a whole, with whatever people find lovely about it, is legitimated by a long religious tradition which holds the social order sacred. In an introduction to Weber's work, Parsons observed that "the basic value-pattern common to all three faiths [Protestantism, Catholicism and Judaism in America] has been at least partially institutionalized at a higher level of generality, and the 'privatization' of religion through denominational pluralism has been extended from the Protestant group to the whole range of faiths."[25] Elsewhere Parsons states that religion "stands at the highest level in the cybernetic hierarchy of the forces which, in the sense of defining the general directionality of human action among the possible alternatives permitted in the human condition, controls the processes of human action."[26] This conviction stems from Parsons's view that secularization is not merely the shrinking of transcendent concerns in favor of worldly concerns, but rather a movement toward greater closeness between the transcendent and the worldly referents of experience. In other words, one should be open to the possibility that the secular order comes to approximate the normative models of religion, and move in the direction of institutionalization of religious values.

*Tillich insisted that only his philosophy was existentialist. Theology would always be essentialist in his opinion.

There comes a time, then, when the sharp distinction between the sacred and the secular no longer holds, when societies manifest a kind of spiritual upgrading. By means of it, nonreligious institutions become vehicles for the dispersion of sacred values and may themselves become endowed with functional aspects of the sacred. Conversely, religious institutions may find a sizable part of their mission fulfilled through social legislation, civil rights action, and other desirable changes in the quality of life produced by any kind of social institution.

Within this refined and larger view of secularization we can discover today a great many movements which, each in its own way, bring back into the civic pattern just those emotional tones and convictions of seriousness that have traditionally been the hallmark of religion. When Durkheim, in addition to the technical definitions he gave of religion, described it pointedly as having to do with "life in its seriousness",[27] he gave a clue to spotting various preoccupations with the sacred in a secular society.

Various contemporary youth movements portray to a high degree the "seriousness" which Durkheim noted, with just that spontaneity of identification, looseness of organization, and emotional commitment which have always been preconditions for sect formation. Various so-called hippie groups who claim no more than a "pad" and the different types of social affiliation and living patterns tried out in communes share the conviction that "simple sacred love" is to be held up against the harshness of the secular world as well as the dryness of the institutional world of religion. Certain elementary values are to be rescued from the clutches of society which has made a mockery of them. Some of these groups lead an ascetic life.

Other groups, old and young, are bent on recapturing transcendental experience by way of expanding or deepening consciousness, the bliss or horror of which is preferable to the flatness or narrowness of everyday consciousness. Such heightened emotions are alleged to produce a knowledge that is not merely registered, but deeply felt with revelatory power. Whether chemically induced by drugs, or the fruit of assiduous meditation, the desirable end state seems to be one of contact with a *mysterium tremendum*,[28] with something sacred in its quality or its impact that will convince a person that he is not merely a fleeting composition of flesh and bones.

Associations with traditional religion also emerge in the parlance of the enthusiasts of transcendence and even in the scientific literature on altered states of consciousness. There is abundant use of such terms as "highest state of consciousness" and "higher awareness," as if to imply a hierarchical ordering of reality.[29] There is use of Biblical proof texts, as when peacefulness is described in Pauline terminology as a "peace which passes understanding." The frequent use of technical terms from Eastern religions and metaphysical systems barely masks the vast religious preoccupation which gives impetus to this seemingly secular endeavor.

Whether individually or in groups, thousands of people with high school education and up, and very likely with some kind of early or present religious affiliation as well, are looking for emotional contact with the transcendent through demonology, Satanism, or witchcraft. They may apply the pseudoscientific trappings of astrology to their lives, with a conviction of seriousness. Though culturally regressive, these pursuits are by definition (and historical association) exercises in contact with the numinous, capitalizing on the emotions of fear and anxiety, which are both elicited and warded off.

The recapturing of emotionality in order to enhance one's capacity for growth or to produce a significant transformation of heart and mind is an important motive of the so-called encounter culture. To be sure, exercises in classical group dynamics or psychiatric applications of group therapeutic methods hold this end neither as their simple goal nor as their method, but a sizable portion of the human potential movement, the weekend marathons, the sensitivity training, and the various "love groups" abound in activities that come indeed very close to religious liturgies, at times with Dionysian effervescence.[30]

Most of these groups do not speak to the socially oppressed, the uneducated, or the outcasts of society, as nascent religious sects have often done. Rather, they purport to speak to well-educated and well-situated people who long to be unshackled from cognitive dominance and social proprieties in order to feel and express a gamut of emotions. Some of these movements have prophets and gurus whose manners and dress are not easily distinguishable from shamans and priests. They may be charismatic. They attract followers or converts. Or they write tractlike books. Emotions per se are hallowed by these groups, and the strenuous attempts of their members to become "genuine" or "whole" strongly resemble the happenings of nineteenth-century camp meetings and the release phenomena of the sawdust trails.

The writings of Norman Brown[31, 32] seem to many of his devotees the sacred text of a religion of eroticism, an approach to life that blends pansexualism with ideas of salvation, with a promise of freedom and discovery of the infinite.

In some serious modern movements there are strong elements of righteousness, moral indignation, heroic tenacity in dedication to the cause, and, if needed, willingness to accept martyrdom. This is true, of course, for all civil rights movements and various political protest movements. I think it is also noticeable in various forms of the women's liberation movement, which is only in part a case of civil rights. Another part of the movement is peculiarly self-transcendent inasmuch as it is driven by the desire to improve not merely the lot of women but to transform the attitudes of all men and women to the whole issue of gender in human nature. That part of the movement often proceeds from religious and theological premises about creation and the essence of creatureliness. It may come from reflection on the nature of love and generativity. It seeks sanctification of life by a radical reassessment of the relations between men and women and is sharply attuned to the kinds of truth that are shrouded in symbols.

While several of the movements I sketched may take recourse to, or receive some impetus from, traditional tenets or formulations of religion, though their activity seems otherwise wholly secular, due attention should also be paid to the marked growth of emotionally intense, spirit-centered sects and churches which place themselves squarely within the sphere of the sacred. Pentecostal groups, Holiness sects, and the Unity

School of Christianity, and many other movements which have been described as a "Third-force Christianity,"[33] are proving to be attractive to large numbers of people from diverse social strata. Of note also are the spirit-oriented subgroups within mainline churches, such as neo-Pentecostal Catholics and glossolalia-practicing Episcopalians. Indeed the increased attractiveness of glossolalia and faith-healing endeavors anywhere signals a rise in the nonrational (or irrational) elements of modern religious consciousness. And finally, there are the various Jesus movements, very heterogeneous to be sure, whose members engage in apostolic confrontations which tend to produce shock effects in the minds of church people as well as secular citizens. The term "Jesus freaks" by which the parlance of the drug culture designates certain members of the Jesus movement teaches an interesting lesson. It is not intended to convey the dictionary meaning of "freak" as curiosity, caprice, or whimsy but the derived meaning of the slang word "freaking out," which is losing one's mind, in this case to be "Jesus crazy." Can anything be more religious than that?

CHAPTER II

Religious Beliefs and Alienation

When one looks back at the voluminous writings about religion by great philosophers and social critics one cannot escape the impression that their minds were often beset by a peculiar cleavage. To the extent that they were in contact with the prevailing religious belief systems of their time and may have participated in the prevailing religious cults, they claimed for their own religiousness a formidable intellectual underpinning which they denied to the populace. Plato, Avicenna, Spinoza, Rousseau, and a host of other influential thinkers made vigorous attempts to demythologize (long before that word became popular) their own beliefs. They insisted on finding intellectual proofs which would allow them to appropriate in their own way the "core of truth" which they recognized in religion, while declaring that the mass of people would always need myths and images in which to couch their beliefs. But while this distinction may be a typical one for nearly all intellectuals, thinkers in the past added a few important things.

The patronizing concession that the common people's need for myth and imagery must be satisfied implies that religion in the main will always be a rather primitive, awkward, and somewhat nonsensical activity, but one that happens to be so deeply entrenched in human nature and cultural history that it is

nearly impossible to eliminate. And to this intellectual judgment historical thinkers added a social value judgment. All of
them felt not only that religion was here to stay, but that religion, in any form, should and must stay, for without it the social
structure would quickly fall apart. In other words, they attributed great instrumental value to religion when they asked:
What integrates society?

I think we can see in these expressed attitudes the rudiments
of estrangement. These great thinkers did not feel at home
anymore in their temples, synagogues, or churches. They did
not like the language they heard there, the pictures they saw,
or the symbolic acts they witnessed. Though they may have
maintained polite contact with their fellowmen, their world of
thought and action had become quite separated from the world
of these others who were a vast and dominant majority. Though
they agreed with the rest of the citizens that values are necessary if life and society are to remain organized, they disagreed
about the choice of values, and indeed on the whole conception
of values. Their own notion of values had become abstract and
thus allowed for dispute and questioning; the common people
found their values concretized in the life and work of the social
institutions, which had hallowed status. None of the persons I
mentioned, not even Rousseau, could be regarded as advocating anarchy. They all believed in norms. Nor could they be
regarded as irreligious: they all had conceptions of, and feelings
of awe for, the infinite, and some of them continued to talk of
God, sometimes quite movingly. Yet they all demonstrated that
it is possible for some people to feel disinherited or to disinherit
themselves from conceptions and practices which are regarded
as the enduring fabric of life and parts of a powerful tradition.
Such disinheritance is one meaning of the word "alienation."

These historical figures remind us that feelings of estrangement are not new. Alienation has always existed, both as a social
fact and as a psychological state of mind or feeling. But it took
centuries for alienation to become a concept and a focal point
of inquiry.[1] Hegel made alienation the central process for his
metaphysical system; the Absolute Mind alienates itself in the
natural world until nature, through evolution, produces con-

sciousness, in man, who can then recapture Absolute Mind in a new synthesis of knowledge. Hegel called the latter process "de-alienation." The word "alienation" here stands for any form of objectification, concretization, and manifestation.

Hegel's contemporary, Feuerbach, used the word "alienation" (or rather its German cognates such as *Entfremdung, Veräusserung, Entäusserung*) to sketch his understanding of the relations between God and man in any religious system, particularly in Christianity. He saw gods as man's creation, as the essence of man absolutized, and estranged from man. The idea of God is thus the product of self-alienated man. I think that in this case, alienation shares with Hegel's usage the meaning of objectification, but it adds the quality of what we would today call projection, the psychological mechanism. Feuerbach went on to say that man's de-alienation from himself is bound to occur when he abolishes the notion of God (in today's technical vocabulary, when he takes back his earlier projections).

Acquainted with these usages of "alienation" by his famous contemporaries, Marx focused the idea differently. He was philosopher enough to see that there is a sense in which every objectification of an idea that springs from man's mind is an alienation. He was also a keen enough social observer to notice that all that man makes in goods, products, money, and capital is not only a metaphysical alienation in Hegel's sense, but something that assumes objective reality apart from and often against him, estranging him from his human essence. These things may ruin his peace, deprive him of spontaneity, or enslave him. And Marx was social critic and activist enough to hold that the economic and class situation of the majority of men in effect degrades them as human beings and at the same time selectively deprives them of cultural satisfactions available only to the privileged groups in society. In Marx we find a whole scale of meanings of alienation, with a scholar's emphasis on socioeconomic alienation and an activist's emphasis on the de-alienation which will come through abolition of the class system and collectivization of the means of production.[2]

More pointedly for Marx, labor is the alienated, rejected class whose eventual de-alienation will not only benefit its members, but in the long run rehumanize all mankind and set it free from its self-imposed enslavements. What is important here is that there is a messianic element in labor's struggle for a place in the sun in the sense that anybody's de-alienation is thought to be everybody's de-alienation. From this angle the Marxist theory of action comes close to liturgical work known in religion: it is essentially corporate, and the mind of the participants is doubly attuned to the self and the immediate reference group as well as mankind at large.

I have described the nineteenth-century origins of the concept of alienation at some length in order to emphasize its profundity and complexity. Today alienation is regarded by some social scientists as an overworked idea, badly vulgarized. Those who feel that it has shifted in time from a social to a psychological category can indeed point to increased allusions to it by modern psychotherapists, psychological investigators of youth movements, the majority of existentialists, and students of cultural "states of mind." But it should not be forgotten that alienation has had psychological meaning all along. Feuerbach and Marx, despite their differences, both used the term to describe a state of consciousness and a set of attitudes, if not feelings, interacting with the workings of social institutions and the pressure from cultural themes. For both thinkers alienation was closely akin to the modern concept of stress, which in the same ambiguous sense comprises both social and psychological events in intimate interaction. Feuerbach saw that alienation as he defined it hurts proper self-regard. Marx saw that alienation begets personal suffering and depravity, destroys families,* and leads to the accumulation of large reservoirs of anger, even if its surface manifestations may for a long time be impotence and apathy.

---

*In *Das Kapital*, Marx cited the situation of the underpaid industrial worker forced to "sell" the labor of his wife and children to industry when machines had made their labor possible by requiring less physical strength and endurance.[3]

Political Alienation of the Oppressed from Religion

By and large, those who built on Marx and Feuerbach saw religion in terms of its institutional trappings and its conservative features. They properly sized up the role religion plays in preserving the present social order and hallowing it—a condition which is obvious and conspicuous in the parlance of the religious bourgeoisie. There can hardly be any doubt that labor's head-on criticism of religion has done much to secularize sizable groups of people. But not all of this secularization can be described as alienation in the sense of a state of mind characterized by disillusionment, distrust, powerlessness to alter the dominant beliefs, and feelings of homelessness, of being an outsider to leading cultural themes. For the emancipated workers and their leaders, it is largely a matter of rationalism. It is refusal to seek refuge in any magical or superstitious belief that diverts attention away from the here and now by focusing on eternity, or that substitutes long-range compensatory satisfactions for immediate ones.

This kind of secularization is a rational debunking by the oppressed of the conspicuous religious beliefs and institutions of the bourgeoisie. Within the Marxist frame of reference it is a case of expected de-alienation, a way in which people finally come of age. And it seems to me that it is based on insight, at least partial insight. It may also be based on good reality testing, as far as awareness of some tenor of social institutions is concerned. It does set the mind free, at least from some kind of bondage. Typically, it leads to a purely social world view, and even if this view in turn may be discovered to have strong ideological underpinnings, its adherents will deny that their undergirding beliefs are in any sense religious.

The latter clause is tricky indeed. Buried in it is the whole question of defining religion. Is any ideology ipso facto a religion? I doubt it. We have seen over and over again in the history of civilization that religion, however defined in any era, is not everyone's cup of tea. And if we are to deal honestly with the phenomena of secularization and unbelief we must take into

account any individual's claim that his beliefs, whatever they
turn out to be, are not religious. I think we should fully underwrite the sagacity of E. R. Goodenough's remark:

> Those who think they know most clearly, for disapproval or ap-
> proval, what religion "is" seem to recognize least what amazingly
> different aspects of human life the term has legitimately indicated.
> We can, therefore, best approach religion by getting in mind the
> various experiences that men have called religion, rather than what
> we think should be given the name.[4]

Though Goodenough wrote these lines as a premise to the psychology of religion, they hold equally for any psychology of
unbelief or irreligion.

Religious Alienation

But the same, century-long era in which rational secularization came about also developed a powerful countertheme, by
selecting from the history of religion an entirely different set of
observations. This countertheme, developed in scholarly and
scientific fashion rather than apologetically, is epitomized in
Weber's work,[5,6] with its painstaking documentation of the active role of religion in changing social institutions and conditions and in creating new belief systems. Weber saw religion as
producing from time to time revolutionaries and radicals who
despised the prevailing social arrangements and experimented
with new departures for living and thinking.

Weber distinguished, as many have done, between priestly
religion and prophetic religion, but he did not equate these
with, respectively, the stabilizing and the change-producing
functions of religion. That contemporary equation is an untena-
ble cliché in view of Weber's thorough work. Asking himself
how religious themes and beliefs can produce social change, he
took from his survey of religious innovations the theme of *radical salvation*. Radical salvation can follow two paths: it can take
the form of withdrawal from felt conflict and avoidance of the
arenas of tension by *mysticism*, or it can assume an activistic
form producing overt rearrangements in life, by *asceticism*.
Either of these can be personal and social at once. But both

mysticism and asceticism need to be qualified, for they are complex attitudes.

The goal of mysticism is to seek contact with the numinous. In the pursuit of this goal, the mystical path accommodates itself to the existing order by finding in it a corporate or private haven—for example, the monastic life or a life of personal meditation. This is thought to bring salvation at different levels: to an individual, to a congregation, and perhaps indirectly to mankind at large through the other two.

The mystical path may be prophetic as well as priestly in its inspiration. Moreover, the optimal distance from the world which is sought through mysticism does not necessarily amount to a total abnegation of the world. The world may remain very important to those who make the mystical choice, but they will not seek to alter it radically here and now, much as they may hope that it will eventually be changed. An element of resignation to the facticity of the world and its institutions characterizes mysticism as Weber used the term.

The ascetic path on the other hand does not lead to accommodation but to intervention in the prevailing belief systems and social institutions. Although Weber recognized the existence of an asceticism that rejects traffic with the world, he focused on in-the-world asceticism and said of it: "In this case the world is presented to the religious virtuoso as his responsibility. He may have the obligation to transform the world in accordance with his ascetic ideals, in which case the ascetic will become a rational reformer or revolutionary on the basis of a theory of natural rights."[7] Historical examples are Cromwell's Parliament of the Saints and the Quaker state of Pennsylvania.

Parsons[8] has seen in Weber's work the emergence of four types of religious orientation toward the need for salvation, by crossing the ascetic-mystical choice with the in-the-world–otherworldly choice.*Thus, there is an in-the-world ascetic and an in-the-world mystical type; and an otherworldly ascetic and

*I am indebted to Parsons for his exegesis of Weber's difficult text in his introduction to Weber's *Sociology of Religion*. But the use I make of Weber's ideas is my own, not Parsons's. I have changed Fischoff's translation of Weber's "inner-Weltlich" to "in-the-world" in order to reduce confusion of "inner-worldly" with the private "inner world" of the psyche.

an otherworldly mystical type. Parsons links this typology with his own theory of action[9] and finds much convergence between the two. While all four types legitimate their salvationist schemes religiously, the two otherworldly types lead away from intervention in the world. The otherworldly mystic finds his niche while avoiding the promptings of his subjective desires; the otherworldly ascetic seeks mastery over the flesh.

THE WEBER-PARSONS TYPOLOGY OF RELIGIOUS ORIENTATION

	Otherworldly	In-the-world
Mystical	avoidance of personal desire	modeling to others an attitude of detachment
Ascetic	personal mastery over the flesh—one's own	personal and corporate mastery over everybody's flesh

The in-the-world types have leverage in producing social change. The in-the-world mystic has this leverage only mildly, but by participating in the world he at least models an attitude of deliberate detachment from mundane concerns. His detachment, if emulated by others, may in turn change the predominant human concerns which have begotten the social institutions in their present form. The real leverage for change is given to the in-the-world ascetic type who seeks mastery over the worldly drift in his own person and seeks to extend this mastery to the whole fabric of living arrangements. Weber saw in-the-world asceticism embedded in the traditions of Judaism, Christianity, and Islam, and epitomized in ascetic Protestantism, notably Puritanism.

And so we have at this point two large classes of critical attitudes toward religion and religious belief. One, epitomized by Marx and some of his adherents, is critical of all religion and rejects it; the other, described by Weber, is critical of certain religious beliefs and certain religious institutions but seeks a religiously legitimized solution to the observed or felt problems. As we have seen, the latter class is very large and intricately subdivided; Weber's own typology was first published in 1922 and is thus certainly not the last word, for new phenomena may meanwhile have emerged.

It seems to me that the second class of critiques on belief is of pointed significance for understanding alienation. In the first place, the guardians of the social order (who are not only the politicians but also the bulk of citizens at large) tend to look at all alienated individuals and groups with great suspicion, fearing that they might undermine institutional stability and damage public morality. Second, it is almost a truism in social science that charismatic and prophetic movements find in the alienated a ready reservoir of potential adherents, who are mentally prepared to make a break in, and from, the establishment.[10] And third, the group comprised by Weber's types represents intriguing cases, not of alienation from religion, but alienation within religion—of religious alienation!

Classical Forms of Religious Alienation Updated

Rather than start with a precise definition of alienation, let us first use the word descriptively and with appropriate fuzziness in exploring the possibilities of alienation in each of the four types, using Weber's own observations as well as modern impressions of the current religious scene.

The otherworldly mystic gets his thrill from private, not corporate, experience. He seeks personal illumination, with the ultimate aim of finding rest in God or the Infinite or some other notion of the Encompassing. Though he is obviously looking for peak experiences in A. H. Maslow's[11] sense and will prize them highly when they come along, his attunement or at-one-ment with the Infinite is not necessarily a paroxysmal affair; he may keep it in slightly lower key much of the time. His basic belief is that God can be found within the human breast, because man, indeed each individual, is a vessel of the divine.

For persons with this penchant the world is, to say the least, a distracting place. It may be worse: dangerous, overwhelming, threatening, demonic. It poses itself obnoxiously between the self and the infinite. It separates. Even most of the religious

things that people do, the religious beliefs to which they confess, and the religious thoughts they entertain stand as a barrier
between the self and God. To the extent that mystically inclined persons emerge from affiliation with religious institutions, are familiar with God-talk, and have been exposed to
some basic religious precepts, their psychological hunger for
something more private, deep, and meaningful points to the
experience of alienation. At some time in their lives, they find
themselves estranged from the old religious customs—they
may see themselves as robots going through the motions of
religious busy work. They come to feel alienated from the religious crowd, particularly from the group they used to be with;
they become alienated from the typical cult and from the ordinary creedal thoughts. The daily compromises which other believers and their institutions make with the exigencies of the
world repel them. They begin to see all these other people,
religious or not, as alienated from God. Corporate religiosity,
attachments to things, and concern with institutions arouse
their indignation. Let us suppose that such mystics have talked
with other people about their growing or new-found convictions. It is plausible that most of these attempts got them no-
where: unable to convince others, they came to feel increasingly impotent and deeply frustrated, particularly by their own
kin (faith group, denomination, congregation, family, and so
on). Their anger and indignation mount, until they reach the
point where their feeling of being misunderstood precipitates
them into blatant withdrawal from participation in the worldly
marketplaces as well as the religious establishment.

Such people may always have had a penchant for withdrawal.
Their object relations may always have been tenuous. They may
always have felt somewhat distant and aloof. They may have
been vulnerable babies. But one should not underestimate the
strains and special frustrations whereby their mystical style
finally came to a head in adolescence or later. When Meister
Eckhart says: "Prate not about God, for prating about Him thou
dost lie,"[12] he is not speaking to avowed unbelievers (who
would not use God-talk anyway) but to his coreligionists, and his
sense of frustration is as keen as his anger is fierce. He feels

thoroughly alienated from the prevailing attitudes of those with whom he grew up and from whom he received his religious nurture. Alienation is not merely having a new belief or a unique value system; the sting in it, the pain of it, come from knowing that one once felt and believed differently and in companionship with other people. In this sense, the estrangement in alienation is literally comparable to leavetaking, to departing from loved ones, and metaphorically to a "little dying."*

For the *otherworldly ascetic* the situation is somewhat different, although the withdrawal tendency may be just as strong. The ascetic's interpretation of salvation is not unity with his God but his moral acceptability to God. His orientation is ethical. He sees himself and all other people as God's instruments to fulfill the plan of creation. To the ascetic, God is not within (which is to him a rather blasphemous or narcissistic thought) but transcendent. God is above his creation, and outside man. His relation to man is one of confrontation and demand; or of love, but then of an unmerited, gracious love, whose mystery is hidden in God himself.

The ascetic's thrill in living comes from knowing that he is discharging his creaturely tasks properly and is gaining in ethical purity. Life is a battle with the flesh, a struggle with the old Adam. Victory in that battle requires constant self-scrutiny lest impure or imperfect motives contaminate means or ends of the tasks at hand. It also requires an ongoing feeling of gratitude for a thousand unmerited blessings.

Insofar as this kind of ascetic is otherworldly, his partial withdrawal from the world is occasioned by a fear of contamination, rather than resistance to distraction. To the ascetic, the world is not merely a nuisance; it is awesome in its sinfulness. The natural self is also awesome, in its seeking after pleasure. The ascetic takes pleasure in a broad sense: sensualness is not necessarily its most important aspect. Pleasure includes the release of pent-up aggressive urges. It includes the hidden love of oneself and the tendency to elevate the self to the divine level.

*Cf. the French proverb: Partir, c'est mourir un peu.

In his arduous self-criticism and his striving for self-abnegation the ascetic of this type will be irked, time and again, by his
own natural self and the manifestations of other people's natural selves. The "kingdom of this world" is seen as a conglomer-
ate of such natural selves, natural enough, but precisely therefore godless. Hence, the otherworldly ascetic will in the first
place give up the world, and thereby extricate himself from
Satan's domain, but he will also look with horror at the compromises with the flesh occurring in religious institutions. He may
come to find his own childhood religion too magical, too consoling, too indulgent toward human frailties, too cozy. He may find
that his own church of origin is getting along much too comfort-
ably with the secular world, entrapped in the laws of the flesh.*

The alienation of the otherworldly ascetic will tend to have
a judgmental quality. It will be oppositional, and it may be
argumentative. His withdrawal from the world and from the
religious establishment will be a demonstrative and perhaps
provocative attempt at separation. When the otherworldly ascetic argues with his secular peers or his churchly brethren he
is vicariously arguing against his own natural tendencies and
takes his own "old Adam" to task. And thus his alienation is
peculiarly distributed: while he may *feel* alienated from his
worldly compromisers, he also *strives* to be alienated from his
old self, or from that dynamic tide in the self which needs
constant checking. In some way, then, the phenomena of the
divided self (in James's sense, not Laing's; see Chapter VI)
qualify how alienation is experienced.

One with clinical acumen who sees in the otherworldly ascetic type a parallel with the obsessive-compulsive personality
may be right in some individual cases. But he may overlook an
important additional feature. The religious ascetic, otherworldly or in-the-world, has a notion of God as abundantly forgiving and almost whimsically loving once he chooses a person
as his instrument. Predestination doctrines have had a particular charm for ascetics, and their effect has not been an unmiti-

---

*A recent study of a branch of the Jesus People movement by Harder, Rich-
ardson, and Simmonds gives an up-to-date picture of a contemporary otherworldly ascetic group in the United States.[13]

gated feeling of chronic doom. If anything, they have had an energizing effect, as Weber noted when he correlated the ethic of Protestantism with the spirit of capitalism, and although the latter is focused on the in-the-world ascetics, the mood component of otherworldly ascetics which I have in mind may be the same in both cases. It is that conscience, which plays such a dominant role in all ascetics, has two sides. It contains not only prohibitions but also approbations. It damns and it praises. It rejects and it loves. Normally it contains prohibitory rules and also techniques for atonement. To act in accordance with conscience therefore gives good feelings, which are evidence of the love bestowed by the persons which became the internalized models during the formative years in which conscience developed. To have an adequate conscience thus entails having a close internal friend or lover.

Predestination doctrines may seem to stress the (merited) divine rejection of the person, but they also propound a divine acceptance (unmerited, and thus seemingly whimsical) based on the divine choice. Thus, if an awareness emerges that one may belong to the elect, or if this grows into a conviction, a new quality of alienation may ensue: that of the chosen remnant which stands apart from the masses, who have either abandoned themselves to the world or are caught in a strenuously religious scramble for merit and self-justification. This aspect of alienation can be captured in the intriguing picture of the anchorite who sits on top of his pillar—not only apart from the crowd but also above it.

Let us now turn to the situation of the *in-the-world mystic*. If the instinctive orientation of otherworldly souls is flight, those who stay with the world are oriented toward fight, or at least some kind of redemptive action. Such mystics accept the world as an inescapable fact but try to redeem it by showing how "God's vessels" live: humbly, incognito, dedicated to spirituality. They may emphasize love in its nonactivistic forms by making themselves available to those who need them or by banding together with like-minded tender-hearted seekers in communal arrangements. They transform their mysticism into a vocation that is visible in the world and is part of the world's total pattern, but they demonstrate at the same time a sublime indifference to the rest of the pattern, acknowledging it factually but refusing to be swayed by it. They may engage in a special communion likely to be overlooked by the prevailing mores and social institutions. Thus, St. Francis preached to the birds, spoke to wolves, and saw sisters and brothers in the heavenly bodies. Dostoevsky's "meek characters" portray a compassionate recognition of other people, social institutions, the state, and the church simultaneous with a pronounced detachment from the rules, mores, and values of society in general.

Feelings of alienation in this religious position pertain first of all to the world, but in a special way. What is distracting for the in-the-world mystic is not merely the world's overt busyness and the fact that it requires social arrangements. The games people play in the realm of Caesar, its rules and premises, are what distinguish the world from the kingdom of God on earth. Caesar's domain may deal with some of life's necessities, but it also stimulates vanity, one-upmanship, avarice, calculation, and pride. One may get a feeling for the in-the-world mystic's alienation by contemplating the famous episode of St. Francis as a young man. In the presence of his former friends among the aristocracy, he deposited his rich clothes and his sword at the feet of his father, settling for a life of cheerful, honest, spontaneous friendliness. Such alienation is not from the world per se, but from the world as symbol of the powers of darkness. While one cannot leave it, one can at least shed its uniforms and discard its institutional trappings to show that one is not *of* it, albeit *in* it.

The deepest questions for the in-the-world mystic are about loyalty and authority, the source of conflict for the young man Luther when he was already embedded as a friar in a powerful religious organization. Which should he obey: the word of God or what institutional religion had made of that word? And to whom did he owe loyalty: to the God of grace or to a pedantic, forbidding vicar?[14]

Luther's case, the events of the Reformation, and much in the history of sectarian movements indicate that the in-the-world mystic's keenest sense of alienation is directed against bureaucratic religion. It is an alienation from the mandarins, the learned, the dogmatists, the structure addicts, the hierarchists, as well as from the slavish obedience with which the populace tends to hail these meddlesome know-it-alls. It is alienation from the symbols of vested power, perhaps based on a wholesale suspicion of all power—except, of course, the interior power of faith which can move mountains, and of the illuminated conscience which will bend a man toward cheerful charity.

Before he discovers his longing for a direct contact with God and before he breaks away into a new sect or attractive religious movement, the in-the-world mystic is very likely to have an increasingly painful sense of captivity. His church of origin, his university, his trade union, the banking system, the military draft, and all the secular powers may be felt as so many prisons which deny him his freedom and negate his dignity as one of God's creatures. He must eventually break out and find his freedom. And when, after gaining his freedom, he does not typically rail at his jailers (though he may scoff at the institutions which produce them), this only shows that he is at heart not a misanthrope, as some otherworldly mystics may be.

Both Weber and Parsons find the *in-the-world ascetic* the most action-oriented type and the most engaged agent of social change. He believes in a transcendent God who has assigned him a role in the scheme of creation. This role is to glorify his Maker, not privately but publicly, wherever he finds himself and whatever station he may occupy. His orientation is both ethical and energetic. He not only judges all things in terms of divine norms; he must also shape people and institutions and public morality so as to approximate those norms. Right conduct in all things is the key, with due attention not only to oneself but also to one's fellowmen. Life is seen as a vocation, and the actual occupational role one plays in everyday life is one way through which to help realize the kingdom of God on earth.

Inasmuch as the Puritan is most often cited as the classical example of this type, one will take for granted that the in-the-world ascetic tends to be a busy person, dedicated to an ethic of industriousness, work, obligation, and virtuousness, and often very practical. Social institutions, he believes can be changed (just as the heart of man can be changed) to conform to divine commands. They are not sacrosanct, but are tools (as man himself is a tool) for accomplishing the creator's goals. Radical salvation is accomplished by the in-the-world ascetic through mastery and competence, by using whatever leverage is available and adding to it his conspicuous energy.

On the face of it, in-the-world asceticism would not show a high correlation with alienation. It is too active, too zestful: very much involved in worldly marketplaces and ecclesiastical labyrinths. The Puritans may become such a dominant group, such a "mainstream," that alienation is the last feature one would think of in their case. But not all in-the-world ascetic movements have been dominant or popular, and even the New England Puritans could not lord it over everybody. Nor could the Calvinists maintain their Geneva theocracy for very long.

I think that modern phenomena in the life of churches exemplify a special form of alienation experienced by persons describable as in-the-world ascetics. Today, this term can be used to refer to members of mainline churches and faith groups, Catholics, Protestants, and Jews alike, who want their congregations to be involved in social action and progressive legislation, in political witness and social criticism, in the profound belief that their faith demands it. By and large, they have found that their principles and convictions as well as their activism meet with enormous resistance in the congregations, whose members opt for stability, sameness, and separateness from Caesar's domain. Although the would-be change agents like to appropriate the prophetic label for their orientation, their polarized attitudes cannot be captured correctly in the words "prophetic" and "priestly." My point is that this intrachurch and intracongregational polarization itself promotes feelings of alienation which become patterned in intricate ways. Often, the conservative elements of the congregations feel themselves ill at ease with the voices and actions emanating from their own national councils or boards. They sometimes form organized countermovements of protest, threatening to withhold financial support or to break away in schismatic maneuvers. They certainly see themselves and their institution threatened by the "radicals" who want to use the church as an instrument for social change. These cases are interesting in the sense that their predicament is not one of institution-specific alienation, as occurs in those who feel alienated from the religious establishment at large or from a particular faith group or denomination. They are, rather, cases of factional alienation, in which members of one group have come to resent the dominance of another faction within the same institution, without hope of solving their problem by leaving their institution of origin and joining another established religious group.

On the other hand, those who proclaim the need for social righteousness and who marshal their faith and their religious institution to its implementation may find themselves at times in hearty agreement with high-level policy statements or plans of national councils, but thoroughly alienated from their brethren under the same local church roof. While trying to act in the best ascetic tradition (with much church history to back them up) they find themselves deeply frustrated. For they have not been able to convince the mass of their co-members; they have not been successful in activating and mobilizing the energies of the congregation and in gaining access to ecclesiastical power and financial resources. They find themselves often imprisoned in the institution of which they are members. They feel themselves locked in by traditional ritualistic exercises. They feel like the adolescent must feel when he realizes, after many experiences, that his parents really live in a different world and cannot be reached. For the teenager at home, the feeling of estrangement from parents and kin is much more painful than some feeling of detachment from cultural ideals and norms. In the same way, those who feel alienated from the congregations they know from all kind of familylike face-to-face contacts are in a much more painful situation than those who merely feel distant from policies pronounced by their national headquarters; those headquarters have always been distant anyway, and have a measure of abstractness.

And so the in-the-world ascetic of today may find himself

naturally and expectedly at variance with the world whose values he rejects and whose themes he criticizes, whether these are competition, consumerism, segregation, utilitarianism, exploitation, vulgarity, sexism, or capitalism. By his basic orientation, the ascetic is well equipped to deal with such issues, at least privately, as a citizen or through various groups dealing with special causes and problems. But what causes him pain is the alienation he feels from his fellow religionists who, according to him, should know better, ought to act differently, and should put their faith to work in tasks and projects that will lead to the kingdom of God on earth. This alienation is likely to come to him as a surprise, not in the sense that it comes suddenly (it usually grows slowly) but in the sense that what he discovers is so grossly at variance with what he thought his religion was all about. Having been trained to hold certain beliefs and to act upon his faith, he discovers that the lessons he learned as a child were academic, without corporate application value.

In turn, the modern puritan who believes in the vocation he has to fulfill on earth, in the state and in the whole social fabric, may find that the means he uses for his corrective action may alienate others who at first might have felt drawn to his goals and ideas. Alienation, once experienced to a significant degree, tends to spread or spiral, particularly in those prone to activism.

Features of Modern Alienation

Alienation has become a cultural theme of great pertinence today. People describe themselves or others, proudly or with derogation, as alienated. Alienation has become an organizing principle by means of which beliefs are affirmed or criticized, conformity is extolled or rejected, life styles are endorsed or discarded, hopes are fostered or defeated—and all of this with considerable feeling and strong convictions. Alienation demands a toll, from the conformists as well as from the alienated. Alienation means bitterness and sadness—somewhere. Alienation means loss of something once held dear—to the conformist and the alienated alike. Alienation may mean mourning—over a lost Atlantis or a lost faith, a lost childhood or a lost naïveté.

Alienation means disorganization—somewhere, in society or individuals. But alienation may also be the beginning of reorganization—for society or individuals. Alienation says something about the temper of our time and in this sense demands a response, first of understanding, then of attitude and action.

Since our focus is on unbelief and its varieties, alienation does not concern us as such, but only as a condition affecting qualities of belief and unbelief, faith and doubt. Some salient varieties of alienation today, particularly among select young intellectuals, have become epitomized in the titles of Keniston's successive books *The Uncommitted*[15] and *Young Radicals.*[16] If the contrast between these titles is not striking enough, the subtitles of these works, *Alienated Youth in American Society* and *Notes on Committed Youth,* respectively, amplify it. The first book deals with the varieties of estrangement, the alienations "from," the losses experienced by those who seem unable to subscribe to beliefs capable of energizing their lives and securing a sense of fulfillment. The second book, published eight years later, describes those who turned from a sense of alienation to a positive set of beliefs that enhanced their zest, enlisted their energies, and propelled them into action to bring about changes in the human environment. The themes of these two books repeat in some sense Weber's distinction between otherworldly and in-the-world attitudes, but the new key words are "withdrawal" and "activism," or "noncommitment" and "commitment."

Since Keniston's work is on youth, his observations are made in the context of transition and development. Time is the important variable: the personal experience of time with its stages of growth, its developmental crises, its stages of identity formation, its losses and gains, its tension of stability versus change. This emphasis on personal time in the evolvement of value orientations is a relatively new feature that sets modern studies of alienation apart from those done in the era from Marx to Weber. It owes much to existentialism, particularly Kierkegaard's seminal idea of the solitary individual who is chronically assessing and reassessing himself in order to achieve honesty about his ultimate beliefs. Though Kierkegaard's dialectical reasoning is not by any means the same as psychological thinking about development, in both cases time is conceived dynamically and change is appreciated as an asset to the full life. Kierkegaard brought faith and honesty close together: he demanded ruthless honesty in matters of faith and advocated a faith in honesty. Purity of heart is purity of thought, and vice versa. Christianity demands an attack on Christendom. Stages on Life's Way never end: all of life is leaving something behind and leaping forward into something new with ever purer motives and ever clearer self-understanding.

While Kierkegaard modeled the existential quest in his laborious writings, he was no doctrinaire existentialist. He eschewed philosophical systematization and was skeptical of all "isms." He distrusted reason when it became pleasing or beautiful. In fact, he always assailed the imperialism of aesthetics with its demand for order, neatness, and harmony. Kierkegaard's existential man first practices, then preaches—in sharp contrast to the existentialist philosophers who give systematic lectures on Being and constantly generalize from the individual to mankind at large. It seems to me that Keniston is aware of this fundamental difference between existential decisionmaking and existentialist philosophizing when he says that the alienated university students he assessed were "native existentialists."[17] They assumed attitudes and sought a posture germane to themselves and their world, with a great deal of spontaneity and a feel for the cognitive value of mood and temper.

Since this century's midpoint existential thinking has evidently "gone native" for large numbers of people, not merely for a handful of college students in the sixties and seventies. The dissemination of existentialist philosophies cannot be the major cause for this trend, although there has certainly been a notable increase in printed texts and formal college courses on the subject. What we see is the emergence of existential themes in the arts and literature, experimentation with existential attitudes in civic life, the use of existential language in self-descriptions, and the formulation of everyday experiences in terms of existential constructs. Psychotherapists have remarked for years that many patients seek them out for guidance in achieving a meaningful existence rather than the reduction of definable symptoms of classical neurotic ailments. The theater of the absurd does not owe its acclaim to philosophical texts that justify it, but to experiences of theatergoers that validate it. Theologies of the death of God are not spurious proclamations of a few intellectual doomsday prophets, but summaries of a basic change toward ultimates felt by millions of people since Nietzsche began tolling the bell nearly a hundred years ago. Erikson's work on identity formation assumed at first with some comfort that most sane people would achieve some stable identity in the third decade of life, after the major identity crises of childhood and adolescence had been weathered. Now, only twenty years later, we find that the third decade of life is still full of turmoil for very large numbers of people. Lifton has begun to speak of "Protean man"[18] to denote young adults who do not embed themselves in enduring belief systems and values, but shift repeatedly from one ideological orientation or life style to another, with sharp breaks and great intensity, but only for short periods. They wish to remain "young" well beyond their years and engage in repeated rebirths, demonstrating a new style of self-process full of experiments and explorations.

The wish to remain young and the acute awareness of being young are patent features of the so-called generation gap. Roszak[19] has pointed out, and I believe rightly, that alienation from the parental generation is a relatively new phenomenon that goes well beyond the traditional process of generational disaffiliation. Parents and children have always been in tension. The values transmitted by one generation to the next are always somewhat modified. And opposition between the generations has always been seen as a fact of experience which no amount of pedagogy can alter. But formerly such generational differences and tensions have typically been borne with patience and forbearing, and sometimes even been welcomed, by the parties on both sides of the dividing line. The experience of difference was only a peripheral part of life, nothing to worry about. Now the dividing line is felt as a gap, and the experience of estrangement has become a central fact in the lives of the young and the old. Moreover, when the generational alienation goes deep, youth forges its alienation into a tool to produce social change,

with the awareness of being a saving remnant which will eventually make all things new for everybody, including the older
generations.

In 1930 Freud[20] wrote about a prevailing sense of unease or
discomfort with civilization (this is a literal translation of the
German title *Das Unbehagen in der Kultur*) on the part of
many people in the Western world. The theme of this influential book is the pursuit of happiness; its emotional tone is one of
profound unhappiness and its outlook one of pessimism regarding the viability of any of the maneuvers people make to obtain
some contentment. In it, Freud took a dim view of religion as
a means for obtaining happiness; yet he acknowledged that the
power of religion to make charming promises for satisfaction
would probably always give it considerable mass appeal. The
years that have gone by since Freud's judgment have proved
that Freud did not merely speak for himself. His judgment has
been shared by many, with the result that religion now tends
to be seen, even by many of its adherents, as one of a number
of ways of coping with the inherent miseries of reality rather
than as a glorious, self-validated, unquestioned truth. There is
a certain kind of alienation in this new attitude too, for something once held as objectively real has been supplanted by
subjective guesswork and private gropings. Affiliation with the
social symbol of that one-time objective reality, the church as
an institution, with its creeds and its cults, was once regarded
vital. Affiliation with the church (in a pluralistic society "the
church of your choice," to be sure) is now merely optional or
functional according to individual needs, and by no means for
a lifetime. Alienation has become operative within the sphere
of religion itself and has become an accepted, if not respectable,
attitude of contemporary individuals toward "their religion." It
represents a shift toward subjectivity, often with the noble intention of listening carefully and analytically to one's personal
needs, checking the gains and losses to be expected from religion's premises and promises, and ascertaining the grounds of
one's faith. Such an attitude can be seen as existential gain. If
greater honesty entails disaffiliation from religion, so be it. Or
if the scorning of Christendom is motivated by a search for a

purer Christianity, so be it. In either case, one makes a private decision and runs some personal risks—precisely the acts which bespeak the existential tenor of our time.

But Freud's prediction about the continuing mass appeal of religion, in one form or another, has also been validated. We started this chapter with an allusion to some of history's great intellectuals who sought for themselves sophisticated proofs for their beliefs, while holding that the masses would always demand the pictorial certainty of images and myths. Evidence for the latter abounds. These are great times for signs, on posters, placards, necklace pendants, and car bumpers. Our visual world is filled with crosses again—Greek, Celtic, Maltese, Latin, or pop-art varieties. And if not crosses, then Ankh signs, zodiac symbols, or Holy Ghost doves. Some of the Jesus people emulate sackcloth and carry sticks—and the latter are not designed to put other people at ease. The sports industry has its Christian athletes, organized to kick, push, jump, or shoot for the glory of God. University campuses have their occasional Crusades for Christ. The evangelists' tents of yore have been replaced by stadiums and exhibition halls—not a sign of dwindling interest and attendance. Whatever these observations may mean, they all bespeak mass movements, many of them designed to counteract estrangement from religion and within religion.

CHAPTER III

A Psychological Perspective on Unbelief

We began this book with Einstein's paradoxical testimony and followed it with an attempt to sketch the major historical developments of religion which could place his utterance in perspective and give it sense—from the archaic sacred cosmos, through the process of differentiation, to the distinction between sacred and secular realms. We looked at the institutionalization of religion and its ties to the state, arriving eventually at the idea of pluralism. We caught a glimpse of the modern phonomenon of civil religion. The central concept of our initial exploration was secularization—what it means and how it comes about. We saw that only one part of it is descriptive of a decline of the authority formerly vested in religious institutions; another part of it is generated by religion itself, particularly by thoughtful reflections on the essence of the Judeo-Christian-Islamic heritage. And we noted that, despite widespread secularization in both senses, there is evidence today of a massive interest in transcendental experiences, charismatic movements, and folk religion which seems to indicate that mankind's old religious quest is not about to die.

The next stretch of our journey was concerned with alienation. Acknowledging alienation as a bridge concept between the various social sciences, I stressed its relevance and usefulness as a psychological construct of some descriptive power. We found alienation to be a state of mind, a particular constellation of consciousness with both self and others as constant reference points, thereby safeguarding ourselves from succumbing to two scientific fictions: the fiction of the single, solitary, self-sufficient, encapsulated individual as well as the fiction of "man the social animal" forever playing roles only. We found that alienation has sad as well as creative aspects. We found that there is not only alienation from religion and religious beliefs and values, but also considerable alienation within religion, which led us to speak of "religious alienation." To grasp the impact of the latter case we cast Weber's typology in modern form and saw how much alienation can contribute to the production of social change, while at the same time it is no doubt a response to perceived social change.

Object Relations and the Search for Satisfaction (A Theoretical Interlude)

Let us now go further into psychological considerations and set forth the major thesis of this study: that both religion and irreligion, belief and unbelief, are to be understood in terms of man's pursuit of happiness. Though reminiscent of Freud's *Civilization and Its Discontents*,[1] the thesis actually pursues another Freudian proposition whose origins go back to *Three Essays on the Theory of Sexuality*,[2] published in 1905. I am choosing from this work a few key ideas which have remained stable through decades of psychoanalytic theorizing—so stable and well entrenched that one could call them the basic assumptions of all psychodynamic thought since Freud.

To put it concisely, psychodynamic reasoning starts with the recognition that behavior is motivated, in part, by relatively enduring drive constellations, among which the erotic and aggressive drives are of cardinal practical significance. These drives, which have a *source* in man's biological disposition and the physiochemistry of the body, also have an *aim:* the production of gratification by the reduction of excessive tension and the avoidance of pain. In a broad sense, gratification of drives is guided by the pleasure principle, even when under influence of the reality principle the forms and timing of gratification are altered. A third parameter of drives is the *object*. An object is anything which functions as the satisfier of the drive, anything with which and through which satisfaction is found. For an infant, the satisfying object may be the mother's breast, the mother as a whole, his own thumb, his comfortable crib, or his security blanket.

Even this very simple infantile situation alerts us to the fact that one can distinguish at least three great classes of satisfiers or objects: (1) *other persons* or parts or representations of them; (2) *the subject himself* or parts or representations of him; (3) *things* in the sense of inanimate objects, situations, and surroundings, as well as invisible things in the sense of ideas and cultural realities.[3]

Thus, we have the following simple scheme:

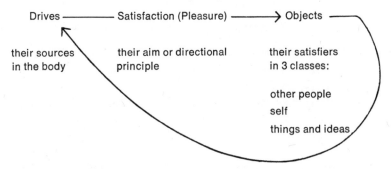

Today what is called "object relations"[4-12] is an elaboration of these basic observations and propositions. Readers may well wonder (they should!) why psychologists and psychiatrists speak so frequently of "objects" when the context of their parlance suggests that what they have in mind is "persons." Why the cold word "object" when a more humane and noble word is available? Who would talk about an object when he means his spouse or, for that matter, his enemy? Who would designate God as an object? I think that this awkward word use is not merely the result of an expression's becoming a technical term, which happens so often in science, but a consciously adopted warning signal that persons attach themselves to other persons for the sake of obtaining satisfactions. This is a very useful warning, for the word "person" fills too many roles to be precise. For instance, "person" is a word in law, ethics, and politics, which describe the legal, moral, and power relations between people, each from a distinct vantage point. These views could distract one from the essential psychological relations. The psychodynamic vantage point is that people function as emotional satisfiers (technically, as drive objects) to each other, and this aspect of interpersonal relations is never to be forgotten by the psychological observer!

The psychodynamic key word, then, in considering any and all relations an individual maintains to his world (including others, self, things, and ideas) is *satisfaction*. But because human beings are very complicated organisms, chock full not only of desires and wishes, but perceptions, feelings, judgments, discriminations, attitudes, values, muscle movements, communication mechanisms, and internal control devices, the directional principle of satisfaction needs far greater elaboration and embeddedness than I have given it thus far. For one thing, is not pleasure severely limited by the actual conditions of the subject and his environment? Of course it is; perhaps the most basic task to learn in life is that growing up means putting pleasure in the context of what is realistically possible. Maturing means learning to act under a new guide: the reality principle. Important as the reality principle is, however, as a new and acquired direction in life, it does not imply renouncing the pleasure principle. What it does mean is postponement of immediate wish fulfillment for the sake of later, wiser, more enduring, more intense, or more adaptive forms of satisfaction. It involves judgments and the establishing of workable compromises between the desired and the possible. It entails thinking about consequences of wish fulfillment: its immediate or long-range dangers or boomerang effects, and the risks of blunting the delight of pleasure through satiation. It may mean putting up with a lesser pain if a great pain threatens to be its only alternative. In other words, when the reality principle becomes established in the course of maturation, a dialectic ensues between the pleasure principle and the reality principle: the quality and quantity of satisfaction are bound to change, but always with the preservation of pleasure seeking and pain avoidance.

For another thing, the satisfaction of drives (and everything that is derived from them, such as needs, wishes, and longings) through suitable objects needs mediation. There are complicated tasks to be done: objects are to be sought, found, sorted out and combined, and tested for their suitability. These activities demand perception and attention, thinking, and various kinds of action. In addition, internal attention must be bestowed on the needs and wishes which push for satisfaction. This task involves considerable introspection, the production and registration of feelings, and the capacity for holding some needs in abeyance in favor of others. Comparisons between present and past situations may give clues as to what to expect. Memory—particularly its automatized part, which guides us unconsciously by myriads of associations and habits—is a central function in all these endeavors. Inasmuch as all these psychological processes are commonly attributed to the ego, whose natural functions they are, our original schema can now be elaborated as shown on the opposite page.

The ego, however, is not merely a collective name for the various psychological functions I have mentioned. The ego is the phenomenological "I," differentiated from others as well as from aspects of the person-as-a-whole which have at times a certain degree of "otherness," such as the id, the body, conscience. In special circumstances, these can be more or less objectified or, conversely, kept out of focal awareness. But the ego is always the action center, the pivotal point of awareness, the nucleus of identity through which we know that we are one and the same person from birth to death, and that we have unified functioning at any one time. The ego has a gubernatorial role to play for the benefit and well-being of the person-as-a-whole of which it is a specialized part. As a product of progressive differentiation and specialization of functions such as all organisms undergo, the ego assumes the roles of integrator, governor, manager, and executive of the person, maintaining his integrity against threats, embedding him in the environment, securing his nurture.

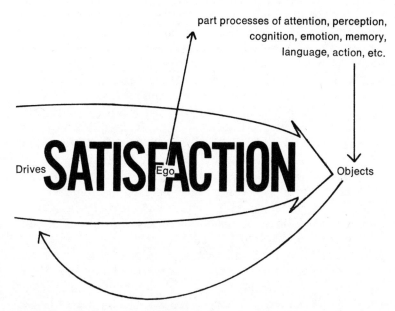

The part processes mentioned in the diagram can be seen as the "tools" which the ego has in obtaining contact with the environment and its objects, and being properly apprised of the internal household of the individual. Vigilance is to be maintained both ways: toward the external world as well as toward the internal environment of feelings, urges, fantasies, the voice of conscience, and the language of the body. Being so closely connected with identity, with the sense of *who* and *what* the person is, the ego is not merely a slave in the service of drives with whose satisfactions it is concerned, but it claims satisfactions for itself as well, particularly by demanding in all things consistency with the self-image, validation of a feeling of competence, and enhancement of a sense of freedom.

But persons are far more complicated than the sketch thus far presumes. From the earliest interaction between the infant and his world through the rest of life, the satisfactions and frustrations obtained from objects leave a kind of psychic residue which is worked over by the progressive differentiation and specialization of which growth consists. In childhood, do's and don'ts of parents become internalized to form the rudiments of conscience, which essentially transforms external controls and advice into an internal control and advice system and thus fosters automatization of action, with reliability and predictability of behavior.[13] The superego, translatable as the phenomenological "over-me," becomes a special, differentiated part of the person. The ego has to reckon with the superego and satisfy its demands if internal conflict is to be avoided. When a person's speech and thinking become organized, and life widens from the home to the world at large, adhortations and prohibitions received from many people, as well as books, movies, and other encounters with culture, become internalized. The ego ideal thereby formed is another part of what the man in the street calls his conscience. Typically the ego ideal contains mature and subtle values more accessible to consciousness, in distinction to the values of the superego which are of earlier origin, more rigid, and largely acquired by nonverbal or preverbal means, through predominantly unconscious processes of learning. At any rate, the ego must also be responsive to the demands of the ego ideal and keep the person attuned to its values, or other internal conflict situations may develop. The two new built-in signal systems have the capacity to produce special affects when their demands are not satisfied: in the case of transgression or conflict, the superego produces guilt feelings and the ego ideal produces shame.

The reader will have noticed that I described the genesis of superego and ego ideal as the product of human encounters. They are indeed the fruits of experienced satisfactions, of experienced pleasure and pain. They are a part of the fabric of object relations, formerly external, but now internalized to form a complex inner world in which the most significant and desirable persons of our individual past are the actors on the stage. The people we liked or feared, those we had to obey, those we emulated and attempted to imitate—everyone in whom we made a strong emotional investment—leave within us their traces and images which affect us profoundly. In this sense, interpersonal relations are also intrapersonal relations, and vice versa, at least historically. But nobody should be chained to his history. Under the impact of reality testing, most of us are constantly revising the residues of old interpersonal experiences in the light of new encounters with people. The toddler's intrapsychic image of his father gradually gives way to modifications, through his successive experiences with father in puberty, adolescence, and the various stages of adulthood. Despite these corrections, early experiences tend to retain a powerful impact, since they represent the first canalization of significant emotional experiences, and in this way set us on a course from which complete backtracking is impossible.

The ego, then, always has to seek workable compromises between the various psychic realities within us and around us. It must be vigilant to both the inside world and the outside world, bargaining with all parties so that no serious conflict with any one party will ensue. It must mastermind the adaptations that will ensure survival and keep the person-as-a-whole in a state of optimal well-being. When the person's integrity is threatened from without or within, the ego must take recourse to salvaging efforts to stave off the dangers. Through the specialized functions of the ego we cope with our world and our selves, seeking a vital balance among all the relevant dynamic factors that affect us.[14]

The pursuit of satisfaction obviously becomes a multilayered and polyvalent enterprise. The integrity of the person depends on the integrations he achieves with his world. Conversely, the integrations achieved with other people, one's self, and things and ideas—that is, the satisfactions obtained through all these objects—are nutriment for the integration of the person. We can now elaborate the basic psychodynamic schema as shown in the diagram on the following page.

It now appears that satisfaction is to be procured for many parties: the drives and all their derivatives, the superego, the ego ideal, the ego itself, and the person-as-a-whole. All of these have to do with the promotion of well-being or happiness of the individual. But no man is an island—certainly not in our

schema. Happiness is found through objects, and many of these objects are constituted in the same way as the subject. They too demand happiness for themselves. They too must be satisfied. Neither the subject nor the object is encapsulated—both are part of the matrices of nature, society, and culture.

It is in this modulated sense of satisfaction that I take the pursuit of happiness as keynote to the psychological understanding of religion and irreligion, belief and unbelief.

Provisional Conceptualizations of Unbelief

It is now obvious that definitions of belief and unbelief change: twentieth-century belief is different from nineteenth-century belief, and unbelief today is not the same as yesterday's. The very fact that overt unbelievers are reported to have grown in number puts each unbeliever in a sizeable company from which he gains much reinforcement.

Biblical writers had much to say about true believers and idolaters. The Book of Revelation has a pungent statement about lukewarm people, whom God would "spew out of his mouth." Tertullian considered the human soul not only religious by nature, but *naturaliter Christiana*. During the Crusades a sizable portion of mankind was called infidel; these people happened to be Turks who, as adherents of Islam, were ready to give their lives for their faith in holy wars. Slightly more liberal was the attitude of Francis Bacon, who said: "It were better to have no opinion of God at all, than such an opinion as is unworthy of him: For the one is unbelief, the other is contumely."[15] These examples suffice to show the persistence of a *vantage point which makes belief (sometimes a particular belief) the norm and declares unbelief a deviant condition in need of a special explanation.* This vantage point is fixed by the linguistic structure of the word "unbelief": as a negation, it seems to imply that belief is the normative state.

What time does to definitions of belief and unbelief is illustrated by modern examples. Kierkegaard's image of the "leap of faith" implies that unbelief is a more natural state than belief, and that the latter requires an explanation. At another level, this image is based on a sophisticated but partisan distinction between religious belief or religiosity in general, including membership in Christendom, and what Kierkegaard saw as authentic Christian faith. That same distinction is demonstrated in the fondness of many contemporary theologians for the neoorthodox slogan that religion is unbelief. Near the turn of the century, William James wrote his celebrated essay "The Will to Believe" in an effort to make a state of belief understandable, if not acceptable, to intelligent people who were prone to take, as he put it, "a different option between propositions."[16] Since James, far more has been written about the psychology of belief than the psychology of unbelief, but it would be rash to conclude that belief is therefore considered the normative condition. On the contrary, many writers, particularly the early psychoanalytic students, seemed surprised at the existence and persistence of religious belief in otherwise reasonable people and therefore found it worthy of special attention and special explanation. Thus, in modern times, at least for some people, the negative term "unbelief" is no longer a term of disapprobation. *The vantage point is shifting from belief to unbelief as the natural or normative condition.*

The psychology of religion cannot identify itself with either of these points of view. If it is to do justice to the phenomena of both religion and irreligion, or belief and unbelief, it finds a better foothold in thought patterns that keep both terms in apposition. Apposition can take several forms. Kierkegaard regarded belief and unbelief, faith and doubt, religion and faith, dialectically. This means that every thesis elicits its antithesis, and no proposition remains fixed. A simpler form of apposition is demonstrated in the intriguing Baconian phrase that "there is a superstition in avoiding superstition."[17] In terms more amenable to investigation one could say that it takes a kind of faith to be an unbeliever of sorts. Browning stated the relation between the two vantage points poetically and with a touch of nostalgia in "Bishop Blougram's Apology":

> All we have gained then by our unbelief
> Is a life of doubt diversified by faith,
> For one of faith diversified by doubt:
> We called the chess-board white—we call it black.[18]

Whatever the particular formulation, the interactional viewpoint of belief and unbelief locates the tension where it matters: within each individual, within each church, within each culture. It is a shabby business to compare a group of believers with a group of unbelievers when we know that within each group, individuals are tormented by questions of belief and unbelief. We can no longer indulge in the game of calling unbelievers all those who do not share our particular posture, whether of self-confessed unbelief, doubt, skepticism, agnosticism, or atheism.

The interactional view also allows us to keep a good grasp on reality, which, insofar as it is interesting, is so precisely by its phenomenal messiness rather than any neatness. Reality pre-

sents such untidy facts as a gradual attrition of church membership in this country in the last fifty years, with a sudden upward
spurt in the ten years following World War II; considerable
dissent within denominations; acts of faith outside the congre-
gational establishments and postures of unbelief within; the rise
of new religions and belief systems or the reemergence of old
ones such as astrology, Satanism, witchcraft, or chauvinistic nationalism complete with creed and cult; renewed interest in the
cabala and drug-induced mysticism; and the rise of underground churches which once more pitch faith over and against
religion. Reality presents the fact that many unchurched persons claim to be believers, not in religious fads or spiritual ec-
centricities, but in mainline Christian tenets. Reality offers the
observation of the tremendous expansion of the religious book
market in the last several decades, not solely in churches but
in universities and on paperback racks.

Another and very important element of untidiness in any
approach to the phenomena of unbelief is conceptual: whether
belief and unbelief are apposed or opposed, much will depend
on the underlying definition of religion. I myself regard the
problem of defining religion insoluble, not because of any presumed elusiveness, spuriousness, or ephemerality of religion,
but because religion is so tied up with thoughts of vastness and
plenitude, capsuled in the German prefix *Ur* and the Latin
omni. I rest my case with the statement by Goodenough quoted
in the previous chapter. Goodenough, like James, kept the *varieties* of religious experience in the picture because he saw
variety itself as an essential feature of religion, much as the idea
of art entails by necessity a multiplicity of media, forms, and
schools.

Granting, then, that definitions of religion will affect any
statement about the apposition or opposition of belief and unbelief, I would like to illustrate the inherent complexities of
unbelief by reviewing in this chapter selectively and provision-
ally a few major psychological thinkers about religion in order
to see where their thoughts would lead. What I wish to emphasize is the immense variety of unbelief, and the tenuous status
of the word "unbelief" in designating the whole span of

phenomena. I will focus on authors whose works have proved
to be seminal.

A very good starting point is Schleiermacher, not only because his major work from 1799[19] is now undergoing a kind of
renaissance, but because he pitched his lectures on religion *an
die Gebildeten unter ihren Verächtern*—to the sophisticates
among its despisers. Here is no quick damnation or cheap denigration of unbelievers; on the contrary, there is the implied
compliment that many unbelievers are eminently reasonable,
cultured persons with impeccable ethics, an asset to their civilization. In essence, Schleiermacher asks them whether they
realize their "utter dependency"—their contingency—and
what they do with the feelings aroused by the human condition.
Their heart is in reasoning, but do they know the reasonings of
the heart?

Schleiermacher made the "feeling of utter dependency" central to his definition of religion. Even if we translate this *feeling*
as *sentiment* or *awareness* in order to do him historical justice,
it follows that for him, unbelief is the failure to admit, realize,
or come to terms with one's utter dependency and, as a result,
organize his life around it. In modern terms, such unbelief is an
intellectual attitude of narcissism in which the individual assumes more self-determination and greater ontological status
than he actually has. This is, however, a metapsychological and
not a psychological statement, for Schleiermacher was well
aware that most of his hearers were not more prone than anyone else to particular narcissistic symptoms. He assumed in his
discourses that many of them were quite exemplary in their
object relations, as we would say today, and he praised their
high-mindedness. He even left the door open to the possibility
that their expressed views of the self were not commensurate
with their private feelings about the self.

In other words, Schleiermacher questioned the limits of enlightenment. An admirer of Spinoza and Schelling, he was quite
enlightened himself, but struggled over the proper role of
humility in an enlightened mind and culture. Obviously he felt
that humility not only preserves a balanced perspective on a
person's status in the cosmos but actually enriches his life and

enhances his human potential. He spoke movingly of a sense and taste of the infinite, a sense of wonder, a longing of the heart, and an attitude of reverence. Trusting that the feelings of the heart are pathways to objective truth, he was bold enough in his other works to try to produce an empirical theology. And thus, one can say that unbelievers are richer than believers in self-respect and dedication to reasoning, but depleted in humility and knowledge of that path to discovery that leads from feelings to thought.

It should be noted, however, that humility has ambiguous status as a condition of religious belief. Psychoanalytic investigators, noting how often religious belief is buttressed by speculations about individual immortality, and vice versa, have correctly pointed to a persistent core of grandiosity in some religious formulations of "life after death." Empirically, some people are humble enough not to demand immortality for themselves, and they may regard themselves irreligious: others, more likely to call themselves religious, humiliate themselves to assure their eventual continuity after death.

Turning now to Rudolf Otto,[20] by jumping over more than a century, we find religion defined as the exercise of a common human talent for dealing with the idea of the holy. The holy is a symbol for the *mysterium tremendum et fascinosum,* for the *wholly other,* for the numinosity that confronts man in situations of awe, terror, grandeur, and overwhelming power. In the later editions of his famous book, Otto assumed that human beings have a disposition or an *Anlage* for numinous experiences, that some people even have a talent for them, and that stimulation and nurture are necessary to turn potentiality into actuality. In the stimulus conditions he included not only religious education (all the obvious ways in which religion is taught), but also the phenomenal forms in which the holy appears (the theophanies of the spirit in nature, art, liturgy, myth, and mysticism).

The crucial implication of this definition of religion lies in the notion of disposition or talent for numinosity. Are unbelievers simply less gifted, poorly endowed with talent for the numinous? Or have they been nurtured less by adequate educational experiences, perhaps been starved of the Spirit's own theophanies? In either case, unbelief would seem to be a lack of something, resulting in statistical data which would show an uneven distribution, just as aesthetic talent and artistic sensitivity seem to be unevenly distributed in any population.

But Otto's thoughts on religion have prepared the soil for another conceptualization of unbelief. His *mysterium* has two dynamic parameters: it attracts and it repels; it causes feelings of bliss and awe. It produces not only an awareness of one's dependency, or even of Schleiermacher's *utter* dependency, but insight into one's creatureliness vis-à-vis the objectivity of the noncontingent—that is, the presence of the numinous. Unbelief, from this vantage point, is not merely a quantitative but a qualitative datum. It might consist in selective blunting of feelings in which the mystery is eliminated from the *mysterium*. One form of unbelief would be the condition of being lukewarm, of having selectively flat affect, with no room for bliss or awe. Another form of unbelief would consist in opting for only one of the *mysterium*'s parameters: if bliss be the option pursued to the extreme, the end product is the Pollyanna who is perfectly at ease with the whole universe because it is so friendly; if awe is the sole option, one ends up in a state of chronic depression and anxiety or in relentless gloom. Neither case elicits the holy: instead, one is either thrilled to death or haunted to death without having to reflect on the ambiguities of his creatureliness. Belief is hardly necessary in these conditions, for the cosmos presents no enigma, no puzzlement, no intrigue, no serious mystery. The individual leaps from his own dominant mood to the composition of the cosmos and finds the two identical, by a grand narcissistic projection, unthwarted by the exigencies of reality testing. Of course, the whole idea of creatureliness is foreign to this projection, for the self is endlessly expanded to the furthest reaches of the universe.

James regarded religion, for the purposes of his Gifford Lectures, as consisting of "the feelings, acts, and experiences of individual men in their solitude, so far as they apprehend themselves to stand in relation to whatever they may consider the divine."[21, p. 31] It is a selective, yet lenient definition, and he used it magnificently in describing the varieties of religious experience. He emphasized the solemnity of reactions to the divine, stressed their enthusiastic quality, and imbued believers with a sense of reality for the unseen. He paid much attention to mysticism and conversion, and as a good pragmatist he tended to evaluate religion by its fruits rather than its origins, putting much stock in saintliness and zest.

James did address himself to the problem of unbelief in the last chapter of the *Varieties,* mainly by opposing science and religion. To him, those who shy away from traffic with the reality of the unseen either have no vision of the unseen, and thus lack imagination, or hesitate to attribute any reality to it, and thus in the spirit of positivism deny its validity. In either case unbelief derives from a narrow conception of the universe and a shallow response to its complexities. James also held that the impersonality of science makes it deal only with the symbols of reality, whereas private and personal phenomena make us deal with "realities in the completest sense of the term."[21, p. 498] Belief may be untidy, ad hoc, and concrete, but the bit of experience it deals with is "a solid bit as long as it lasts."[21, p. 499] Unbelief on positivistic grounds may be orderly, general, and abstract, but what it deals with are "but ideal pictures of something whose existence we do not inwardly possess."[21, p. 499] But James's great stress on motor activity would make him also say that in the end a man's beliefs appear in what he does (with all possible contradictions among his doings) rather than in the ephemeral accounts of his verbalized world view.

In *The Will to Believe,* which preceded the *Varieties* by several years, religious belief is defined as a momentous and a forced option between hypotheses, guided by the double law of knowing the truth and avoiding error. Belief here is seen as risk taking, committing oneself, choosing, venturing, exercising the will; in essence, acting in accord with Pascal's wager argument. By implication, unbelief would be characterized at first blush by a lack of commitment and venturesomeness. But James indicated that one can, at times, passionately decide not to decide —that is, be determined to leave the question open—in which case one also shoulders some risk of losing the truth. In other words, a deliberate and passionate agnosticism can be very close to religious belief, despite its surface appearance of unbelief. This commitment to open-endedness is precisely what Rieff[22] has singled out as the attitude of faith in classical psychoanalysis. We can thus complement Bacon's phrase that there is a *superstition in avoiding superstition* by the proposition that there can be a *faith in avoiding faith*.

Before turning to Freud, it would be well to pay attention to Ernest Jones, who, although a minor psychoanalytic student of religion, formulated the strategically important thought that "what one wants to know about the divine purpose is its intention towards oneself."[23] Though not a definition of religion, this statement implies that a substantial element of belief for many people is thoroughly personalistic: the belief in a personal God who has intentions toward his worshipers, whom he regards as individuals. In this conception, God and man engage in object relations, have mutual concerns, and invest in each other; it is desirable that they are known to each other at the level of motives and intentions. The aspect of God correlated with this belief is known to theologians as providence.

In this perspective on belief, unbelief might consist of any balking at providence, any lack of interest in the terms of one's own contingent destiny, any rejection of the mutual trust that is a necessary condition for engaging in object relations with the divine. Since Jones saw the divine personalities as analogues of human family figures, by projection, and considered the God image essential to religion, unbelief can be a reasoned as well as an irrational or neurotic objection to the kind of object relations assumed in the providential model of belief. A reasoned objection might focus on the childish origins and the atavism of the cosmic projection of the family model and rejecting it, or it might denounce the public or doctrinal formulations of providence as myth. Neurotic objections may stem from personal distrust in any providential benevolence anywhere in the universe and thus lead to a depersonalization of any God image.

In Freud's definitions of religion,[24-34] the God models most often used are the progenitor and the father image of divine providence. One seeks access to such power as a possible aid in one's own felt helplessness. Constructing a phylogenetic sequence, Freud[24] hinged much of his definition of religion on what people do with their infantile feelings of omnipotence. In the animistic stage, people are given to a frank use of omnipotent thinking, expressed in rituals and magical acts which exert power. In the religious stage, man cedes omnipotence to his gods but retains some of it for himself in order to influence these gods to act in his favor. In the scientific stage, man relinquishes his omnipotence and resigns himself to the superior forces of nature, except for that trace of it which undergirds his belief in the power of his mind to cope with reality.

Since phylogeny is repeated in ontogeny, religious belief is by definition a maturational or developmental phenomenon. It lies on the hither side of that unwavering, cold-blooded reality testing which is the ideal of positivism, and of that sober resignation to the superior power of nature in the face of which one dare not ask for personal favors. By conjecture, some unbelief, then, is a rejection of childish propensities or an abandonment of natural wishes for protection and solace. This kind of unbelief requires self-scrutiny, intellectual honesty, and the courage of one's unpopular convictions.

But it is implied in Freud's approach to religion that many forms of unbelief can be at the same developmental level as belief itself. As a clinician, Freud knew of periods of doubting in the faithful; he knew of the dynamic concomitance of faith and doubt as expressions of ambivalent feelings. Some of his patients engaged in compulsive blaspheming; others had obsessions about God and Devil, or loving and hating their God. Some religious persons merge the image of their father with their image of God; others separate these two and split their positive and negative feelings between them. At this level, unbelief can be just as primitive, neurotic and drive-determined as belief. In fact, it may lack the finish which adheres to a more consistent and integrated system of religious belief particularly when the latter is so much in the public domain that subscribing to it has adaptive value.

There is a third ground for unbelief. Publicly upheld religion, buttressed by authoritative doctrinal formulations, exerts in Freud's view a peculiar form of thought control.[26] Its propositions are held to be beyond scrutiny. Belief is close to taboos. Science, however, knows no taboos. Therefore, some unbelief, particularly if coupled with a positivistic spirit, can be appreciated as a liberation of the mind from the fetters of taboo. This kind of unbelief can have a certain nobility as well, for since taboo is feared precisely to the extent that the forbidden act against which the taboo is erected is also desired, such a liberation of the mind implies a disciplined overcoming of desire. Meditation, conversion or self-education could enhance such a state, which in some ways resembles the ideals of Stoicism, and whose outstanding features are clarity of mind and intellectual vigor.

Implicit in Freud's thought on religion is a fourth form of unbelief. Religion, like everything else, is subject to transformations. Freud recognized differences between primitive and sophisticated religion, both anthropologically and individually. He considered his friend Pfister an intriguingly sophisticated religionist. One could thus ask whether religious development can proceed to the point at which it eliminates itself or becomes something else, like a philosophy, an ethical stance, a *Weltanschauung* or an existential posture, with creed and cult receding into the background. I think this is a fascinating problem; it puts some forms of unbelief in that special category of modern experience which some theologians have described as the post-Christian attitude. It may be linked with a God-is-dead theology, and it may even approximate that special state of faith which Kierkegaard saw as the overcoming of religion.

The last student of religion I turn to is Goodenough,[35] whose work is deeply influenced by both Otto and Freud. From Otto he took the idea of the holy, especially its aspect of the *tremendum*. Edified by Freud's thoughts, Goodenough saw the *tremendum* not only as the external and cosmic x, chaotic in appearance, which controls the universe, but also as the internal and personal x, also chaotic, of our motives, childhood fixations, and sense of guilt. Both are equally mysterious and powerful—awe-inspiring in a very potent sense. Man defends himself against the terror of both *tremendums* by throwing protective blankets over them (the blanket of repression, the curtain that hides the holy of holies, the veil that covers the unrevealed, and so on) and paints on them, in concert with his fellowmen, pictures of his beliefs about the hidden content. Myths, creeds, symbols, gods, doctrines, moral rules—these are all projections produced by the individual and his tradition, appearing as ideograms on the blankets.

Goodenough goes on to say that modern man tends to be more acceptant of the *tremendum* than his forebears, and has a penchant for inscribing his curtains with hypotheses instead of dogmas. His interest in meaning is coupled with running pragmatic tests of meaning, and he tends to answer questions with new questions rather than with definitive answers. He is at home with an agnostic stance: he may be aware of some ultimate in the sense of a substrate or order, but will not personalize it. Like the mystics who chose the *via negativa* he dwells on question after question, seeking an ever higher quality of questioning. He does not like closure on any question. The important point which Goodenough makes is that such an ever questioning attitude need not be positivistic; it is, at least in some cases, a modern way of keeping sacred things sacred. "Prayer for modern man is replaced by eager search, which is a form of prayer itself."[35, p. 181]

Goodenough's ideas put appropriate strain on the definition of belief as well as unbelief, and in this sense fit the temper of our time. Some unbelief can be understood as disbelief in the validity or relevance of certain ideograms on the protective blankets; indeed, some ideograms are primitively pictographic. Some unbelief is skeptical whether any ideogram will ever fit the intangible ultimate whose essence is intuitively grasped and felt to be ineffable. Some unbelief recognizes that there has always been a lively trade in blankets with various designs, but questions whether blankets are necessary or useful at all.

Holding fast to this imagery of Goodenough, one can bring unbelief in interesting appositions to belief. For instance, one can now recognize that some belief may be little more than an aesthetic appreciation of some ideograms on some blankets.

Some belief may consist in the conviction that certain ideograms match the hidden reality under the blanket—it is a belief in adequate matching and goodness of fit. Some belief can be understood as hanging on to the blanket itself, much as the toddler carries his security blanket with him while he is fully dressed and not cold. Some belief is reading and rereading the ideograms as intriguing puzzles to be deciphered. Some belief is a compulsion to invent new ideograms that are more meaningful or clarifying than the old ones. Some belief is playing the game of blankets, without any sense of a *tremendum* anywhere.

In the perspective gained thus far it is apparent that unbelief is at least as diversified as religious belief and that Goodenough's warning about the dangers of rigidly defining belief would pertain to defining unbelief as well. To paraphrase Goodenough I thus propose that we can "best approach religious unbelief by getting in mind the various experiences that men have called unbelief or irreligion, rather than what we think should ideally be given those names. We do not yet know precisely what unbelief *is*, just as we cannot pretend to know what religion *is*."

It seems to me that the terms belief and unbelief and their cognates, however one defines them, are quite empirical. Though they tend to be used frequently with judgmental intent and with considerable praise or blame, we must first recognize in all fairness that just as beliefs and unbeliefs are transmitted or inculcated, so are the approbations and disapprobations attached to them. Each term has a long history. The two terms as well as the experiences they denote are culturally transmitted alongside each other. They are taught as a pair, just as truth and falsehood, beauty and ugliness, and good and bad are pairs of ideas. But what kinds of pair are they? Are the members of the pair opposites? Are they positives and negatives? Are they presence and absence of something? Does each term in the pair have an independent status, a "thickness" or substance of its own? Are they like two sides of a coin? Or are they variable expressions of an unknown tertium quid?

We shall consider those questions in the chapters that follow. The previous sketch, though using a specific and limited methodology, has already shown that there is at least a great variety of unbelief. Our provisional conceptualizations will need many qualifications, for they are too sweeping as they stand now. Each kind of unbelief merits a pursuit in depth, just as each kind of religious experience and religious belief warrants psychological exploration. If belief is personal, so is unbelief. If belief has depth, so has unbelief. If belief is respectable, so is unbelief. If belief offers satisfactions, so does unbelief. If belief is embedded in object relations, so is unbelief. If belief is enmeshed in a system of thought, so is unbelief.

CHAPTER IV

Dealing with Dependency and Autonomy

"Men have left GOD not for other gods. they say, but for no
    god; and this has never happened before
That men both deny gods and worship gods, professing first
    Reason,
And then Money, and Power, and what they call Life, or
    Race, or Dialectic."[1]

This complex statement by the poet T. S. Eliot is a combination
of several important ideas. One is that man can decide to drop
the notion of God altogether, either by relinquishing it if he
formerly had some attachment to it or by not heeding it if he
has heard of the availability of a divine object. A second idea,
apparently more viable to Eliot, is that emotional attachments
can shift, by the mechanism of displacement, from traditional
numinous objects (such as gods) to secular symbols (such as
reason or money). This idea also implies a relinquishing of gods
as satisfying objects. But Eliot's third idea is that in some of
these displacements the new objects, though not called gods,
may nevertheless by held with such fervor that attitudes and
practices toward them amount to worship. In other words, if
numinous values become detached from their proper symbols

they may be reattached to improper symbols toward which the individual behaves in reverential ways, with the result that creed and cult begin to crop up in strange places.

Coming to Terms with Dependency

I am not sure that such happenings are as new as Eliot thought they were. More than a century before him, Schleiermacher faced nearly the same situation. His first lecture to the "cultured despisers of religion" was an apology, which he began by acknowledging that "from times immemorial faith has not been everybody's thing. . . ."[2, p. 17] He granted that his hearers were full of the wisdom of the age and had risen considerably above the petty concerns of everyday life; they knew the sayings of wise minds, their homes were full of the songs of poets, and they were absorbed by the ideas of humanity, art, and science. Apparently, he considered his hearers affluent too: "You have been so successful at making your earthly life rich and variegated that you are no longer in need of eternity, and after you yourselves have created a universe you are well above thinking of what created you."[2, pp. 17–18]

It is the old story. An enlightened gentleman, who happens to be imbued with a strong sense of his creatureliness, calls his equally enlightened contemporaries to task for having lost touch with the ground of their existence. But the old story is time-bound; each era deals with the theme in its own way. In Schleiermacher's time the "despisers" of religion were mostly the intellectuals, who seemed to assume that religion was widespread among the masses of the lower classes and the uneducated—and probably good for them as well. In our time, alienation from religion is no longer a class phenomenon and the forms of unbelief are just as pluralistic as the forms of belief. Even so, the questions remain: Why do some people's beliefs pivot around a deep and prolonged sense of dependency on a transcendent arrangement, however conceived, while those of others seem to be organized around the theme of self-sufficiency, vested in themselves or in their fellowmen? What goes into the feeling of creatureliness and under what conditions might it be absent? What makes for heteronomy, and what makes for autonomy—as felt?

Even the most preliminary exploration of these questions will show that the issues are surrounded by controversy. Much depends on the assumptions one makes at the metaphysical or developmental-psychological starting points. Schleiermacher discovered in himself and in most of his fellowmen a primordial feeling of dependency, to which he gave total credence as a cue to the psychic reality of the self as well as the metaphysical status of the universe. Dependency is the basic definition of man, both in his infancy and during the rest of life. He assumed that people have a direct awareness of this inherent quality of their existence and draw certain inferences from it. Those who feel it strongly and in whose mental makeup emotionality plays a dominant role will develop a characteristic humility, which automatically sets limits to feelings of and strivings for autonomy. They are instinctively aware of the differences in scope between themselves and the universe on which they depend. The more feelingful they are, the more they will seek an emotional style in relating themselves to the gigantic, powerful, and nurturing cosmos that sustains them. They will probably personalize the cosmos, humanize it by endowing it with intention, purpose, and meaning, if not a sense of warmth. And since their culture is bound to make god concepts available to them, they are likely to believe that the universe itself is the handiwork of a maker who sustains what he has made through infinite care. If they are habitually more rational they may shy away from personalizing the universe or, for that matter, personalizing its assumed source of origin. They may settle for a more abstract idea of a prime mover, a ground of being, an *ens realissimum,* or a *natura naturans.* Modern minds might think of a great, self-sustaining process. Knowing the platitudes that surround many homespun gods, they may sincerely speculate about a god-behind-the-gods or a *deus absconditus,* and thus distinguish between their own belief and the popular beliefs of their time.

In all these elementary forms of belief, Schleiermacher would spot, with rejoicing, that the essential qualities of dependency and humility were acknowledged. To him, people so thinking are truly human, for they are neither putting themselves on a par with the universe nor arrogating themselves above it. They are doing their feeling and thinking from an enduring awareness of their limited scope, which extends to all the important dimensions of life: limited power, limited knowledge, limited authority, limited stature, limited freedom. In the depth of their being they are heteronomous. This does not mean, however, that they are necessarily meek characters who allow themselves to be run over by their fellowmen and habitually defer to others for initiative and authority. They may play the boss at home, lord it over others in society, and strive for power and status like everybody else. But somewhere in their being there is a set of brakes that may bring these strivings to a halt at crucial intersections of life, as long as the red light is on. Such intersections may be the life crises from which no one is spared: death, bereavement, illness, bitter disappointment, or intense conflict and frustration.

Although he was not too explicit about it, Schleiermacher assumed that something can happen in personal development and through cultural influences to the root feeling of dependency and the associated feelings of humility and reverence. He dealt mostly with the cultural influences. The era of the Enlightenment, of which he himself was a child and most of whose products he prized highly, had shown him that people can forget, ignore, obliterate, or openly protest against the feeling of dependency in themselves and others. Impressive scientific conquests can be made which enhance fantasies of eventual mastery of a good many vicissitudes of life. Rationality may be exercised so assiduously that little room and energy are left for explicit recognition of the irrational or nonrational aspects of reality. Heads of government and other quasi-divine symbols of authority may be made to topple, thus shrinking the amount of exposure to dependency-inducing and humility-demanding social experiences. Art forms and language forms may emerge, as they did in Schleiermacher's time, in which man becomes the center of attention with heightened feelings of self-esteem and respect for human capacities and potentials.

Taboos on curiosity and investigation may be lifted. The
sphere of the sacred, already differentiated from the secular,
may begin to shrink. Aristocrats now gain ample access to satisfactions formerly reserved for kings. And the aristocrats of the
mind, no longer working in monasteries or other controlled
institutions but practicing as private citizens in their homes or
entertained as guests in salons, find marvelous outlets for their
creativity, reaping intellectual or artistic satisfactions that have
a more enduring quality than money, good luck, and the whimsies of health or illness. The enlightened mind also turns the
spotlight on religion, public and private, and finds much or all
of it odd. It is full of superstition; it has authoritarian trappings;
it keeps man enslaved to his circumstances by diverting his gaze
from earth to heaven. It promotes surplus humility or stimulates excessive and unnecessary dependency.

Whatever the specific perceptions and criticisms, the enlightened mind may come to accentuate the other aspect of man: his
competence. In fact, did not an ancient religionist, in his odd
theological phraseology, call man the "crown of creation?"—
"Well, here I am, knowledgeable, civilized, moral, and capable
of further improvement by using my talents. Many things depend on my initiative: I have some autonomy. Life does not feel
as if it were an exercise in dependency relations. I may have felt
dependent as a child, but no longer."

To Schleiermacher such thoughts, if persistent, would
amount to both a lack of something and an abomination. There
would be a deplorable lack of "feeling and taste for the infinite",[2, pp. 43-113] an absence of that "longing" (Sehnsucht) by
which man knows emphatically that he is only a part of a larger
whole. Life would be impoverished if it had no room any more
for that aesthetic, feelingful viewing (Anschauung) of the
grand universe. Worse, with these experiences gone or diminished, there might be no ground for reverence (Ehrfurcht) and
humility (Demut). There would be a decline of patience, and a
general blunting of feelings. That total condition is Schleiermacher's picture of a state of unbelief. It is akin to the Greek
descriptions of hubris and the Jewish idea of chutzpa, although
Schleiermacher did not accentuate its inherent cockiness as
much as he did its diversionary and distractive character. He

saw his audience, the "cultured despisers," mostly as preoccupied people in pursuit of humanistic values and cultural refinements—and thereby missing out on something basic.

The obvious psychological observation which must now be made is that Schleiermacher may have overlooked the deep satisfaction obtainable in the state of unbelief which he described. He did acknowledge that his self-confessed unbelievers had pleasures, and he did not want to minimize the pleasurable nature of cultural engagements. But he insisted that acceptance of one's utter dependency upon the larger arrangements of the universe and especially on a God-Creator or God-Provider promotes deeper, more lasting, and more genuine satisfaction.

What are the satisfactions of the autonomous stance in life? That question can hardly be answered for a generalized individual, apart from his social milieu and the mutual object relations in which he is embedded and engaged. Nevertheless there would seem to be some common ground. For one of the more conspicuous satisfactions of the enlightened, conscious culture-bearer is the feeling of being in the vanguard, becoming emancipated from unnecessary dependency on outworn traditions, popular superstitions, dubious authorities, and hackneyed forms of thought. Enlightenment does give zest. It stimulates curiosity and satisfies it, step by step, when new discoveries or conquests are made. Enlightenment also provides a challenge: it requires good sportsmanship to play a noble game based on the premises of competence, talent, and the courage of one's convictions. Nothing succeeds like success: each venture that promotes self-esteem leads to a new assertion of self-esteem which may build up chains of momentum and exhilaration.

There has always been fun in what used to be called "free-thinking." The unraveling of mysteries and especially the exposing of timeworn mystiques are gleeful activities. The first boldness one takes in speaking out against entrenched traditions is itself emboldening, especially when the emphasis is one of attack, which marshals aggressive energy into the flourish of argument. An excellent illustration of this peculiar glee, which came to the surface in Schleiermacher's own time, can be found in Thomas Paine's *The Age of Reason:*

. . . it is by his being taught to contemplate himself as an outlaw, as
an outcast, as a beggar, as a mumper, as one thrown, as it were, on
a dunghill at an immense distance from his Creator, and who must
make his approaches by creeping and cringing to intermediate beings, that he conceives either a contemptuous disregard for everything under the name of religion, or becomes indifferent, or turns
what he calls devout.[3, p. 30]

. . . Yet, with all this strange appearance of humility and this con-
tempt for human reason, he ventures into the boldest presumptions;
he finds fault with everything; his selfishness is never satisfied; his
ingratitude is never at an end. He takes on himself to direct the
Almighty what to do, even in the government of the universe; he
prays dictatorially; when it is sunshine he prays for rain, and when
it is rain he prays for sunshine; he follows the same idea in everything
he prays for; for what is the amount of all his prayers but an attempt
to make the Almighty change his mind, and act otherwise than he
does?[3, p. 31]

As these passages show, there are not a few sadistic satisfactions
to be gained from reinterpreting one's opponent's self-confessed humility as only a dressed-up form of arrogance. There
is glee in wielding the surgical scalpel deftly and incisively into
the necrotic tissues of that much extolled "utter dependency."

Paine's language, however, is not as calm and reasoned as the
title of his pamphlet would have it. Paine's work is indeed that
of a pamphleteer, whose aim is to do what is now called "consciousness raising." Whatever it may do for Reason, it plays
heavily on the emotions of the readers, and it constitutes a
considerable outpouring of the writer's emotions. Much as I
have always admired his spirited activism and the dare-devilish
quality of his work, it must be said that it has the earmarks of
alienation: estrangement not merely from formal creeds but
also from the major social institutions and traditional values in
which these were embedded. Estrangement also from nation
and local culture: Paine the Englishman acted in the manner of
a French revolutionary citizen and emulated America. Much of
his public argument is also a running internal argument with his
alter ego: the old self of his youth and his erstwhile beliefs. He
was always emancipating *from* something, but what he eman-

cipated *toward* tended to remain vague and abstract: doing good, taking the world as his habitat, and believing in man.

Paine's rhetoric was no less bossy than the priestly teaching he vilified. There is a good deal of one-upmanship in his style. And why did he go on capitalizing the words Creator and Almighty when he so strongly insisted that "Independence is my happiness"?

What Is Humility?

We should take another look at that important pair of terms: dependence and independence. Schleiermacher saw dependence linked with humility; Paine saw much religious dependency linked with bold presumptuousness under a veneer of humility. Is humility really typical of religious belief, and at a low ebb or absent in unbelief? There are several vantage points on this question.

The first vantage point is offered by the church historian Sidney Mead. It puts the light beam not merely on the factual and honest recognition of difference in scope between the small individual and the vast universe, but it focuses on the dynamic function of that difference:

> . . . no man is God. This is what I understand to be the functional meaning of "God" in human experience. Whatever "God" may be —if indeed being is applicable to "God"—a concept of the infinite seems to me necessary if we are to state the all-important fact about man: that he is finite.[4]

The function of the infinite, the universe, or any god is not merely to be there, but to teach something, namely that *man is not it.* Even if there were no infinite, man would still need the conception of it in order to discover something important about himself. Man is not God—but the implication of that statement is that man has an uncanny urge precisely to play God, to assume that he himself is infinite, and that he is the center of the universe. Did not Margaret Fuller pompously affirm just these human tendencies when she said in utter naïveté "I accept the universe"? And what else can one do in response but repeat Thomas Carlyle's marvelous quip: "Gad, she'd better!"[5]

Mead's statement brings the issue to focus on narcissism. Man is born as an omnipotent, demanding creature whose grandiosity knows no bounds unless society and culture set some boundaries. For Mead, the important question is not at first the clinical question of whether a particular individual happens to think highly or lowly of himself, but the metapsychological question of whether there is some way to stem the tide of everybody's rampant, natural, instinctive, and primitive narcissism. Schleiermacher and Mead proceed from different images of man. Schleiermacher felt that humility and dependency are at heart natural to man, but that some one-sided cultural pursuits tend to obliterate them. Mead seems to feel that man is naturally grandiose, but that religion and, in the wider sense, culture provide ideas which temper that grandiosity by making him aware of his proper scale and scope. For Mead, unbelief in the elementary proposition of the infinite which determines one's contingency runs the risk of producing human monsters who will trample the rest of mankind under foot. Mead's is clearly a post-Stalin and post-Hitler imploration, a dire warning.

The second vantage point is Freud's. While we will deal with Freud's ideas on religion and its alternatives at length in subsequent chapters, there is a passage in *The Future of an Illusion* that demands our attention now. It contains a shrewd observation about humility:

> Critics persist in describing as "deeply religious" anyone who admits to a sense of man's insignificance or impotence in face of the universe, although what constitutes the essence of the religious attitude is not this feeling but only the next step after it, the reaction to it which seeks a remedy for it. The man who goes no further, but humbly acquiesces in the small part which human beings play in the great world—such a man is, on the contrary, irreligious in the truest sense of the word.[6]

What a surprise, after reading Schleiermacher! Humility engendered by knowing one's small scope vis-à-vis the large universe is now seriously proposed not as an earmark of religion but of

irreligion. True unbelievers are, or may be, humble souls. And
Freud even used in the original German text the same word
that Schleiermacher liked so much: *demütig*. What light does
this proposition shed on our problem?

The kind of humility Freud has in mind in this passage is not
an instinctive but an acquired attitude. It is a product of reality
testing. It is the result of a long process of growth and accultura-
tion during which the infant and, successively, the child and the
adolescent discover that omnipotent thinking leads to delusion,
that gratifications are to be apportioned, and that frustrations
are the order of the day. Humility is born from renunciation of
the natural, primitive wish for instant and total gratification.
Humility is coupled with a sober reflection on the decisive
power of the reality principle over the driving power of wishes
that abide by the pleasure principle, leading to an awareness of
the compromises and bargains that must be made.

Humility, then, is a result of the eventual overcoming of
narcissism, or at least of its grossest forms. It is "acquiescent"—
it is a calming down from a state of urgent demandingness. It
is a matter-of-fact, sober, mature, and in its own way noble
attitude that accepts the universe for what it is: vastly superior
in power to any individual, and without personalistic qualities
of benevolence or malevolence.

For Freud, this humility stands in stark contrast to any religious belief, for the latter always involves some reneging on the
attitude of renunciation. The religious soul goes on demanding,
like an infant; he seeks wish fulfillment here and now through
fantasy formation in which he secures satisfactions which reality
as such does not provide. He turns the universe into an embell-
ished reality by considerable tinkering and artistry, in the service of finding a remedy for his unbearable sense of helplessness. In discussing religion, Freud always used the word
"helplessness" to describe the original feeling tone of man's
awareness of his smallness in the face of the universe, reserving
the word "dependency" for relations among people, such as the
dependency of an infant upon his mother, or of a weak person
upon a stronger person.

This insight throws into bold relief the dubious status of the psychological attribute of humility. Much that passes for humility is demandingness after all, as a good many saints knew centuries before Freud. Reverence and humbleness, two words that are easily pronounced by religious believers, may quickly acquire a functional usage in a larger extortionist plot through which people bargain for satisfactions, sometimes of a very selfish or childish kind. Pious humility tends to be embedded in a set of ulterior motives through which the world gets twisted out of shape in order to conform to an individual's desires. Pious humility is not submission to the unalterable features of reality, but to the whimsies of a fantasized Father-Creator who is to be charmed while one purports to obey him.

While pious humility may indeed promote humble men, socially and culturally speaking, it does not always foster the humbleness of renunciation, psychologically speaking. Some degree of narcissism is maintained, particularly by religious propositions that tinker with man's finiteness by holding out promises of immortality. For Freud the civilized citizen and the humane man, starting with humility as a desideratum of personal integrity and maturity provided a light in which religion appeared not only as folly, but as childish insistence on external support for the task of living. Religion satisfies too well, too quickly, and too defiantly in the face of a bleak reality which contains much evil. In contrast, the truly humble person must insist on abstinence: first, because reality demands it, but also in order to come to know himself better. Abstinence and self-discovery go hand in hand in the psychoanalytic process of healing and pedagogy. But there is a third reason for practicing abstinence, and that is its ennobling impact. The humble abstainers from religion refuse to duplicate love objects by inventing gods— they only cathect men or ideas, and with these they will have to come to terms in scrupulous honesty and without displacement. Nor can they use gods as objects of hate. What counts is the relationship with the Oedipal father—not his heavenly substitute, which would allow one to divide or split one's love and hate between the two.

For Freud, then, humility consists of a beautiful abstinence. In contrast to this somewhat Stoic ideal the special humbleness which makes believers prostrate themselves before their gods is suspect, if not phony. The dependency on the providential father-god (which Freud took as his model of religion)* is a sought dependency, a product of coping with the stress of having to grow up. From this vantage point, religion is a stylized and socially acceptable way of resisting nature's demand for growing up. Within its framework, some dependency can be maintained and even extolled: intrapsychically by cathecting God, and culturally by finding a niche in the shelter of church or temple.

But is the true humility which Freud advocated free from narcissistic bliss? Does it not also contain the seed of pride, in the sense that the avowal of abstinence may become an exercise in glorious competence? And does not Stoicism, which advocates harmony of the individual with the necessary workings of the world, have its own god-behind-the-gods? What is the status of fate or *Anangke?* While it is true that fate demands no worship and can hardly instill a cult, let alone allow itself to be cathected as an object, it does pose itself as a pivotal point of dependency. Fate reigns—it is so powerful that it leaves no alternative to obedience.

The third vantage point on coming to terms with dependency is James's. The term "humility" is not central in the *Varieties,* but there is an important cognate word: "surrender." At the end of his book's second chapter James cited with approval a German verse which beautifully captures the spirit of the reality principle and Freud's emphasis on renunciation:

> You must abstain! You must abstain!
> So goes the everlasting refrain. . . .[7, p. 51]

At this juncture James remarks that "when all is said and done, we are in the end absolutely dependent on the universe."[7, p. 51] The universe requires of us that we make sac-

*Implicit in Freud's criticism of religion is the notion of God as a love object. Reflections about the nature of God and man's needs for transcendent ideas may lead to the conclusion that the idea of God should indeed not function as a part in the whole of the universe (object) but as the principle of the universe (whole).

rifices and surrender ourselves to it. But what a difference it makes whether we surrender because of an imposition of necessity, with or without complaint, or whether we surrender in positive espousal of the principle of dependency! James then italicized his strategic remark that "religion . . . makes easy and felicitous what in any case is necessary."[7, p. 51] James attributed great functional significance to this feature of religion which makes it "an essential organ of our life."[7, p. 52]

There is no hedging here on the idea of dependency. Dependency is neither despised nor extolled; it simply follows from the nature of the universe and man's status in it. Dependency is inescapable: it is a fact of life. Religious beliefs make felicitous what is necessary, and they do so by the influence they have on our feelings. For James, religion was always more a matter of feeling than of thought anyway, and thus the important practical question is whether people accept their dependency and make their surrenders joyously or grudgingly, zestfully or passively, with a sense of meaning and purpose or in a mood of mere resignation, perhaps with great bitterness.

James did not by any means imply that all religion is happy, healthful, and zestful or that it gives predominantly libidinal satisfactions. He described at length the religion of the "sick soul" and the "divided self" and exposed with care the role that sadistic impulses play in religious preoccupations with evil and in some tyrannical forms of conscience. The satisfactions which certain forms of religion give may consist largely in the placation of a demanding superego that insists on *righteous* relations rather than *pleasurable* relations between man and God, and man and man. Acceptance of dependency in the "felicitous" way that religion offers is not always sheer fun. Satisfaction is not always drive gratification. Religion may satisfy the superego, ego ideal, or ego, but occasionally at a heavy libidinal price.

By inference, postures of unbelief or disbelief may ensue from various critiques of religion, but they too, like belief, must be proven by their fruits in the emotional tones in people's lives. Does unbelief enhance happiness and, if so, what kind of happiness? Does it give zest; does it bring out man's best potentialities? It certainly does, in some cases. There is a time in the life of men in which the rejection of religion—that is, the rejection of one's own previously held beliefs and what one holds to be the religious beliefs of other people—is felt as an experience of liberation. It frequently occurs after adolescence, in the years of young adulthood. Many motifs may play a role in such a rejection, and these amount to forms or types of unbelief.

Increased rationality may be one motif. Entering into adulthood is often accompanied by an attempt to take stock of the proportion between rational and irrational elements in one's life and values, with the conscious desire to expand the scope of rationality. One engages in a process of demythologizing, discarding old formulations of truth and adopting new ones which seem to fit better the cognitive temper of one's current phase in life. This can be a pleasure-laden process: it satisfies the yen for discovery and a desire for neatness and clarity in one's intrapsychic household.

Another motif in unbelief during this phase of life may be protest against the traditional belief systems of the parental generation whose dominant roles one is now gradually taking over. Coming of age means something like starting anew, this time on one's own, developing one's own premises, and playing the game by one's own rules. This requires some demolition work so that some psychic "urban renewal" project may get started, with a sense of purpose, zest, and dedication. One embarks on a project, and this may require not only abstinence from old comforts but active opposition to established projects which have had ample opportunity to run their course and now appear dead or doomed or bad. There is no profit in underestimating the enormous gratifications which such a project orientation can give, at multiple levels of meaning. It entails obvious satisfaction to aggressive impulses if the emphasis is on vilifying the parental generation's myths and failures. But the demolition work can also be seen as a means to a constructive end, and in that case the energetic engagement in the project may receive push from a noble fusion of libidinal and aggressive urges. Emphasis can also be placed on the righteousness of the project, in which case the ego can receive friendly nudges from the superego if it fulfills the latter's moral demands. And the emphasis can be on the joy, the momentum, the efficacy, and the thrill of the engagement itself, in which the ego's talents and functions are exercised or tested, leading to an increased feeling of competence or autonomy.

Coming to Terms with Autonomy

Indeed, a major motif in professed unbelief during the third decade of life may be the exercise of autonomy per se. But before we consider autonomy, a warning must be sounded. It is a peculiar feature of religion and much philosophy that their articulate spokesmen, the theologians and metaphysicians, have a great penchant for radicalizing the terms and propositions that are dear to them. Schleiermacher was not content to speak of dependency—he felt that he had to speak of *utter* dependency, *total* dependency, or *radical* dependency. Historically, the idea of sin has been radicalized into the concept of original sin; the idea of grace into the concept of irresistible grace. Dependency has been radicalized into contingency, with only one alternative: noncontingency. The distinction between the creator and the creature has been formalized into an ultimate and total difference in ontic status, power, scope, and other qualities. These are all examples of high-level thinking purporting to deal with ultimate realities. It is noteworthy, in contrast, that such radicalization has rarely occurred with the ideas of independence and autonomy as human attributes. The closest attempts I know at radicalizing these ideas occur in the book by Stirner (pseudonym for Caspar Schmidt) *Der Einzige und sein Eigentum* (The Individual and His Property, 1845) and the later works of Nietzsche, but both authors met with widespread resistance to their attempts. Without denying that there are religious and metaphysical reasons for the selective radicalization of some key words describing the human situation, the selectivity itself demands our attention. It makes autonomy and independence minor propositions, turning them into contravening factors of a lower order of reality, and often tainting them with sinfulness, evil, or falsehood.

But is this ranking and rating of terms by ontological weight commensurate with the ordinary, day-by-day experience of reality? Is ultimate dependency in the same class as autonomy in everyday experience? I think it is not, for in ordinary life (which may include considerable reflection) autonomy is matched with dependency, not with *utter* dependency. Autonomy and dependency are a pair, to be conceived relativistically.

The exercise of autonomy has always been a viable human option. Even Schleiermacher was open to it, although he was greatly concerned with drawing narrow limits around it. For Freud, autonomy is bound up with that special humility which abstains from the excessive and artificial dependency offered by religion. For James, surrender is intimately connected with the *will* to believe which is the fruit of man's own autonomous decisionmaking.

I remember vividly what a joy it was in my own young-adult years to pursue the possibility of transposing the traditional, Biblically based Calvinism of my childhood to the philosophical framework of Spinoza. That attempt itself was an exercise in autonomy, for it meant moving out of the game of revealed religion and faithful obedience to its premises into a new, self-chosen game ruled by the precepts of venturesome reasoning, by applying my own reason as well as I could in a spirit of freethinking. But apart from the autonomy of the act, there was also an encounter with a vision of man that allowed for considerable autonomy, largely due to Spinoza's tendency to identify willing and thinking. For me, God remained as large and constitutive as ever, but he lost his anthropomorphic features and became a process in which I could participate not by his whimsy but out of his—and my—necessity. This was an uplifting and invigorating vision—all the more so because its ethics were far from lax and thus gave additional challenge to the integrity of the relations between my ego and my superego. Maybe what fascinated me more than anything else was Spinoza's basic assumption of persistence in everything: "Each thing, in so far as it is in itself, endeavors to persevere in its being."[8]

If we can come down to the level of discourse at which rela-

tive dependency interacts with relative autonomy, as I hold
they do in daily experience, we will find a valuable guide in
Erikson.[9, 10] In Erikson's vision of individual human development, stages of mental growth are marked by thematic problem situations which demand a solution. Dynamic factors from
the nascent self, one's body, the introjected parental images,
the actual processes of family interaction, and the world of ideas
and culture combine to push the child, as it were, to the limit
of his current growth plateau, enticing him to make the spurt
or take the leap necessary to find a new integration at the next
higher level of development. In a broad way, such cardinal
variables as dependency and autonomy are not confined to a
specific age or state but run through the whole series of growth
stages which Erikson has mapped out. In fact, Erikson makes us
aware of a very important caveat in any theoretical approach
to the problem of dependency, by stating that "... dramatizing
the dependence of children on adults often blinds us to the
dependence of the older generation on the younger one."[10]
There it is: there are at least two kinds of dependency. One is
the dependency of relative helplessness in which the young
depend on the old for nurturance, as the weak depend on the
strong, and the have-nots on the haves. For the young, moreover, this relative dependency has a timetable which limits it
to a temporary phenomenon. The other kind of dependency
consists of the mutuality of object relations in which self and
other of all kinds, ages, and status serve one another's needs, for
good or evil. Parents need their children and depend on them
for their satisfaction; spouses need each other for the well-being
of both. But the powerful boss also needs his underlings, and the
sadist needs the masochist, as the tyrant needs the meek.

The mutual dependency of object relations has been recognized with perspicacity and daring consequentialness by some
religious mystics. Said Angelus Silesius: "I know that without
me God could not live one moment."[11] And the poet Rilke
caught the same theme when he asked: "What will you do, God,
when I die?"[11] And a Russian lad is reported to have asked:
"Does God know that we do not believe in him?"[12] How could
an "utterly dependent" creature come to such thoughts about

his creator? And how could an unbeliever have so much sensitivity to any deity? I think this is possible, first, by playing on the two kinds of dependency which I sketched, and by treating them as two intersecting lines or dimensions. "Utter dependency" and the mutual dependency of object relations do not run parallel. They produce surprising junctures, at which it is possible to combine as well as contrast the two. In the second place, the thought of the creator's dependency on his creature is made plausible, and rather beautiful, I think, precisely by any man's capacity to introject the image of God and live with him now more or less personalized and as having certain intentions, as an intrapsychic lover.

Even if one considers the remarks of Silesius and Rilke as arising from a mystical and somewhat rare borderland situation of religious belief, they do throw some light on possible borderland forms of unbelief. To put it bluntly: Is adherence to deism, which stages God as a cosmic clockmaker whose well-made contraption keeps the cosmos and all its contents spinning in predetermined cycles, a form of unbelief? Is adherence to the Leibnitzian computer God, whose mathematical genius has ordained the cosmos to a preestablished harmony, a form of unbelief? Or, for that matter, is any mere acknowledgment of a Prime Mover or First Principle a form of unbelief? To put the question differently: How much personalization of any God is needed to make belief religious? Or, still differently put, where is the borderline between religious beliefs embedded in creed and cult, and philosophical beliefs which function as assumptions or hypotheses, even though fervently held?

Religious belief demands more than the assertion of principles. It states more than hypotheses. It holds that somehow and somewhere there is mystery—a mystery that has a certain thickness and positive content, the mystery of "something there," as James said. This mystery, moreover, not merely elicits cognitive assent but orchestrates human feelings and produces action. Says Erikson: "Religion . . . elaborates on what feels profoundly true even though it is not demonstrable; it translates into significant words, images, and codes the exceeding darkness which surrounds man's existence, and the light which pervades it beyond all desert or comprehension."[13] Erikson has also pointed out that an important dimension of all faith and belief is whether the object of belief is held to be benevolent or malevolent. In either case, the object of belief is not merely conceptual but is invested with quasi-personal qualities of warmth, trustworthiness, animosity, steadiness, or reliability and endowed with intentionality. Mysterious as the object may be, it is associated with caring or threatening, friendliness or unfriendliness; at any rate it is seen as somehow "involved" and not an indifferent presence.

These aspects of religion point to another form of unbelief. With a strong penchant for rationality, one may reject the idea of attributing benevolent or malevolent intentions to the object of belief. One may reject any personalization of the object of belief, preferring to believe in principles of order or force of a general sort, without pointed intentions toward oneself. Such cognitive assent to a nonintentional principle of order or force, and a belief in its necessity, may be coupled with the courage to accept things as they are and as they come, subordinating oneself to "the scheme of things" in the knowledge that one is dependent upon it. In other words, the ontic, "utter dependency" may be accepted as an inescapable fact of life, but one refuses to elaborate that dependency by projecting upon it the dependency of relative helplessness that we all know from childhood and from the social inequalities in which we are embedded. Within the metaphysical sphere of utter dependency such a position would leave ample room for autonomy— and the courage to accept things as they come is itself a concretization of that autonomy. Indeed, a spiral may ensue in which autonomy and courage are mutually enhancing, each being both cause and effect of the other.

But autonomy, as much as dependency, has a personal history, as Erikson has been at pains to describe. In infancy the child will have experienced his helplessness in terms of either basic trust or basic mistrust in the (largely motherly) arrangements on which he is dependent. If trust is the prevailing attitude and hopeful cheeriness the dominant mood as a result of this early experience, a disposition is given that may last for life and that will subsequently color the way new information and experiences will be appropriated. Erikson sees in this early patterning of emotional experience one root of religion:

> Trust born of care is, in fact, the touchstone of the *actuality* of a given religion. All religions have in common the periodical childlike surrender to a Provider or providers who dispense earthly fortune as well as spiritual health . . .; and finally, the insight that individual trust must become a common faith, individual mistrust a commonly formulated evil. . . .[14]

To the extent, then, that a person prizes the psychodynamic continuities in his life and has no cause to disown his past, his fantasies and speculations about the ultimately real or the "something there" on which he knows himself to be dependent will naturally have associative links with parental caring (or rejection and neglect) and partake of the emotional quality of human object relations. Dependency may thus not only become a proper abstract idea to assert, given the scale differences within the cosmos, but actually *feel* good, pleasant, or blissful. Or, if basic mistrust was the original canalization of affective experience, dependency will feel dangerous, threatening, and awesome in its evilness because the cosmos, like the early parental figures, is endowed with malevolent intentions against which one must be on his guard.

But after infancy, things change. The next phase of life is so constructed by the confluence of inner states and outer relationships that the child will want to stand on his own feet—or at least practice what that phrase means in his as yet rather helpless and dependent situation. He wants to exercise choice and to claim a say in things. He will try to demonstrate autonomy, and to feel that he is a little powerhouse. These stirrings become acute when control over the body, especially the sphincters, becomes possible—and is socially demanded! "Holding" and "letting go" are the two conflicting modalities of experience that one must now learn to keep in appropriate apposition. Much of the acquisition of sphincter control, including the character traits practiced by the style of the child's efforts, centers on the questions: Whose will prevails—the child's own, or the parents'? Whose timetable and rituals will prevail—the child's own, or those provided by the culture? Who is to be obeyed—the self and the body, or the powerful caretakers and trainers? Maybe the deepest question is whether biology or culture shall prevail.

The anal phase is not the final stage for the practicing of autonomy. It gives only the first opportunity, but all "firsts" in life produce canalizations of experience and affects which elicit powerful habits and produce psychic structures which will leave their impact for years to come. As Erikson describes it, the risk in this stage is that under inadequate guidance there may be too much confrontation with arbitrary experiences of shame and nagging doubt. Traits of obsessiveness may develop, bespeaking an overly demanding superego in the making. Self-consciousness and sensitivity to social exposure may develop, bespeaking an early ego ideal which constantly confronts the child with his smallness, weakness, or ineptness. In coping with these negative internal messages the child as he grows up may adopt certain strategies to preserve some self-respect in the face of his denigration: stubbornness, shyness or slyness, suspiciousness, or a vindictive dedication to law and order.

At any rate, the experiential residue of this critical growth phase tends to link autonomy with patterns of obedience and internal states of shame or doubt. Autonomy can easily become cockiness, competitiveness, willfulness, or stubbornness, or it may be kept under the lid of dependency, in an atmosphere of chronic insufficiency feelings and low self-esteem. Both sets of traits are so common that one sometimes wonders whether anyone can resolve the issues of the anal phase in a harmonious balance, much less elegance (if the word "elegance" will ever fit the language game of sphincter control). At any rate, Erikson's observations and constructs do provide us with important clues about dependency and autonomy and their roles in belief and unbelief.

First, we shall have to repeat that in everyday experience autonomy and dependency are relativistic, proportionate terms. Life is a seesawing motion between the two, each being a correction of the other. We find thrill in autonomy as we realize our dependency, and vice versa. The old saying that what goes up must come down may be a good illustration of the physical law of gravity, but it is a poor adage of psychological experience. What is down may go up, for self-esteem and competence often have a self-stimulating character. And the seesawing movements between autonomy and dependency, as *felt*, may very well take place within and along with intellectual assent to the principle of utter dependency as a basis for religious belief. But they may equally take place in a context of vigorous unbelief or disbelief in any deity—whether the latter be rather abstractly formulated or greatly anthropomorphized.

Second, we must reckon with the likelihood that seemingly abstract propositions and ideas of some weight and seriousness are not as abstract as they may sound. It has been endlessly pointed out that the words "knowing" and "conceiving" have archaic roots in which the meanings of "thinking an idea" and "holding in erotic intercourse" coalesce. There are very few pure thoughts of exclusively intellectual order. We know a lot in our guts, through mood and emotional apprehension. Imagination is a powerful function in life, and by means of it existentially important ideas become personalized, pictorialized, portrayed, or symbolized. Our inner life is full of pictures and voices. And in the unconscious, ideas merge freely with people, so that one may symbolize the other.

This means that states of belief and unbelief are commonly laden with a rich inheritance of people and their ministrations to us when we were young—that is, when we were very dependent and made our first assertions of autonomy. It means that we cathect ideas as we do people: we do not merely contemplate them in consciousness, but we love or hate them, hold them benevolent or malevolent, embrace them or are on our guard against them.

The import of this insight is not that belief and unbelief are rather personal and subjective matters. One hardly needs any special insight for that platitude. It is, rather, that belief and unbelief are embedded in, and ideational portrayals of, our actual human object relations. Statements of belief and unbelief "feel right," just as the important persons in our life feel right and good to be with. This recognition brings the experience of relative dependency and autonomy again closer to the ideas of absolute dependency, total helplessness, and strict contingency which are advanced at the abstract level of theological and metaphysical thought, despite the conceptual distinctions we made between them. For the higher rungs on the abstraction ladder are supported by the same side pieces to which the lower rungs are joined, and the whole ladder stands on the ground of experience.

Let us take a more personal look. Schleiermacher's insistence on utter dependency, Freud's emphasis on helplessness, and James's advocacy of surrender probably derive some of their force from the way these men experienced and solved the conflict between relative dependency and relative autonomy in their lives. Schleiermacher seems to have viewed the idea of utter dependency positively, embracing it as much as he embraced the religious community of which he was a part. The idea felt right and good to him. Freud seems to have realized the idea of helplessness factually and to have accepted it stoically, trying to counteract it by holding out for considerable autonomy, including that proud self-discipline whereby one abstains from easy pleasure seeking. James knew that ontic dependency was inescapable, but he was concerned with learning to like it. The raw idea of it seems to have been hurtful to him, but he found that religious beliefs could make "easy and felicitous what in any case is necessary." Nietzsche, on the other hand, came to assert in his later works the idea of autonomy so strongly that the world wondered about the megalomanic roots of this thought in the philosopher's personal life. And some notorious paranoiacs like Rosenberg and Hitler liked the thought of autonomy so well that they used it to fan their own and their compatriots' hangups into a vast delusional system.

Third, Erikson's ideas about identity formation allow us to see dependency and autonomy as relativistic and interlocking partial strivings, as well as to understand something about the selective emphasis each receives in the lives of individuals. Erikson reveals both the personal and the social dynamics of the process whereby one or the other option becomes accentuated.

For identity is built from positive and negative identity fragments: identity implies that certain things are accepted and
other things are rejected, both with a sense of conviction, pleasure, satisfaction, and righteousness. Moreover, identity is
achieved and constantly elaborated in an incessant play of social
forces. Self and other are being compared and differentiated
ever anew in the interplay between the generations and the
"stages of man."

The process of identification in the nuclear family alone,
along the lines I indicated, contains a large number of possibilities or positions. If each person has a father and a mother after
whom he can pattern himself, he has two choices. If each parent
offers him a set of positive and a set of negative identity fragments he has $2 \times 2 = 4$ sets to choose from. And if pronounced
dependency or autonomy traits of each parent are associated in
various ways with the positive or negative identification fragments (the good or bad father and, the good or bad mother)
which are the building blocks of the person's identity, the
theoretical choices are $4 \times 4 = 16$. Given this large number of
options (already simplified by focusing only on the object relations with parents) available for each person, the vast congruity
of basic belief systems between parents and children is amaz-
ing.

On the other hand, if we take dependency or autonomy as
independent variables and consider either a characteristic trait
of a person (and possibly his guiding principle in working out
a philosophy of life or a religion) a multitude of meanings
derived from object relations will cluster around dependency
or autonomy. Such meanings will form patterns whereby
propositions of belief or unbelief are approached. They will
qualify beliefs and disbeliefs in many ways, and they will give
loaded words special connotations. We already noted that
Schleiermacher and Freud perceived very different things in
the one word "humility."

A modern complication of these subtle meaning clusters is
introduced by the uncoupling of dependency and autonomy
from traditional gender roles. To the extent that dependency
has been linked in the past with feminine behavior and au-

tonomy with masculine traits, the reassessment of gender roles
now taking place under the influence of modern feminism may
reduce the old polarization between the two postures. But this
may also lessen the comfort of the first-level traditional canalization by sex and augment the felt ambiguity.

Obedience, Then and Now

Traditionally, dependency has been associated with obedience by a great many social and psychological links. The worker
tipped his hat for his boss; the soldier saluted his officers. The
Hausfrau obeyed the rules imposed by her paternalistic husband; monks and nuns obeyed their superiors. Laymen obeyed
their priests and ministers, and everybody obeyed God. Children obeyed parents, and almost everybody obeyed the government. Obedience was not only a fact of life, but it was considered a virtue as well, which needed constant practice. It was
rooted in the special belief that the order of society was sacred
and that tinkering with authority was a sacrilege. Obedience as
a virtue is embedded in the sacred-cosmos view of the world in
which authority is hierarchically distributed from God down to
emperors and popes, princes and bishops, police chiefs and
priests, and so on to employers, teachers, and parents.

Erikson has described Luther as caught, nearly for a lifetime,
in serious conflict about obedience. The most nagging question
in his life was: To whom do I owe obedience? It is the pivotal
experiential question that deals with the implications for action
of dependency and autonomy. For Luther, as for many others,
the virtue of obeying had to be commensurate with the virtuousness of the authority to be obeyed. Therefore, the converse
of the question is also relevant: Whom should I defy? Or, in
more practical terms: Whom can I defy safely? In Luther's case,
the unresolved anal components of his conflict drove him to
pair obedience with defiance, in ambivalence. It also drove him
to struggle intensely over the purity and virtuousness of his love
objects: How could he obey his father if his image of that man
contained so much evil, which cried out for defiance? And how
could he obey God if his image of God contained so much

harshness and cruelty? And so, the natural distinction each person makes between the good and bad qualities of his father became for Luther an irreconcilable pair of opposites: a good father separated from a bad father. Similarly, he could obey God only after eliminating from the divine image all traces of the "bad father" by projecting these onto the image of the devil. The paradigm was: obedience to the good father and defiance of the bad father in the name of that greatest of all psychic goods; conscience.

But conscience is, in a classic psychoanalytic phrase, the precipitate of abandoned object relations. What conscience prescribes and proscribes has much to do with the love and hate we have had for the persons on whom we depended for satisfactions in the early stages of life. And the distribution of those loves and hates extends to the ideas and the rules which these persons portrayed. Conscience primarily guides and judges the self, by bestowing love and hate on all the thoughts and feelings we experience in the pursuit of satisfaction. It sorts and sifts the obedience and defiance patterns.

What happens when obedience is no longer considered a virtue to be practiced in any and all encounters with external authority? Since Luther's day the distinction between external authority and the internal authority of conscience seems to have widened, with the result that obedience to conscience in disregard of external authority has become a viable, and at times noble, option—to some more virtuous than the old virtue of obeying the powers and principalities. Conscience has achieved a great deal of autonomy in our cultural estimation of it. It makes demands on the self for obedience to its rules, while also exhorting the self toward defiance of flagrantly contrary demands imposed by the external world. Some forms of modern alienation can well be understood and appreciated as conscience-induced defiance, as an ethical warding off of foreign impositions which, if obeyed, would make the person unloving and unlovable in his own eyes.

As Mitscherlich[15] has pointed out, the dominance of the father has waned for centuries as Western society has moved from feudal-agricultural arrangements to the modern industrial corporation pattern. The importance of father images and father symbols has declined; as the title of Mitscherlich's book puts it, we now live in a "society without the father." Patriarchal and paternal patterns are seen as archaic residues, no longer suitable in an age of participatory management and strong appeal to individual self-determination. This observation enables us to forecast a change in the structure of conscience, or register a change that has already taken place in some people. It is a change in the direction of multiplicity and pluralism, increased selectivity in the building blocks that compose conscience. If fathers and father symbols such as God, Caesar, pope, generals, policemen, employers, or teachers are no longer as dominant as they once were, they are also less likely to serve as admired identification figures to whom one is totally devoted. They are all likely to be split up into multiple good and bad fragments, and as a result the identifications are becoming more partial, selective, and fragmentary. Even in childhood and adolescence, peer influences may become stronger in proportion to parental influences. As a consequence, obedience is less likely to be total obedience to certain persons or person symbols but may incline toward a selective obedience to specific principles extracted from many different encounters with greatly varied love objects.

As I have sketched it, such a development does not amount to a watering down of conscience or the relinquishing of obedience. At its best, the new trend may elevate conscience to a high-minded guide which does not demand slavish conformity but fosters loyalty to select principles which are held with positive feelings and conviction. But such a good outcome would depend on great integrative capacity of the personality, stimulated by basic trust and enhanced by adequate practice of the partial dependencies and the partial autonomies that form the dignity of man. But the new process of conscience formation has its dangers. At its worst, conscience may become so fragmented that it fails to help the ego with guidelines for behavior. Pluralism played to the hilt may produce a conscience that is composed of snatches of allowable and forbidden things, in odd mixtures that lack consistency and order.

Much of today's contending about beliefs and disbeliefs seems related to the function of obedience in a complex society in which the old, hierarchical ordering of authority has lost its halo and the vestiges of traditional authority have become suspect. And belief, as well as unbelief, is heavily determined by the primary choices one makes between dependency and autonomy. The author and film critic James Agee wrote in one of his letters to Father Flye: ". . . I am a frenetic enemy against authority and against obedience for obedience's sake, and against 'society' insofar as 'society' is content with itself."[16]

Flatfooted obedience is no longer a virtue; the modern emphasis is, rather, on selective disobedience. These trends seem to come to a head in the increasing modern posture of civil disobedience. In turn, civil disobedience teaches us something about life's basic parameters of dependency and autonomy. Whatever the essence of civil disobedience may be, it thrives on selectivity. Its occurrence is testimony to the fact that in modern experience, dependency and autonomy are no longer regarded as fixed attributes pertaining to the person as a whole. Few people today are describable as obedient or disobedient for the duration of their lives. There is no longer any virtue in obedience as a character trait. We now find that both dependency and autonomy are qualities which are apportioned and variously distributed *within* the personality. They pertain to the structural divisions within the self. In psychodynamic theory we have learned to speak of the autonomy of the ego—not to denote its measure of power vis-à-vis other people, but to describe its relative strength in dealing with the urgency of the person's drives, the demands of the superego, and the enticements of the ego ideal. Similarly we are learning to speak of the relative autonomy of the superego and ego ideal, the relative autonomy of drives. In clinical practice we find that the superegos of some persons are "utterly" dependent on external reinforcement—they need constant buttressing by social control devices, special milieus in psychiatric hospitals, or specially arranged transitional object relations that offer opportunities for new identifications with both the persons and the values these stand for. In other cases, we find superegos with great autonomy, which may need to be analyzed in order to achieve somewhat greater tolerance or to make the person more aware of its loving features.

After this lengthy analysis of the challenge that the ideas of dependency and autonomy present to each person—yesterday, today, and tomorrow—I can do no better than present the following review of treatment goals in psychoanalysis, recently presented by my colleague Ernst Ticho: (1) establishment of mature personal relationships; (2) overcoming narcissistic self-centeredness; (3) increased tolerance for frustration, with good knowledge of one's limitations, and capacity to endure the anxiety, suffering, and depression that are part of ordinary living; (4) a more tolerant, integrated, and loving superego; (5) a sense of identity, with the attendant awareness of one's goals and responsibilities and of how to integrate them, and (6) the undoing of repression.

> At the end of analysis there is not only freer access to the infantile mainsprings of love and hate but also access to infantile dependent tendencies. The freshness of experience and the spontaneity of childhood—just as the initiative and activity of the phallic phase, and the enthusiasm and idealism of adolescence—will find sympathetic response in us and give richness and depth to our feelings.[17]

CHAPTER V

Coming to Terms with Mystery

Quite a few authors whose works achieved wide circulation during the past decade have taken our society to task for its overwhelming dedication to technology and technical expertise, and to the thought that competence in making or organizing something will eventually abolish all or most human woes. They have also pointed out that a great many young men and women, in particular, have begun to see the dehumanizing effect of technology when it becomes the dominant value orientation. And so technology, formerly invested with great expectations, begins to lose its halo precisely when it becomes institutionalized into a technocracy and allowed to roam the human habitat like the sacred cows of India.

Roszak[1] speaks of *technocracy's children* who, "miserably educated as they are, bring with them almost nothing but healthy instincts." These healthy instincts are critically discerning; they lead to protest against and rejection of a world view that extols nothing but competence in physical and human engineering. In *The Greening of America* Reich[2] sounds the same tune of rebellion against and rejection of the state of mind which, with omnicompetence, habitually seeks to dominate all experience in order to demonstrate its mastery over the world. In Marcuse's[3] *One-Dimensional Man*, industrial society is on the one hand taken to task for the surplus repression it has imposed. On the other hand society is expected, by virtue of the affluence it has brought, to stimulate a need for liberation from excessive repressiveness. Man can then be set free to pursue wider erotic satisfactions which have little to do with competence and technology.

The list of observers who have thus criticized today's prevailing values can surely be multiplied. It includes almost all existential philosophers and playwrights. Much of the critique of the technological world view and what it has done to man's mind comes through obliquely in the theater of the absurd.[4] In a world of overwhelming technical competence and collective know-how, what are the values and feelings that make life human and worth living? Do frequently repeated moon explorations add one whit to human happiness, or do they even vouchsafe what little happiness there has been on the long trek of humanity, when one notes that the same technical competence douses the world with napalm? Small wonder that alienation, protest, and revolutionary ferment exist in millions of people. Small wonder that millions of others experience emptiness, depression, and nihilistic laissez-faire. In Beckett's[5] play *Waiting for Godot* nihilism is not discussed as a willfully assumed philosophy of life, but portrayed as a half-anguished, half-bored state of mind to which one simply finds oneself captive, unable to resist or defend. It is just there, and one cannot blame anyone for it. Similarly one cannot shed tears over a condition which is so absurd—not absurd as judged by the standard of anything meaningful that should be upheld, but as manifestation of *The Absurd* in its autonomy.

Observations of this order by men who feel the pulse of a culture, an era, or a generation demonstrate something about belief and unbelief. They show that the world cannot be neatly and simply divided into a camp of comfortable believers, sure of their beliefs, and a camp of equally comfortable unbelievers, sure of their unbeliefs. Rather, most people, at least in today's world, are between beliefs and unbeliefs and find themselves contending about loyalties and struggling for clarity between the options.

Novak[6] has eloquently described the modern conundrum:

increasing numbers of people today seem both to believe and to disbelieve, with divided allegiances. The crisis of belief, once quite shocking, is now matched by a crisis of unbelief, equally shocking in terms of the searches it produces. The phenomena of the generation gap do not by any means suggest that all young people think alike and that all people over thirty have homogeneous beliefs. Rather, between the young and the old there is an accentuated contending or vying between one option and another in values, life styles, and basic outlooks on life, with each of these emphatically held and demonstrated.

Those who are against "the establishment" are by no means all young and not by any means all anarchists. Rather, the establishment (to the extent that it has some homogeneity at all) is surrounded and embattled with animosity by spokesmen for alternative patterns of power, justice, and other values, albeit on diverse grounds. Some proposed alternatives would lead to equally awesome establishments. In the bewildering pluralism of our time, then, the task of identifying oneself is not limited to espousing certain beliefs and rejecting everything else in unbelief. It is, rather, an anguished process of coming to terms with all the major beliefs, unbeliefs, and disbeliefs to which one is exposed, as well as the vehement strife between man and man and within every solitary breast. Most of us are most of our lives between all kinds of belief and all kinds of unbelief, in shifting patterns. What Lifton[7] has recently described as the Protean personality—based on observations of people in their early twenties who shift from one belief system or life style to another, seriatim, by short-lived experiments with abrupt conversions—may be only an exaggerated surface manifestation of a deeper instability of belief characteristic of most of us, anywhere along the age scale. We have an awareness of being "between the times," in an interim period between eras, and between the many beliefs and unbeliefs of yesterday and tomorrow.

The Rediscovery of Mystery

It is noteworthy that yesterday's hyperrational, positivistic, and technological world views have elicited a kind of protest in which the very word that was scorned and rejected by the builders has been chosen as the cornerstone for another project. That word is mystery. Technical reason does not like mystery —it prefers manageable problems, and sets out to solve them, one by one. The story of human reason is a glorious series of advances on the territory of mystery in which the latter has shrunk considerably, if not deemed to have been eliminated decisively. Mystery has now been delegated to the diversionary sphere: we can read mystery stories in which the "whodunit" question is logically answerable from the start and all that matters is the reader's stupid imperceptiveness which dooms him to a few hours of suspense. Or we can look benignly at all the funny things that the people of yore (surely not our kind of modern people) did in the great archaic mystery cults of Sumeria and Greece, and the folksy medieval mystery plays. And so we may satisfy our originological curiosity, as Erikson[8] would call it, with the exhilarating feeling that we have come a long, long way—away from mystery. Except for a few irritating unpredictabilities that remain, such as the next move of Russia, of which Churchill is reported to have said in 1939 that it is a riddle wrapped in a mystery inside an enigma.

The works of Martin Buber[9–12] are laced with references to mystery: the mystery of being, the mystery of encounter, the mystery of what he calls "the realm of the between"—the narrow ridge between the objective and the subjective where I and Thou meet. These are all philosophical and anthropological formulations of mystery. As a Biblicist, Buber also speaks freely of the mystery of God, and the mystery of the beginning when heaven and earth were created—neither from something nor from from nothing—one does not know how. Another existential thinker, Gabriel Marcel,[13, 14] has been at pains not only to restore recognition of mystery in the modern mind but to develop a concise phenomenology of mystery. Marcel makes a distinction between problem and mystery, which I will paraphrase as follows. A problem is a challenge to the intellect, eliciting a detached objectivity by means of which it can sooner or later be solved. Problems are posed, and formulated, by the human mind itself and made manageable to its cognitive premises. A mystery, however, cannot be approached in this way. It cannot be "solved." It demands recognition, and it elicits personal involvement in an encounter that brings the person face to face with its presence. Says Marcel: "A mystery is a problem which is entrenched upon its own givens, which invades them and by that token goes beyond being a problem."[13] The idea of mystery implies the notion of power. It is related to the idea of value. Mystery poses itself; it touches the human being. It belongs to the sphere of the Thou. Mystery remains, even when all problems one can think of will have been solved.

Kafka[15, 16] saw mystery—unfathomable and overwhelming mystery—in the powerful way in which undefinable systems impose themselves on the lives of individuals. Whatever one associates to the veiled fantasy images of Kafka's *Castle* and Court *(The Trial)*, one ends up feeling that he has only made a guess or taken a stab at something essentially dark and ungraspable. The very essence of castle and court is mystery; one cannot solve it, one cannot get closure on it. And the existential question that arises in dealing with those oppressive mysteries is: how can one prevent himself from becoming frantic and paranoid?

Marcel has also pointed out that one cannot approach mystery with a technique in attempts to come to grips with it. *Homo faber* stands with useless hands before mystery. The same message is strongly implied in Buber's descriptions of the mystery of encounter. *Doing* is of no use vis-à-vis mystery—what counts is *being*. These are familiar existentialist phrases. They say, often much too ponderously, what we all know from experience, namely that there are certain situations and occasions in life which elude the grasp of reason and flout the dictates of logic. And these are precisely the thrilling, uplifting, or tragic experiences.*

*I used in an earlier paragraph the word *uplifting*. I confess that in my own emotional household this word is the closest rendition I can give of the technical philosophical term *transcendence*. The trouble with transcendence is that many of its users have fallen into the habit of not bothering to specify from what and to what anything transcendent transcends. The word is much too intellectual and thus becomes quickly a cliché in technical writings. In my own case I have found phenomenal aptness in translating it into *uplifting:* raising aloft.

No matter what we may think and feel *about* a great work of art, in the last analysis it eludes our grasp. Instead, it grasps us, and all we can do is exclaim. The so-called mystery of being is not a philosopher's invention—who has not at some time in his life contemplated, with awe, whether he really is or whether everything including himself is only a chimera? Mystery is present in realizing that one is alive, and notably when one is in love. The popular song goes: "Ah, sweet mystery of life!" and those words do not mean that life or love is a puzzle or a problem. Strip the romantic "sweet" and one is still left with an experiential thickness beyond comprehension. And so one sings.

In his *Varieties of Unbelief,* Marty[17] remarks that the originality of modern unbelief, as compared with older forms of unbelief, rests to a great extent on reluctance to deal with transcendence. He finds that the predominant emphasis is on people's immediate experience. For example, the question of God is apt to be quickly shoved under the rug by the attitude: Whether God in general is dead or not, he is dead *for me,* and that's that. Marty's statement needs some amplification. Emphasis on immediate experience may also take the form: Whether God in general is dead or not, he is alive *for me,* and that's that, without further cogitation, let alone inquiry into his transcendence. It is enough that "He walks with me, and He talks with me. . . ." And as one can see every day, emphasis on immediate experience, in the sense of getting some kick in a dull or meaningless life, leads to the concoction of quite a few strange transcendents in witchcraft and astrology cults, in Satanism, and in fantasies of unidentified flying objects. While thoughtful people may question whether those occult items are worthy specimens of the transcendent, I would hold, sadly, that they are seriously regarded as transcendent by their devotees. And so one sees on the one hand a reluctance to deal with the transcendent, on the other hand great zealousness in fabricat-

---

The reader should feel free, as I do, to think of moments in his childhood when he was lifted up by his mother or father, in mutual joy or in an effort at consolation. Or when he was raised up so as to look over the heads of a crowd, to see the action.

ing something transcendent or in looking for transcendence where there is none. To apply Marcel's distinction: some things that pass for mystery are little more than trivial puzzles or misplaced problems.

The Mystery of Evil Reappreciated

The rediscovery of mystery and the role it plays in human life does not pertain solely to mysteries that are positively intriguing or enchanting. Some people will focus on love, life, being, or the encounter and feel thrilled by the mysteries they discover; others disclose how they stood face to face with the abhorrent, how they felt dread, and how they discovered the raw reality of evil. Since evil in all its forms has been omnipresent from the dawn of civilization, if not from the world's creation, one cannot say that evil itself must be rediscovered, now or in any previous era. People have always lived with it and felt surrounded by it, with a consistent urge to protect themselves from it or seek its mitigation. And often, while seeking to mitigate evil, people have found themselves augmenting it again by inappropriate matchings between means and ends.

But what must be rediscovered from time to time is the mysterious quality and status of evil. For despite the patent occurrence of evil events and situations in the lives of any group and any individual at any time in history, evil is not always seen as mystery. In optimistic times when everyone shares a keen sense of progress and feels competent to tackle the problems that beset society and individuals, evil may tend to be seen as "a problem"—one of those left over from previous times which proved to be obstinate, but which one hopes could be solved or dispelled if only enough people would be willing to put their heads together and develop a plan. And since some concrete evils have indeed been warded off or lessened—for instance, some forms of infectious disease, much physical pain, and periodic mass starvation owing to crop failures—such optimism is not entirely groundless, if vigilance and diligence continue to be exercised. There are ways of reducing poverty; there are ways of reducing cruelty; there are ways of preventing some

wars. It has been possible to prolong life amid the onslaught of
ravaging diseases. It is possible to foster a spirit of cooperation
rather than cutthroat competition.

But progress is rarely linear and almost never comprehen-
sive. It seems that for every concrete form of evil mitigated a
new form springs up. And some forms of evil are so perennial
and culture-free that they are taken to be paradigmatic of *all*
evil. Death is such a paradigm, as are the feelings of hate and
the urge toward aggression. And all three are today no longer
regarded only as outside forces which will sooner or later in-
trude upon an unsuspecting individual to overwhelm him, but
as inside forces as well, which beset him from the cradle to the
grave. Even if exterior rearrangements were possible to prolong life, foster love, and curb aggression, most of us today are
convinced that an interior constellation of these same forces
holds us in their grip, in a doom from which no one can escape.

And so, even the most blatant optimist, the most zealous
do-gooder, and the most skillful denier of reality will have a
hard time upholding the belief that evil is only an as yet unsolved problem, an odd misconception, an unfortunate mistake,
a temporary flaw, or a neutral negative, like the absence of
good. And the instrumental theory of evil, which holds that it
functions as a spur to accomplish the good and to instruct us
about a weakness that can be overcome, is no longer respectable, let alone popular. To thoughtful people it has always been
suspect, anyway, for it has all the earmarks of a pedagogue's
trick.

Freud was no optimist and no denier of reality when he
contemplated the situation of mankind. He spoke persistently
of the helplessness of man in the face of the overwhelming
powers of nature (and sometimes of culture). In his groping
thoughts about the death instinct he saw organic life perpetually emerging from the inorganic but always pulled back by the
inertia of matter, so that each individual life in man and beast
is like the hesitant flickering of a small light describing a short
arc in the vastness of darkness. Using the same imagery, others
have speculated about the possibility that each of the little lights
is at least a spark of some Great Light which maintains itself

somewhere in the universe, and will eventually illumine everything. Such a thought may be consoling and ennobling, but it cannot rule out the darkness, large or small, in which that Great Light shines. If darkness could be entirely dispelled, light would no longer be light. No metaphor about light can abolish the reality of darkness—in fact, it presupposes that reality.

Mystery and darkness have much in common. They are not merely annoying puzzles. They are not merely the absence of clarity. They have an oppressive thickness that envelops and overwhelms us. They elicit dread. They crop up in unexpected places and at unforeseen times. They pose themselves mightily and inescapably. And some mysteries, such as the dark "problem of evil" as the philosophers call it, pose themselves without the least glimmer of light at the end of the tunnel. Our time knows this and affirms its tragic implications. Some latter-day Satanists and witchcrafters even extol it.

Mysterium Tremendum et Fascinosum

One of the best works ever written about mystery and its impact on man's experience is Rudolf Otto's[18, 19] celebrated book on the holy *(Das Heilige)*. Its subject matter is not mystery as such, but the various qualities of reality and dimensions of experience which are elicited when the holy is encountered. For Otto, the holy is a special category of reality and experience, just as beauty and morality are such categories; they are all special in the sense that they are original and irreducible aspects of human life. In the language of Kant, they are a priori categories, with unique and independent qualities.

For our purposes, the most fascinating parts of Otto's work deal with the phenomenology of the holy. What happens, what is given or experienced, when a person is in the presence of something he regards as holy? Knowing that most readers would tend to equate the holy with gods, but wanting to keep his focus broad enough to include all manifestations of the sacred, Otto designated the objects of his refined descriptions as the *numen, numinosity,* and *numinous experience.* The original meaning of the Latin word *numen* is the divine nod of the head whereby a deity accepts an offering or gives approval to his worshipers. By derivation, it has come to stand for anything divine, sacred, spiritual, magical, supernatural, or primordially energetic and creative.

Perhaps the most basic aspect of numinosity is its presence—the way it poses itself in any encounter. The philosophical question of whether numinosity is in the eye of the beholder or whether it emanates from the numen is, of course, an important one, but Otto asks us first to be open to the phenomenology of numinous experience. In it, whether the numen appears of its own accord or whether it is invoked, its presence determines the relation between the beholder and his numinous object in such a way as to reverse the usual power relations between subject and object. The numen grips; it casts a spell. It constitutes itself. It is overwhelmingly there and thereby sets the stage for the relations between subject and object. The subject feels himself small in comparison with the greatness of the numen. Before one knows the specific qualities of the numen and before one can name it, it poses itself mysteriously, ambiguously revealing and concealing itself to the beholder.

Why is the holy or the numen a *mystery?* Because our first reaction to it is silence, muteness, dumbness. It forces us to "shut up"—at least for a moment. The Greek root *mys* in the word "mystery" means shutting the eyes or mouth, both because mystery has the power to overcome and because its essence is secrecy.

We have here a description of mystery which rings true to the richness of experience. What Otto describes has nothing to do with mystification or mystique, which to the cool-headed man are pejorative words for muddled thinking, promoting unnecessary secrecy. It has nothing to do with the taste for the arcane and the occult which has had its occasional fads. Mystery is a borderland situation in which something both powerfully reveals and powerfully conceals itself, and its self-concealment is a feature of its essence. Our incapability of "solving" it in the way we are able to solve any puzzle or well-formulated problem is not due to inadequate thinking or poor training. Mystery alludes to the experiential and perennial fact that some very important aspects of reality stubbornly resist analysis. The mystery of creation, the mystery of the universe, the mystery of God, the mystery of love, the mystery of death, the mystery of evil—one can eliminate them from one's problem list only at the price of truncating human experience. Even if one chose to go through life with blinders, the mystery of death will introduce a final day of reckoning in which those blinders will be useless. On this sober point, the theater of the absurd and many existentialist short stories seem to agree with the more elaborate affirmations of the pious and the romantics.

Otto went on to describe the mystery of the holy as being profoundly ambiguous. Its effect is double-sided: it attracts and repels. In Otto's fanciful Latinisms, the holy is a *mysterium tremendum et fascinosum.* Its mystery is *tremendum* in the sense that it evokes tremor, shuddering, or shaking, the typical accompaniments of dread. The uncanny elicits a special feeling, best rendered by the English word "awe," and its derivations "awesome" and "awful." It causes fear and trembling by its darkness, hiddenness, and overbearing powerfulness. But the mystery of the holy is also *fascinosum:* it attracts, it intrigues, it fascinates—and it also elicits a special feeling: *bliss.* As the *tremendum* wards off, the *fascinosum* simultaneously beckons. One fears to approach it, yet feels powerfully drawn to coming close to it. It is important to note that the attraction-repulsion dimension of the numinous is not perfectly correlated with its revealing-concealing dimension. One can be attracted by the revealed as well as the concealed aspects of the numinous, as one can be repelled by its manifestations as well as its hiddenness. Similarly, the emotional states of bliss and awe are not neatly matched with, respectively, the revealed and concealed sides of the numinous. The most important features of Otto's phenomenology of the holy are its dynamic ambiguity, its combination of contrasts, and its capacity to induce complex cognitive and emotional states.

The cognitive state induced by the holy includes the awareness of the subject's creatureliness. In any encounter with the holy, the parties assume definite roles: the subject is the creature, the holy is the creator; the subject is of smaller scope, the holy of larger scope; the subject's power and energy are less than those of the holy. All the subject's experiences are relativistic, since, in the encounter with the holy, they are measured against the vastly superior or absolute attributes of the holy. At this point, Otto takes Schleiermacher to task for his radicalization of man's state of "utter dependency"—if utter dependency were the primary datum, the feeling of the dependent self would be the nucleus of self-awareness and the whole idea of the holy could be seen as a defensive fiction brought in to ameliorate the dependent human condition. In other words, Otto spotted the psychologism, or at least the grave danger of it, in Schleiermacher's work. For Otto, the starting point is neither man nor the holy in isolation, but the total reality of two parties in an encounter. It is *in the relationship* to the holy that man becomes aware of his creatureliness as well as the divine "otherness."

Otto's phenomenology thus unfolds into a parallel series of relations and interactions between man and the holy. They are not stimulus and response, or need press and satisfaction; they are what Otto calls "moments" of experience, from which I want to abstract the following correspondences:

Experiencing Man Subject of Experience	The Holy/Numinous Object of Experience
Self	Wholly Other
Creature	Creator
Awe, dread	*Tremendum*
Smallness	Majesty
Quickening	Energy, Source of Life
Wonder	Mysteriousness
Admiration	*Fascinans*
Self-devaluation	August, Grandeur
Profane	Holy

Though all knowledge concerning the numinous starts with experience, it cannot be entirely explained by experience. In fact, the experiencing subject tends to attribute to the numinous itself the ultimate origin and the initiative for his encounter with the holy. Mystery is not conjured up—it poses itself.

We have noted that writers who have proceeded from a sense of wonder for mystery have not always displayed equal interest in the whole scale of mysteries with which man is presented. An empirical selectivity seems to be at work: some people are preoccupied with, say, the mystery of love, while others are preoccupied with the mystery of evil. Polarities of good and bad, life and death, love and hate, pleasure and pain, seem to run through the gamut of mysteries and may affect the practical choices people make. In Otto's descriptions of the mystery of the numinous, these polarities are combined into a patterned whole of dynamic ambiguities and interactions. For Otto, the mystery of the holy elicits both awe and bliss, approach and avoidance, rejoicing and guilt feelings, trust and fear, quickening and self-effacement, faith and doubt, all in complex interaction. The ability to grasp such a pattern of dynamic interactions is part of Otto's modernity; his is a twentieth-century model.

Is There a Talent for the Experience of Mystery, Numinosity, and the Transcendent?

In the later editions of his famous book,[19] Otto assumed something like a disposition or talent for numinous experience, with the implication that there is individual variation in the strength of such a disposition. Some people, such as Moses, Mohammed, St. Augustine, and Luther, have a genius for experiencing the holy; others have only a weak awareness of it. And like all talents, a stimulating environment is needed to bring the talent to fruition. Nature and nurture cannot be separated. Moreover, it follows from Otto's phenomenology as well as his epistemological assumptions that the numen itself is active in eliciting man's experience of the holy: something in outer reality corresponds to the subjective experience. The holy has manifestations; it comes through in theophanies, which mean literally "appearances of the divine."

For the sake of the following argument, I assume a great deal of similarity and parallellism between the three categories of experience which I have thus far used: numinous experience, the experience of mystery, and the experience of the transcendent. They are not identical; each category has sprung up in a special context of discourse. But mystery has been described by those interested in it in very much the same way as Otto described the holy, and the transcendent is frequently described in terms of God, the All, the mystery of being, or some other "ground" of reality which is acknowledged with reverential feelings.

What truth, then, is to be given to the idea that a disposition or talent may exist for experiencing the holy, mystery, or the transcendent? Are there any clues to the psychology of such experiences? On what might belief in the holy, mystery, or the transcendent be based, and what might constitute the corresponding unbelief or disbelief? There is a promising vantage point on these questions in psychoanalytic object-relations theory, particularly in the observations and formulations of Winnicott.[20, 21]

As a pediatrician and psychoanalyst, Winnicott has paid close attention to children and their mothers and how they interact with each other, with their bodies, their selves, and the world which they share. He has made astute observations of infants and children at play, in solitude or in company, and has made important theoretical contributions to the understanding of infant and child development. Like nearly all students of early human development he has tried to trace the process whereby the "me" (infant as subject) and the "not me" (mother and others as objects) become differentiated out of the matrix of the original mother-fetus and mother-neonate symbiosis, and how the nascent self becomes articulated vis-à-vis the world or outside reality. The process of differentiation has a bearing on cognitive development, for the infant is from birth on faced with the problem of the relationship between what is objectively perceived and what is subjectively conceived. Behind that terse formulation lie some distinct fragments of developmental-cognitive theory, as yet poorly integrated, but rich in potential.

One theoretical fragment holds that the infant mentally takes in bits from the world just as he physically takes in food from the world. He "introjects" these bits much as he eats food. Similarly, the infant gives off, or "projects," to the world his mental residues just as he physically eliminates his waste products by urinating, defecating, or spitting. He engages in these two processes, however, not as an isolated unit, but in a special context which normally prevails in infancy only, when the mother is maximally adaptive to her newborn baby (for instance, by being ready to nurse him when his stomach demands nursing). Her great sensitivity to the timing of her infant's needs and the promptness and richness of all her ministrations allow the infant to think that her breast is part of himself, controllable by his wishes and urges. When he thinks "milk" the breast is there, or on the way to him, with little delay. The special environment that the mother creates in this hyperadaptive period is not yet seriously frustrating. Within the self, a protoconcept emerges, probably composed of many sensory phenomena and feelings, of milk-breast-mother. It is likely that this rudimentary bit of thought is a hallucinatory image which contains vivid traces of taste, smell, temperature, texture, vision, and kinesthetic impressions. It is as if the breast is created by the infant over and over again, out of his needs and from his capacity to love. For by this time he is already practiced in loving, having been in the closest vital contact with his mother before parturition. Says Winnicott:

> To an observer, a child perceives what the mother actually presents . . . but the infant perceives the breast only in so far as a breast could be created just there and then. Psychologically, the infant takes from a breast that is part of the infant, and the mother gives milk to an infant that is part of herself.[21]

What happens when the hyperadaptive period is over and the mother begins to impose delays in gratification? The infant now has wish-fulfilling hallucinatory thoughts which provide substitute satisfactions that come to stand in distinction to the actual gratifications which the mother and others provide at their own schedules, dictated to a much greater degree by the requirements of the outer world. Subjective, pleasure-oriented thinking becomes differentiated from objective, reality-oriented perceiving. "Me" becomes distinct from the "not-me," as "inner" from "outer." Mothers and other objects become "good" as they satisfy, "bad" as they frustrate. In addition to the internal objects (such as breast and other fragmentary symbols of the mother) which came about by introjection and magical, omnipotent thinking, external objects appear. Such external perceptions elude magical control; they may be good or bad, pleasant or unpleasant, satisfying or frustrating, or combinations of these qualities, alternatively or mixed. They may be frequently present or only sparsely so; they may be close or somewhat distant. But they all appear in their immutability, beyond the infant's manipulative control, albeit his projections upon them may color, change, or distort their objective reality. For instance, "bad mother" memories and feelings, stemming from earlier introjections, may become projected on the now differentiated, real mother and thwart accurate perception of her.

And so a difference grows between what is subjectively *conceived* and objectively *perceived*, and a distinction emerges between the subject with its limits and the object with its contours. It is the difference between mentation under the pleasure principle and mentation under the reality principle. Slowly, interaction between "me" and "not me" becomes possible, with constant mutual checking and correcting, so that inner world and outer world are experienced each in their uniqueness and both in their mutuality. While much will be added to this basic pattern in years to come, the person will retain, indeed elaborate, the capacity to keep the two worlds in appropriate and useful apposition, deploying his attention in an inside as well as an outside direction, and seeking a proper balance between the two. This includes the capacity to compensate for experienced deficiencies in the outer world by drawing on the richness of the inner world, and vice versa.

The other theoretical fragment that Winnicott offers derives from some homely observations. Infants use parts of their own body to stimulate and satisfy another part: they use fingers and fist to rub against the lips or to stick into their mouths. After a

few months, they tend to become strongly attached to a piece
of their blanket, a soft toy, a rag doll, or some other special
object which they keep close to their bodies, often their mouths.
Sometimes they suck a finger while the rest of that hand holds
the special object. Such action often occurs before the child falls
asleep or when he is overtly frustrated, fidgety, anxious, or
depressed. It took a Winnicott to emphasize the corollary of this
obvious observable situation: that the mother and the rest of the
family seem to realize instinctively that the baby's special object stands in a very precious, intimate, and intense relation to
him that has (in my words, not Winnicott's) an almost sacred
connotation. That odd piece of blanket or that much-fingered
rag doll is to be kept near the baby as his possession. It should
not be laundered as often as his clothes and bed covers, for it
is unlike all the other objects in the baby's world: it is his property, his cherished symbol. Perhaps it combines many fragmentary elements of the total mothering situation and elements of
his nascent selfhood, but for the child it is not an internal object
in the sense of a mental image or an external object at par with
all other things in the world. The mother does not argue
whether her infant has a right to that special object, or whether
it is internal or external to him, and the whole family takes a
ritualistic attitude toward it without questioning right of possession or propriety of choice.

Winnicott infers that the transitional objects and all the go-
ings on around it (which he calls the transitional sphere) are the
origin and first practice of illusion. In my words, *the transitional
object is the transcendent;* it is beyond the ordinary division we
make between the mental image produced by the mind itself
and the objective perceptual image produced by the real world
impinging upon the sensory system. Illusion is neither hallucination or delusion, nor is it straightforward sense perception.
Illusion also includes mystery: since it is beyond the merely
subjective and the merely objective, it has a special object relationship endowed with many surplus values about whose
legitimacy one does not bicker. Its validation lies in the encounter with the special object itself. And illusion also includes the
holy: the special object is held as something sacred and so re-

garded by third parties also. It may become a fetish. It is held reverentially. One's dealings with it may become rituals. In the transitional sphere a language emerges which takes certain attitudes for granted as expression of a unique verity, which cannot be reduced to mere "subjective nonsense" or "cold, hard facts of perception."

The transcendent, mystery, and the sacred are not equivalent to the so-called security blanket of the infant merely because they have primitive origins. The security blanket is only the beginning of an infinite playful relation between mind and world, and the first illusion focusing on the first possession will typically disappear in a few years. Some of the infant's early illusions will lead to disillusionment, but in the meantime a sphere and a manner of relation have been created in which things are not merely what they are perceptually, and not simply flimsy imaginings either. Winnicott himself sees in the transitional sphere and the transitional objects the beginnings of human play, and the origins of religion and art, but to the best of my knowledge he has never articulated their contact with religion as I have. His statements on this point have remained programmatic.

Movement from the pleasure principle to the reality principle is a lifelong endeavor. Relating inner world and outer world produces some strain. Winnicott has pointed out that relief from this strain comes from an intermediate area of experience whose inner or outer reality is not challenged. This intermediate area, and the actions engendered within it, are *sui generis*. Nevertheless, as Winnicott has also suggested, only a fine, thin line divides the illusory intermediate reality of religion and art and the hallucinatory projections and delusional ideas which indicate madness. Adequate reality testing is needed to keep the transitional sphere properly bounded, and its content and language consensually validated.

As Winnicott has described the special characteristics of transitional objects, the infant assumes rights over the object, with the agreement of his parents. Yet there is some abrogation of primitive infantile omnipotence. The object is cuddled and excitedly loved, or mutilated. It may not be changed, except by the infant himself. It must survive instinctual loving and hating. It must seem to give warmth, to move or do something to show it has vitality and a reality of its own. In addition, the infant's playful dealings with the transitional object find some clues in the mother's attitude: she also initiates play and deals with certain objects in a special way. She too adopts a language, a ritual, and a mood of playing in which she elaborates the transitional sphere. In other words, the style and content of the transitional sphere are not entirely the child's own creation *de novo*. There is external reinforcement and outside encouragement or initiative. As Erikson[22] has said, all ceremonies begin with the greeting rituals which mothers spontaneously adopt upon revisiting their infants after a short separation.

And so the difficult question of a disposition or a talent for the numinous resolves in the more manageable observation that reality is not simply split between an inner and an outer aspect, but permits an intermediate sphere in which one can have various degrees of practice, usually at first a joint practice of mother and child. The transcendent, the holy, and mystery are not recognizable in the external world by plain realistic viewing and hearing, nor do they arise directly in the mind as pleasurable fictions. They arise from an intermediate zone of reality that is also an intermediate human activity—neither purely subjective nor purely objective. They derive from transformations of the subjective into something original, as they derive from transformations of the objective into something special. Their peculiar reality, which is both imaginative and concrete, is clarified by regarding works of art: the painting transcends both the dream and the three-dimensional visual world; the marble bust is not merely an idea or simply a piece of rock.

Art is obviously not prized by everyone to the same degree. Artmaking is not everybody's forte, and art appreciation is specialized. A certain vision, a certain touch, a certain mode of contact, a certain kind of object relationship, requires a practiced eye, an openness to wonder, the capacity to be arrested by the illusion of a world on a flat plane in a frame or a moving form in marble or bronze.

As art creates a third world, which transcends pure idea as

well as pure matter, so religion, to cite Erikson's words again, ". . . elaborates on what feels profoundly true even though it is not demonstrable: it translates into significant words, images, and codes the exceeding darkness which surrounds man's existence, and the light which pervades it beyond all desert or comprehension."[23] One can hear in Erikson's words the echoes of numinosity, mystery, and transcendence.

Belief and Disbelief in Mystery

But not everybody who is aware of what feels to him profoundly true and who knows of the darkness and light of existence will feel constrained to elaborate his feelings in religious ways, by religious beliefs, through religious practices. Some people do not need to play or like to play; they may not have been encouraged to develop the transitional sphere. Instead, they may have been goaded to notice only the outer perceptual world with its facticities and its inherent laws, some of which have proven to be discoverable. One may become a realist with profound loyalty to the immutable features of the natural world and to its determined processes without need to elaborate his relations to it in the religious manner. The outer world can be approached with a no-nonsense attitude that sets out to solve its puzzles and problems. In fact, the outer world is so large, so grand, and at times so splendid that it can command great devotion and loyalty. Freud felt "humble" toward it. Einstein's phrase "I am a deeply religious unbeliever" seems to capture his loyalty and his close bond to nature in the word "religious," while abnegating the relevance of the ritualized transitional sphere to him in the word "unbeliever."

Conversely, the transitional sphere and the relation to transitional objects may remain undeveloped because of overactivity of the inner world of dreams and hallucinatory wish fulfillment. The private world may remain too full of instinctual products. The unchecked fantasy may be too gratifying. No external objects are necessary: the internal objects derived from fragmentary incorporations suffice for a modicum of well-being. But since life in such a completely autistic privacy is hardly possible, it is more likely that frequent projections occur which falsify the outer world of the senses beyond recognition. Self and world become dreamy habitats, subject to magical control and omnipotent manipulation.

One may call this alternative "sick" if one wishes. It is the world re-creation in fantasy of the pure pleasure ego, in which pleasant fictions are substituted for unpleasant actualities, unalloyed by the demand of reality testing. It should at once be acknowledged that the history of religion and the history of mystery cults and even the history of philosophy have shown great indulgence toward the fantasy products of the pure pleasure ego. The so-called supernatural has been a receptive screen for all kinds of projections. Illusion in Winnicott's sense has often shaded over into hallucination or delusion. Many entities have first been conjured up by the unbridled imagination and then spotted as actors in the outer world: vampires, demons, incubi, phantoms of the dead, or in our technological age, unidentified flying objects. Souls have taken wings, virgins have become mothers, and gods have been seen sitting on clouds with books in their hands. In a word, the religious heritage is tainted by excessive fantasy formation and at times flagrant disregard of the obvious features of outer reality.

The fantasies inherent in religious history, with their underlying psychodynamic implications, result in highly subjective or idiosyncratic beliefs which ride slipshod over the evident messages of the outer world. Obviously, much religious psychopathology follows. Schreber's[24] *Memoirs of My Mental Illness* describes in detail that author's belief that he had become God's wife, and that he participated in a cosmic scheme which would radically change the sex differences among people. In one of his psychotic episodes, Boisen[25] believed that the Day of Judgment had arrived as he saw all humanity streaming "like in a vast circulatory system" from all corners of the earth in order to be judged. Swedenborg[26] had visions of heaven and hell full of pseudoscientific minutiae. From time to time someone proclaims he is Jesus and starts acting in line with his unchecked fantasies of Jesus. The recent mutilation of Michelangelo's Pietà in Rome's St. Peter's Church by a man with a long-handled hammer is an up-to-date example. And many a dear soul goes on believing that a literal room has been reserved in his name in a heavenly mansion. Such autistic beliefs, although some of their implicit ideas have a foothold in Biblical metaphors or derive their words from hallowed phraseology, are corporately transmitted. It is eminently sane to disassociate oneself from such concepts, or to decry them in patent disbelief or unbelief. Aware of all this, who would not like to be, as Einstein, a "deeply religious unbeliever"—reserving the adjectival phrase "deeply religious" for the awe that the grandeur of nature may inspire in him, for the humility which necessity elicits, or for the reverence with which he has glimpsed the mystery of being in an encounter with some other person?

The same judgment, by and large, must be brought to bear on magical thinking and magical practices. Belief in magic also derives from hyperactivity of the pleasure ego and a very weak tie with outer reality. Magic manipulates power—a power of narcissistic origin projected onto the world and then charmed, conjured up, or maneuvered in such a way as to reappropriate it for self-aggrandizement or for cutting down one's enemies. The blatant disregard of outer reality, so patent in magic, not only makes magical acts silly but inflates the self with each repetition by furthering the enslavement to the pleasure principle. Whatever is deemed to be transcendent in today's renascence of witchcraft and Satanism does not arise from the playful and delicate transitional sphere, but seems a crude projection of the "bad mother" imago, tantalized, bitterly fought, and battered about in a fictionalized "outer world." And whatever is held to be mysterious in these cults is not Otto's *mysterium tremendum* or Buber's mystery of being, both of which elicit wonder and reverence, but bungled mystifications which flout the laws of the outer world. Again, disbelief or unbelief in magic is an elementary sign of sanity—but the persistent hold of magic on the masses and the occasional lapses into magic by individuals of the mature elite show how difficult it is to abrogate belief in magic entirely and consistently. Even an otherwise sane person, perhaps even a dry realist, when anxiously awaiting the results of an important examination, may find himself "knocking on wood" or being careful not to step on a crack in the pavement.

The outer world, which I have thus far identified largely with nature, has nevertheless a very important nonnatural dimension: culture. The dimension of culture transmits to each individual an enormously complex set of ideas and acts, accumulated over generations, many of which are now presented to him in vivo, particularly by his significant love objects. Each individual is exposed to a barrage of notions which include ideas about human selfhood, the world, the ideals of maturity, religion, and art, and indeed all kinds of special uses of Winnicott's transitional sphere itself. Playing, believing, practicing the imagination, admiring beauty, wondering about mystery, and having thoughts about transcendent realities—for all these activities the culture provides codes and norms and words and values, in addition to live portrayals of their practice by members of one's group. Each child is born into a cultural world already linguistically full of philosophical abstractions, religious propositions, artistic styles, and so on, and their plausible alternatives or opposites, together with the rules of the various language games one can play with these words. And each culture, subculture, and family presorts the accumulated stock for its children in accordance with its preferences—that is, its beliefs.

Thus, a child grows up not only in a welter of beliefs and disbeliefs but is inculcated to believe and disbelieve selectively. One of the best empirical demonstrations of such complex patterning of beliefs and disbeliefs has been made by Rokeach[27,28] and his co-workers. Using various scales to measure the strength and cohesiveness of belief systems, they found that the preference of one person for another is powerfully determined by mutual congruence of beliefs, and that beliefs in turn have the double dimension of being held as similar (and close) to those of "friends" and contrasting with (and distant from) those of "enemies." To know what beliefs one is opposed to is apparently an important co-determinant of any belief one holds. Beliefs and disbeliefs are arranged on a continuum of similarity: for the open mind, with many gradations; for the closed mind, with a greater penchant for dichotomies.

Logically, then, belief in mystery will be influenced by the climate of the times and prevailing opinion. Apparently mystery and the search for something transcendent are becoming respectable again, as the wave of positivism is subsiding. Beyond the fads and fashions and the occult experiments of the lunatic fringe there are earnest attempts to recapture contact with the *tremendum* and to give due weight to life's "peak experiences" for the kinds of truth that neither the solipsistic mind nor the outer world in its factualness can give. Much explicit attention is being paid to the transitional sphere, notably by explorations in depth of the role of play in life (following Huizinga's[29] *Homo Ludens*) and by renewed interest in celebration. Within organized religion the key word is liturgical renewal, which will, it is hoped, allow believers to recapture the full affect that should be commensurate with their beliefs. Within the sphere of psychological therapy and pedagogy much is made, under various names and schools of thought, of prompting people toward lively, multisensory engagements with one another, so that they may experience in wonder the mystery of being and personhood instead of meekly pigeonholing themselves into social roles. Logical reasoning and good reality testing are being augmented by efforts at contemplation, not only to achieve greater mastery over one's mind and body, but primarily to enrich consciousness by contact with a transcendent reality dimension and to widen the scope of what can be perceived in one's self and one's world.

But what seems more heartening than contemporary culture's renewed acceptance or active advocacy of these things is that the beliefs thus engendered are likely to become existential beliefs. As Rokeach has pointed out, some beliefs directly concern one's own existence and his identity in the physical and social world. These tend to be held centrally in the personality, so that they become prime organizers of other beliefs of a lesser order. Certain elements in the youth culture portray this vividly. Beneath the frills of dress, emblems, and odd diets one can find in many young people a determined effort to organize life around the humanistic ideal of openness to self and openness to others, or around religious belief in brotherhood and charity.

The very fact that conversions are reported to occur with some regularity suggests a desire for a change of heart—in the central beliefs, and not merely for a rearrangement of the more superficial values and peripheral beliefs. Keniston's[30] young radicals were seeking congruence between the deepest beliefs of their parents, with which they were greatly identified, and the life styles that should logically follow from these beliefs. They sought to match truth with consequences, by and large by substituting for some of the subordinate and derived beliefs of their parents a different pattern of second-order beliefs which would seem to fit better with the key convictions. From a clinical viewpoint, these positive strivings in the youth culture suggest that its members have had, by and large, a good and wholesome early life experience, with "good-enough mothers," in Winnicott's term. They have an obvious capacity for satisfying object relations, at least with selected men and women. They have made positive identifications with some of the major beliefs and values of their parents. In fact, Keniston notes that the alienated radical students he studied emulated their mothers in many ways and admired their intelligence, intenseness, and artistic and other gifts, although they found much to object to in their mothers' dominance patterns and possessiveness. It was their fathers who appeared weak to them. The students' stories in response to the Thematic Apperception Test showed what Keniston calls the theme of a Pyrrhic Oedipal victory: "the younger man who defeats the older man, but only to be overcome himself by some extraneous force."[30]

In other segments, however, the culture also shows a great preoccupation with the occult and produces odd patterns of syncretistic beliefs. It comes as a shock to most liberals and to the upholders of religious pluralism that today fundamentalist versions of Christianity appeal to many young people, including youth from Jewish homes. I put the preoccupation with the occult and the lure of fundamentalism together in one paragraph because in both instances one finds much concretization of darkness and evil, much polarization between good and bad or God and devil, and an apparent longing for authoritarian leadership. In both cases, the operational emphasis is on suggestion and control of the individual by the group with, at times, hypnotic effects. These phenomena are surely far from playful and far from rational; the predominant affects which they employ, moreover, are anxiety, a sense of persecution, and feelings of guilt and shame. In a recent comment on those preoccupied with the occult, Ehrenwald[31] suggests that such regressive attitudes may be produced by a spectrum of upheavals, involving persons with psychotic and severely neurotic disorders, otherwise acculturated persons with rarefied interests in the parapsychological, and cultists, sectarians, and faddists. Ehrenwald proposes that many of the more psychologically healthy cases involve a reaction to "myth deprivation." Commenting on the influence of demythologizing, he says: "If you deprive mankind of its daydreams, of its primal or Ur delusions, man has to look for something else to fill the void." Although this statement fails to distinguish between various kinds of myth (which may range from the sophisticated recreations of Sophocles down to the loose fantasies that lie behind palm reading and the use of tarot cards), there may be some truth in the assertion that the anxious zeal of these devotees is a response to deprivation. Deprivation of myths is not necessarily a component. Deprivation of activity, practice, and stimulation of the transitional sphere may be crucial, along with adequate exposure to other players engaging in ceremony, ritual, worship, or celebration on the basis of shared beliefs.

Mystery and De-Alienation

Throughout the modern descriptions of mystery by Otto, Buber, Marcel, and others runs an epistemological theme: knowledge of "the other" is a precondition for knowledge of self, and vice versa. Only as we encounter others in their "otherness" do we know ourselves in our selfhood. The same theme is implicit in the later work of Maslow,[32] who held that peak experiences and the Being-cognition that accompanies them are the hallmark of the truly self-actualizing person.

The conception and ontological status of "the other" obviously affect belief. For Otto, who dealt with the experience of the holy, "the other" is clearly God as a transcendent "wholly other." For Buber the Biblicist, "the other" is God, but for Buber the humanist, "the other" is also other human beings and the community. Marcel would also recognize in "the other" a transcendent, divine being as well as another human being who transcends, when encountered, the subjectivity and solipsism of the solitary individual. These are all applications of the Hebrew thesis that the knowledge of God co-varies with the knowledge of man. Only by knowing God can man know himself, and only by knowing man can one know God. This epistemology, which undergirds the whole Judeo-Christian tradition, is rich enough to allow for the possibility that "God" may be discovered in encounter with other human beings, or that "God" resides in the righteous community.

As Bertocci has shrewdly observed, a decided effort has been made in Maslow's works to put this concept in strictly humanistic and naturalistic terms, without reference to any supernatural dimension. "He has dispensed with the farther side of the More in James' supernaturalistic overbelief. He has accepted the experience of conversion without interpreting it as human-superhuman interaction."[33] Despite differences between Maslow and the religionists, the self-actualizing person has his moments of transcendence and conversion in that he is not solely driven by deficiency motivation but acts (at times) by growth motivation. In other words, he transcends himself; his Being-cognition is a lucid, revelatory awareness of the essence of self and others gained through heartfelt engagements. It seems to me that Maslow's very term "Being-cognition" implies the idea of the mystery of being, inasmuch as this special awareness is beyond the ordinary recognition of quotidian things and facts and events. Maslow's is only a somewhat truncated variant of the old Hebrew epistemology.

In all these formulations, whether theological or humanistic, there is an implied reference to alienation and de-alienation. They all proceed from the observation that ordinary life, ordinary consciousness, the ordinary social ambiance, and the ordinary themes of culture can have a profoundly alienating effect. Despite all his alertness, knowledge, and coping endeavors the individual runs the risk of knowing neither himself nor his fellowman well. He remains caught in social roles, he is liable to all kinds of prejudice, he functions as a cog in the vast machinery of society and culture—and he learns to accommodate himself to these givens and even, if he can, to eke out a modicum of contentment in his captive state. This is the state which Marx and Feuerbach and Hegel called alienation.

The other implied message in this chapter is that mystery has the power to overcome alienation. Whether it be Otto's *mysterium tremendum,* Buber's mystery of being, or Maslow's special Being-cognition, openness to mystery boils down to allowing oneself to be gripped by "the other"—God, man, or community. In this sense, coming to terms with mystery is coming to terms with one's self.

CHAPTER VI

Coming to Terms with Options

When one surveys the works of William James, a number of typical Jamesian terms gradually enter his stream of thought and become signposts of the master's presence: *pluralism, varieties, options, richness, more.* They all bespeak James's aversion to monism of any sort, his revulsion to any dogmatism, and his suspicion of any reductionism. He liked to have choice and to exercise choosing. For James, the outstanding feature of experience is richness, as the outstanding feature of the universe is its colorful diversity full of surprises. Even his word picture of the human infant conveys a recognition of the plentiful: "To the infant, sounds, sights, touches, and pains, form probably one unanalyzed bloom of confusion."[1] Thus did he speak first in *The Principles of Psychology.* Later, in the *Briefer Course,* this phrase became the now celebrated " . . . one big blooming buzzing confusion."[2] The world of James is not a miser's world, and the language of James is not a skimpy idiom.

For James, the old problem of the association of ideas quickly became the "stream of thought"; the psychology of religion became, as the subtitle of the *Varieties* says, a study in human nature; and reflections on belief gave rise to the term "over-belief." It is as if in James's mind everything that is considered becomes enlarged. When everybody, on Darwin's impetus and

123

in Spencerian fashion, searched for the developmental origin of anything, James called attention to the outcome, the fruits of a process or action, and pointed to the crucial difference between the results of one act and another act. When everybody talked determinism, James showed the virtues and the necessity of indeterminism. When positivism had made reality manageable by shrinking it, James set out to make reality more intelligible by expanding it. When everybody collected hard scientific data fit for mathematical treatment, James recorded lengthy and unwieldy biographical statements and direct impressions, not scorning the anecdotes of everyday life. Long before the existentialists and somewhat earlier than the methodical phenomenologists, James held out for unadulterated experience. His real man, the subject of psychology, is a real person, with real experiences, in a real world on which he has a real influence. His beliefs make a real difference; his religion is a real attempt to deal with his real existence in a real universe.

Small wonder then that James's basic ideas have remained alive long beyond the moment of their formulation and are as relevant today as they were three-quarters of a century ago.

Willing to Believe or Disbelieve

If the material of the previous chapter is still on the reader's mind, he may—nay, should—be arrested by the following phrase: "The universe is no longer a mere *It* to us, but a *Thou*, if we are religious; and any relation that may be possible from person to person might be possible here."[3, p. 27] Is it Buber speaking, or Otto? No, it is the voice of James, in 1896, in his lecture *The Will to Believe*. Leaving justification *by* faith to the theologians, James wrote in justification *of* faith, pursuing the psychological, philosophical, and moral viability of "a voluntarily adopted faith."[3, p. 2] And so he related faith, one of his lifelong preoccupations, to willing, another process which fascinated him during his whole career.

This approach, which should not be misread as ending up in whimsical voluntarism, makes believing a project, to use a favorite existentialist term. It holds that every person is entitled to engage in a project, through which he comes to terms with life's essentials *for him*, on which he can put his stakes, through which he may fulfill himself by taking hold of reality as reality appears and applies to him. A man takes a notion or gains a vision, he sees a choice and makes a decision, and in abiding by his decision, in courage, he finds out who he is, or rather, who he becomes. Today, such a sketch of the process of identity formation seems acceptable enough, barring the need for greater detail. And the embeddedness of that process in person-to-person relations is also readily acknowledged. The important formative relations are I-Thou relations. But James goes much further: Could not the quality, the essence, of person-to-person relations be isomorphic with a person's relations to the universe? Does not the universe have a "face" for each of us, does it not show us its "features," for comfort or fear, like or dislike? Are there not similarities between what we believe about persons and what we believe about the universe? If we succumb to the temptation of dealing with other persons as *its*, are we prone to regarding the universe as an *it* also, or vice versa?

The *Will to Believe* is an oddly titled essay. Is believing really a matter of willing? Can one simply will to have an opinion? Pascal's wager argument for the existence of God may trip a person into ordering his life around the belief that God exists —but are the argument and the chance taking it induces the wellsprings of any such gambler's belief, or was the belief there earlier, on other grounds, so that it could lead to rationalization in terms of gambling odds? Beliefs are induced by "fear and hope, prejudice and passion, imitation and partisanship";[3, p. 9] they vary with our socioeconomic situation. Imitation is a particularly potent determinant of beliefs, for James recognized that often "our faith is faith in someone else's faith," especially in "the greatest matters."[3, p. 9] We are bound to believe in the beliefs of those people we feel bound to. The will to believe thus seems a flimsy notion: we do not have that much inner or outer freedom to arrange our beliefs. What James was after is not so much a purely voluntaristic choice between beliefs, as the "right to adopt a believing attitude in religious matters, in spite of the fact that our merely logical intellect may not have been coerced."[3, pp. 1-2] The essay merits the title: "The Right to Believe."

Any right to believe includes the right to disbelieve. Disbeliefs too are determined by fears and hopes, prejudices and passions, imitations and partisanships. They too are conditioned by socioeconomic situations and are embedded in identifications and imitations, so that one can paraphrase James by saying that our disbeliefs are often expressions of faith in someone else's disbeliefs. James the pragmatist puts it very nicely: we disbelieve, as a rule, anything for which we *have no use*.[3, p. 10] What we have no use for may be simply out of our pale, outside our frame of customary assumptions, or contrary to our habitual style. Or more forcefully, we may have no use for certain facts, theories, or beliefs because they would be in conflict with other facts we appreciate, theories we uphold, or beliefs we cherish. One can hold disturbing facts and values at bay by using the mechanisms of denial or suppression. One can choose to be myopic. But for how long and at what cost?

> Our passional nature not only lawfully may, but must, decide an option between propositions, whenever it is a genuine option that cannot by its nature be decided on intellectual grounds; for to say, under such circumstances, "Do not decide, but leave the question open," is itself a passional decision,—just like deciding yes or no,— and is attended with the same risk of losing the truth.[3, p. 11]

This thesis of James's militates against indifference. It is both a psychological and a moral thesis. It says that people choose between options (and thus hold beliefs) because they are motivated to do so (by whatever inner needs and outer pressures). It implies that not choosing warps human nature, and is at bottom a disguised way of choosing anyway. To put it popularly, one can risk sins of commission as well as sins of omission, and one is accountable either way. The thesis is moral also in the sense that we have to fulfill our duty toward our cognitive nature: "we must know the truth; and we must avoid error,— these are our first and great commandments as would-be knowers. . . ."[3, p. 17]

The twofold duty of believing truth and avoiding error leads to an immediate, crude typology. In certain people the pursuit of truth is paramount and the avoidance of error only a secondary function. These are the affirmers, adventurers, hearty believers, and enthusiasts who hold positive opinions, for whatever reasons and on whatever grounds, even if they may have to change their opinions from time to time. There are also people whose main concern is the avoidance of error, letting "truth take its chance."[3, p. 18] Cautious, critical nay-sayers, their minds are vigilant for the purpose of avoidance. Though they may be believers, their watchfulness overtakes their enthusiasm and narrows the scope of plausible propositions. Quite a few religious dogmatists are of this ilk. But many nay-sayers are likely to be articulate disbelievers in mass opinions and to assume the posture of unbelievers when faced with traditional affirmations of enthusiastic believers. As James put it, they do not want to be "duped,"[3, p. 19] but in their constant fear of pitfalls they may assume too glibly that most other people *are* being duped by the beliefs they hold.

This little typology will have a ring of practical truth to most psychiatric ears. Excessive and accentuated examples of the two types can be seen in the hysterical and obsessive-compulsive personality organizations respectively. A closer look shows divergent superego functioning: in the hearty believers the accent lies on the engaging "do this and do that and I love you" side of conscience; in the cautious minds disposed to disbelief the emphasis is on the forbidding "don't do this and don't do that or I will hate you" side. Conscience is both friend and taskmaster, but these roles are differently proportioned in different people. The friend's or taskmaster's roles of conscience also pertain to the ego ideal: in hearty believers the ideal is richness with risks; in cautious spirits and skeptics the ideal is purity and safety. Early interpersonal experiences and object relations are likely to engender ego factors which predispose a person toward one or the other side of the typology. The believing enthusiast, at the risk of being too gullible or somewhat cavalier in his reality testing, seems to proceed from a position of basic trust. Being duped is not his foremost concern, for things have turned out all right for him in his years of dependency, and his very beliefs may have given substitute satisfactions when reality seemed grim. For him, the mental act of affirming and the physical act of embracing are of one piece. On the other hand, the fear of being duped, which is so prominent in the skeptic and the cautious critic, must have deep roots in early disappointments which promoted a sense of distrust and defensive vigilance. If love is felt to be conditional rather than absolute, belief will be felt as conditional too, dependent on criteria of purity, exactness, tit-for-tat reciprocity, and careful reality testing which guards against disappointments.

But the duty of believing truth and avoiding error can be discharged only when a person sees genuine options before him. The will to believe or the right to believe demands a setting in which choice is possible as well as necessary. James approached the act of choosing by means of his concept of genuine options.[3, pp. 2-4] A genuine option has three qualities. It must be a *live* option, a hypothesis that is personally relevant and plausible, given a person's personality and cultural milieu. For instance, in America many persons have had a live option to be either Catholic or Protestant, while the choice between being a Muslim or a Hindu has been a dead option. Second, the option must be a *forced* option and not an avoidable one. For instance, the filling out of bureaucratic forms demanding a check mark at the traditional triad "Protestant, Catholic, Jew" is a forced option for any of these religions, since it excludes irreligion; but when the box "None" is added, this option is avoidable. Third, the option must be a *momentous,* not a trivial, one. The momentous option demands a significant stake, a commitment; it presents a weighty opportunity whose acceptance or rejection entails some risk. Thus, the genuine option is live, forced, as well as momentous for the person who is to choose and so embark upon a belief. Dead options, or avoidable and trivial ones, may present us with interesting intellectual exercises but place themselves outside the sphere of belief.

Several classes of queries and demands pose genuine options and in so doing may elicit the will (or the right) to believe. Moral questions are of this order. What is good or bad cannot be ascertained by outside criteria; moral issues elude logical demonstration, sensory proof, and scientific verification. Moral issues can be approached only by moral stances—that is, by moral beliefs—and these are decided by our will. James also felt that personal relations or "states of mind between one man and another" pose genuine options. His own example is the question: "Do you like me or not?"[3, p. 23] If one is not allowed to dodge such a question, it can only be answered by belief, often by an added belief in the reciprocity or mutuality of the liking or disliking—a trace of faith in someone else's faith. Some large-scale social situations also pose genuine options to the will to believe. When a mugger accosts a helpless victim in the streets of a city while dozens of bystanders watch without moving a finger to help, one must infer that each watcher believes no one will join him in concerted action. Even worse, each bystander may believe that all others will act like fighting dogs in which the whole pack will demolish itself. *Homo homini lupus!* The option is momentous, live, and forced—and one cowers before it. But in cowering one makes a genuine and momentous choice.

Finally, James recognized the question of religious faith as posing a genuine option and a momentous choice. The choice for or against religion cannot be fully determined by logical argument or scientific proof, although logic and science may qualify the formulation of religious belief and the details of its tenets.

For the purposes of his essay, James defined religion as making two assertions:

[1] . . . the best things are the more eternal things, the overlapping things, the things in the universe that throw the last stone, so to speak, and say the final word.[3, p. 25]
[2] . . . we are better off even now if we believe the first affirmation to be true.[3, p. 26]

Religion is a momentous option: anyone who chooses for it is bound to gain by belief and to lose by unbelief. Religion is a forced option: one cannot wait for more data, wait for some sort of proof, or postpone a decision about it until there is more light. The choice is always *now*, for waiting and postponing and en-

gaging in skepticism are themselves ways of deciding for the
present between the options. Though in trying to postpone the
choice one would avoid error if religion were untrue, one would
also lose its good if religion were true. Both the believer and the
unbeliever play stakes. The believer says: "I'll try, and shoulder
the consequences." The skeptic or unbeliever says, in James's
words: "Better risk loss of truth than chance of error."[3, p. 26]

Though James stood on both philosophical and psychological
ground in his case for the will to believe, the crux of his argument is best caught in that marvelous psychological capsule:

> Dupery for dupery, what proof is there that dupery through hope
> is so much worse than dupery through fear? I, for one, can see no
> proof; and I simply refuse obedience to the scientist's command to
> imitate his kind of option, in a case where my own stake is important
> enough to give me the right to choose my own form of risk.[3, p. 27]

There it is: the will to believe is the right to choose at one's own
risk. Everything live, forced, momentous, and genuine is risky.
The will to believe proceeds from a sense of autonomy and an
act of spontaneity. The will to believe, indeed any act of will,
affirms our identity and at the same time shapes it further, not
by whimsical choices between frivolous options but by thoughtful choices between momentous options.

James hastened to add another psychological detail. Religions
tend to represent the more perfect and eternal aspects of the
universe in personal form. While such representations may be
animistic, and then decried as primitive or childish, they may
well be experienced in mature ways. The earlier quote from
James is relevant: "The universe is no longer a mere *It* to us, but
a *Thou*, if we are religious." Any relation possible between
persons can be transferred to our relations to the universe.
James spotted and stated this similarity or congruence on the
condition "if we are religious," thereby linking it to religious
belief and the religious world view. Psychoanalytic reasoning,
and maybe James himself as well, had he thought of it, would
assume the same possibilities of congruence in states of unbelief
or disbelief. World view, self-view, and view of others are
dynamically related. What we know about infant and childhood

development suggests that all three views become articulated from birth on, in close interaction with one another. When one takes the momentous option of believing the universe to be a gigantic machine, one is likely to see the human body, that important part of the self and others, as a machine also. Possibly even the mind is viewed as a machine. In fact, logical consistency demands such a view, and the behaviorist fallacy has at least the merit of logical consistency.

But not all beliefs are the result of genuine options and momentous choices. Some choices are playfully or sloppily made, between avoidable or trivial options—"just for the heck of it." Not all choices result in existential beliefs. The synthetic function of the ego is not always so strong that perfect consistency prevails. One may indeed choose to be inconsistent, at least for a while, and live several lives at once, as it were. Certain views can be compartmentalized, and a person can engage in several different projects simultaneously. Not all behaviorists ignore consciousness and mentation in their spouses, their children, or themselves. Exemplary positivists may be ardent lovers and admirers of art. Comte, their founding father, was not above assuming the role of high priest in a homemade system of religion. All these things are possible by compartmentalization and diversification. What Lifton[4] has described as Protean man amounts to a life style of hopping from one choice between momentous options to another, with startling flip-flops. One wonders, though, how momentous these options are to the makers. Indeed, the modern existentialist notion that life is a project can easily predispose a person to engagements in various short-lived projects. Much in today's culture seems to be moving into just that fragmented direction. The idea of choosing one lifelong vocation in a profession, trade, or career is being displaced by opportunistic flexibility in selling oneself to the next highest bidder. The word "task force" is on everybody's lips, and that word itself implies short-term views of short-term problems leading to short-term projects. Work and play seem to diverge: as industrial work is allowed to deteriorate into a dull, stupid, monotonous grind of forty horrible hours per week, recreation must be stylized so as to appear to be a different world altogether for the remaining hours. Thus, fragmentation abounds, and with it one is prone to choose between several sets of options at once, for the different compartments of life, dispensing with consistency. In James's parlance, one could describe these trends not only as fragmentation of choices but as trivialization of options (and life) as well.

It is also noteworthy that professed beliefs may come about by frantic and ill-considered choices in which the will to believe, which for James included foresight into long-range consequences, deteriorates into whimsicality. Many current commentators on the recent Jesus movement[5-7] are impressed by the quickness of religious conversions which, moreover, seem to demand hardly any preparation, very little soul-searching, and hardly a well-considered choosing. They are too quick and too slick. On the other hand, many professed disbeliefs and unbeliefs give way in existential moments, when there is dire need to consider their consequences, or when they suddenly do not seem to fit the exigencies of the situation. Logic and consistency are easily dethroned when the pace of life changes, when a repression gives way, when a mood changes, or when the unexpected occurs. We all know, sometimes from self-experience, that for the same person in different phases of life there may be cocktail party disbelief and foxhole religion. Whatever choices we have made so far, deathbeds and gravesides tend to make revisionists of all of us.

The Divided Self

We have noted that the self can be divided, at least in the sense of its holding inconsistent, contrary, or compartmentalized beliefs. Such divided selves are found so regularly, and with such great frequency, that we balk at calling them all pathological. Though we may uphold the ideals of the integrated self and integrated beliefs, realism would demand that we resign ourselves to the fact that millions of people fall short of the mark.

But in certain divided selves the division is felt as agony, and agony can produce a strong impetus toward religious belief.

James considered that situation extensively in his *Varieties of Religious Experience.*[8] He went to it by a detour, first describing what he called the religion of healthy-mindedness. This is based largely on a direct and persistent pursuit of happiness, organized around the belief that happiness is life's goal, the Creator's intention, and the essential spirit of the universe, whose parts work together in harmony. Such belief is so strong that it overrules the contrary evidence of misery, pain, suffering, and anguish, and ignores the patent presence of evil. James's descriptions suggest the existence in some people of a temperamental predisposition toward healthy-mindedness and optimistic religion which allows suppression or denial of unhappiness at a basic emotional level. Consciousness in these people is instantly purged of negative affect when circumstances would induce anguish, depression, anger, or bitterness. Moreover, the intrapsychic defenses against negative affect tend to be reinforced by metaphysical speculations or selective belief systems which hold that all is harmony, that man can be in tune with a universe which is a whole of unmitigated beauty, truth, and goodness, and that "all things work together for good to them that love God." (Rom. 8:28). James took over Francis Newman's typology of once-born and twice-born people in describing such optimists as once-born persons, who in his time were exemplified by followers of mind-cure movements, Christian Scientists (then just beginning), adherents of the Gospel of Relaxation, and members of the "Don't Worry" movement. "It is but giving your little private convulsive self a rest and finding that a greater self is there."[8, p. 111] The preferred methods in upholding the optimistic belief are suggestion, relaxation, concentration, and meditation.

It is not difficult to spot these penchants today, or at any time, for if Newman and James were right, there will always be people with cheerful and optimistic temperaments who are either refractory to feeling the presence of evil or who will, the moment such feelings emerge, counteract them by tinkering with the stuff of the universe and the thrust of experience. The modern word frequently used in this connection by commentators on the current religious scene is "escapism." Christian

Science, Scientology, the Unity School of Christianity, a good many meditation cults, Moral Rearmament, and, as Bellah[9] has pointed out, a large part of American civil religion testify to this temperament. Once-born souls believe in goodness; reality that seems to fall short of the mark results from faulty human habits, lack of perspicacity, or a weakness of moral fiber, and it can be easily repaired by firm moral leadership from elders with positive suggestion and inspiration or by training in idealistic thought.

The healthy-minded are James's stepping stone to the "sick soul" and the divided self, those twice-born people who live life laboriously, always feeling that something is basically wrong with themselves and the universe—the whole universe "groans and travails," and they themselves suffer or muddle with it. Compared with the once-born, twice-born people have an anhedonic emotional temperament. A whiff of melancholy, a feeling of failure, a sense of misery, or a touch of nausea besets the crannies of their awareness and gives their lives a special existential "feel."

In striking cases, the sick soul shows a preoccupation with the omnipresence and overwhelming power of evil which colors his inner life with anguish, loathing, or despair. Religion may mellow these affect states and mitigate their sting somewhat by offering a partial solution to the problem of evil, but deeply felt despair and nausea tend to promote hopelessness and cynicism about religion as well, and thus the sick soul's situation may eventuate in protracted unbelief or disbelief. In fact, if unbelief and disbelief can ever be clearly defined, without ambiguity, it is in just these "exasperated cases,"[8, p. 148] as James called them, who are refractory to any belief whatsoever, except the assertion of meaninglessness. Their affirmation of the omnipresence of evil is so total that not the faintest light of goodness, beauty, or truth seems to shine anywhere. There is no outlook on salvation, neither today nor tomorrow. If all possibility of rescue seems ruled out, the very idea of religion is annihilated also, for "rescue work" lies at the functional core of all definitions of religion.

But not all sick souls are so extreme. Many do find rescue in added beliefs which proclaim the possibility of salvation through renewal, rebirth, restitution, redemption, or regeneration. Some deliverance can be found not only for the individual in his extremity but for the whole cosmic scheme as well. One needs to be born twice. The natural self born from the mother is only a preliminary or provisional self; it needs to be renewed and reappropriated in a nonnatural perspective that will alter its experiential quality. Twice-born people move through a complex situation: they must first pluck up the courage to cry for help and then find an answer that will be at least as loud and clear as their crying. It goes without saying that all soteriological religions, Buddhism, Christianity, Islam, and a good deal of Judaism have always spoken to such twice-born people. And less conspicuous soteriological elements can be easily detected in most other religious systems.

It appears that the major option for twice-born people is to either unify the divided self or remain stuck in inner discord. James focused on situations in which the first option is taken, and it led him to an elaborate discussion of conversion. Subsequently, he dealt with the fruits of conversion or rebirth under two headings. One is saintliness, in which attitudes and conduct are rearranged in the direction of asceticism, "strength of soul,"[8, p. 273] purity, and charity with a sense of freedom from the once prominent, problematic self. The other is mysticism, which moves from this-worldly to otherworldly concerns by means of higher insight, deeper knowledge, and keener unity of the individual with the fabric of the universe. But James was well aware that many people remain discordant with themselves for life, and that conversion is not the only way to unify a divided self. Some shifts in ideas and beliefs remain transient, without producing enduring transformations; some discordant beliefs undergo pseudounification by regressive maneuvers in which difficult or demanding parts of the belief system are simply given up. For instance, one may throw a puritanical heritage overboard as so much useless baggage and settle for a frankly hedonistic orientation without compunctions.

Since the self can be divided in different ways, its unification may require different techniques or experiences. What are some of the major patterns of divided selves? Which are the main divisions relevant to belief and unbelief? Today, the notion of the divided self is no longer a fringe idea but is widely regarded as an apt description of millions of modern men and women in advanced industrial societies. And among today's existentialists the term "alienation" crops up again (mostly in obscurantist fashion, I am afraid) in describing the divided self as estrangement of a person from some alleged core of his being.

One group of divided selves can be conceptualized by deep and enduring conflicts between the ego and the id. Historically, much of the romantic movement and the preceding Sturm and Drang period can be seen as cultural expressions of a perennial tension between reason and feeling, cool thought and hot wish, order and disorder, constraint and impulse. Schelling's typology of the Apollonian and the Dionysian temperaments or life styles, elaborated by Nietzsche, hinges on the same basic distinction between the clarity of orderly, quiet reasoning and the darkness of turbulent, noisy drives. James often described situations with such a strong inner cleavage as cases of a divided will, using the word "will" as a shorthand term for all motives.*

Obviously such a fundamental distinction, if it produces much intrapsychic tension, tends to put its stamp on beliefs. St. Paul's law of the flesh and the law of the spirit is but one ancient example; moreover, it is not offered as a choice between a set of equal options, but one that asserts the marked superiority of the second over the first. The romantic writers and artists believed in the superiority of the ideal over the real, showing a noted lack of what realists call "common sense." Eissler's[10] psychoanalytic study theorizes that Goethe's finished works show a remarkable transparency of themes and word choice which express neurotic beliefs derived from his conflicts over the incest taboo and the Oedipal situation. In such a case, the Apollonian and the Dionysian commingle. Longings for union with the ideal nurturing mother foster belief in the Virgin Mary and

---

*In Kierkegaard, the penchant for subsuming all kinds of diverse motives under the term "willing" is even more pronounced, but his view of the various lines of division within the self is far more subtle than that of James.

have led to the great Mother religions of the past. The need in celibate priests and monks to distinguish between "spiritual women" and "carnal women" has been an important contributor to Mariology.

Religious beliefs, while typically upholding the taboos which society needs, also provide temporary and stylized exemptions from such taboos through symbolic acts or cosmic projections, and in this way heal the schisms between ego and id. Parricide and infanticide are strictly forbidden in ordinary life, but in sacred rituals such acts may be performed or their remembrance kept alive through symbolic repetition or verbal accounts, with the congregation's vicarious engagement.

A modern religious form of the ego-id cleavage can be found in the polarity which besets many churches: are beliefs to be attuned to the predominantly wishful hankerings of the individual private soul concerned with its own salvation, or are they to be enacted on the plane of outer reality for the improvement of actual human relations and the abolition of social injustices? Much fundamentalism derives from the wish to protect a deep longing or a cherished promise from the intrusive influence of sober reality assessment which may jeopardize doctrinal tenets. Classical statements of the apparent conflict between religion and science tend to express conflicting beliefs, in which each party sees the other as putting too much stock in either "blind" faith or "cold, dry" reasoning. Such divisions of belief do not occur only among people. Divergent beliefs are so commonly juxtaposed within one's divided self that few readers will hesitate to acknowledge that their beliefs often interact alternately as belief and disbelief. If we can and do seesaw between opposed beliefs, this is tantamount to vacillation between opposed disbeliefs. Standing at the edge of the Grand Canyon we may believe ad hoc in a personal or purposive Creator; the next week, back at work, when constructing a statistical table, we deem it better to believe in chance and are ready to argue with anyone who would disturb us with God-talk.

Clearly, important beliefs are held with tenacity because behind them lie vital object relations with people whose love we dare not risk. Shifts in beliefs may entail reorganization of the ego ideal; because we are conscious of the interpersonal origins of the ego ideal, new beliefs mean giving up old loyalties (and love objects) in favor of new ones. One's adoption of a different ethos, however defensible rationally, is therefore often taken as a personal offense or a breach of faithfulness by the individuals who served as the original models for the ego ideal. But apart from the reaction of others to any marked shift in our beliefs, the self has intrapsychic obstacles to overcome, feels divided within itself, and may experience shame over giving up or revising the old heritage. The young Jew who becomes intrigued by Christianity, the daughter of a liberal Protestant family who begins to turn to a fundamentalist's Jesus in a group of authoritarian and hortatory followers, or the Catholic who is about to marry a staunch Protestant—all these people will have intrapsychic problems regarding feelings of disloyalty in addition to the social and interpersonal problems they have to face. The ego has to negotiate a new position with the ego ideal, or strong new identifications with great gratification are needed to modify the ego ideal itself.

We can admire other people not only for the beliefs they hold or the ideals they follow, but also for the beliefs they are against, or the disbeliefs and unbeliefs they assert. We tend to despise what our heroes despise: we incorporate the pet peeves of our models and make them our own. One form of loyalty is to hate what our loved ones hate. Therefore, we may find ourselves painfully disloyal when we are entertaining beliefs which father or mother rejected. It amounts to betrayal: we befriend our friends' enemies. Although I speak of such situations in quasi-interpersonal terms, let me again stress the intrapsychic nature of such troubles: they are felt as qualities of a divided self. Problems of this sort occur with great frequency in the mission field, when conversion from one faith to another involves far more than learning a new catechism and engaging in new rituals or adopting a new life style. The social disruptiveness of such conversions often accompanies subjectively felt threats to the person's sense of well-being, to his sense of oneness. The aroused feelings of shame and disloyalty can be borne only when they are counteracted by great gains in deeper satisfactions or when the new loyalty is directed to an altogether more worthy or admirable object who is felt to have a greater claim on the person's devotion.

The same is true in cases of disbelief and unbelief. The child of ardent disbelievers who is charmed by some religious faith, or the militant atheist who turns to patently religious beliefs, is likely to feel torn within, even if his loved ones and friends assume a tolerant attitude toward his new explorations or others think he is "getting soft." He himself may feel that he is dishonest toward his old self and unfaithful toward his own best precepts, and his convictions may be contaminated by cultural concepts that accentuate his pride. It is the prevailing notion that faith is archaic and reason modern, that religion is superstition, and that agnosticism or atheism is a sign of emancipation. Such quasi-evolutionary value judgments are often taught by those who identify themselves as unbelievers, since it is one way for them to rationalize the choice they have made between the options as they saw them. As mentors of the young, they thus put a special burden on admirers who find themselves drawn to religion. The latter's gropings for religious beliefs will be interpreted as primitivization or regression, producing feelings of shame. Because it takes much time and thought to overcome such opprobrium many noted scientists, I think, have waited until their advanced years to make public statements about the religious beliefs to which they have felt drawn or the vestiges of religion which they have maintained.

A third form of the divided self derives from strong conflicts between the ego and the superego. Its essence is dramatically captured, with an ironic reversal, in the famous lines from Goethe's *Faust:*

Faust:	. . . who are you then?
Mephisto:	Part of that Power which would the Evil ever do, and ever does the Good.
Faust:	A riddle! Say what it implies!
Mephisto:	I am the Spirit that denies![11]

Good or bad—these are the perennial judgments made by the superego, and they impose on the ego a sense either of well-being or of dejection and guilt. Mephisto, being devilish, starts from where he feels most at home, with badness, but finds that he has to say *No!* even to that propensity. Most citizens of the world, aspiring to be angelic, start with good intentions which make them say *No!* to a lot of things they would like to do naturally. In either case, an inner, emphatic *Yes-saying* or *No-saying* to what a person thinks or does or entertains is the primary function of the superego, which aims to keep the self on the track of morality. Is the self good or bad, or a mixture of both, and in what proportions? This question can make certain selves feel divided.

Compared with the ego ideal, the superego is usually seen as the earlier part of conscience. It too is enmeshed from the start with object relations and identifications. The parental do's and don'ts which govern the early years of life and guide the person through the oral, anal, and Oedipal situations leave their traces in the form of internal rules which gradually come to control the person from within, habitually, and with a good deal of automatization. Obedience eventually rejects bowing to external pressure and follows a voice within the privacy of the self. But the mental, dynamic links with the original parental voices remain: every *do* done and every *don't* avoided connotes a parental smile, an *I love you* that has primitive emotional impact of great immediacy because it stems from largely preverbal and unconscious incidents of learning; every *do* undone and every *don't* done is linked with a parental frown or threat of punishment, an *I hate you* of similarly raw impact. At the root of the superego lie puerile efforts at massive and not very discriminating identifications with the parents ("I want to be like Daddy"), whereas the ego ideal of the older child is based on more selective and partial identifications ("I like the teacher's smile" or "I like Father's decisiveness").

Just as obedience to the superego enhances self-esteem and gives the unifying feeling of being loved, transgression of the rules of the superego produces guilt feelings and lowers self-esteem. The superego is both friend and taskmaster. When transgression produces self-hatred and elicits an urge to punish oneself, the ego then feels "no good" until it finds ways of rehabilitating itself before the superego's demands—for instance, through confession, acts of penance, retribution, or other maneuvers of placation. A sizable portion of "high demand religion," as practiced by conservative churches and sects, finds its perennial appeal in the psychological role of "taskmaster."[12]

Beliefs are related to the superego in several important ways, primarily by forming a large part of the superego's actual content of ideas and demands. Many of the rules we incorporate are (or are derived from) the beliefs of our early, affectionate caretakers. In becoming moral and self-controlled, we tacitly assume the beliefs and moral ideas of our parents and other early love objects. Both "an eye for an eye and a tooth for a tooth" and God's alleged infinite love for repentent sinners are moral precepts embedded in religious views; both happen to be also very diverse ways of experiencing man's object relations with his gods. Thus, much of what we believe or disbelieve is enmeshed with parental approval or disapproval. In this sense, beliefs and disbeliefs are profoundly emotional, symbolizing parental love and hate as well as primitive self-acceptance and self-hate.

Beliefs are also part of the superego's sanctions when transgressions occur and, conversely, of the superego's acclaim of the ego when its adhortations are obeyed. In what ways shall a taskmaster punish when his worker performs badly, and in what ways shall a friend tighten the bonds of friendship when his companion appears to be of one mind with him? In a word, what are blame and praise? The answer is that they are largely a matter of beliefs—pedagogical beliefs. The enforcement of parental do's and don'ts proceeds by conscious or unconscious consideration of what the child deserves upon good or bad behavior: merit or demerit, reward or punishment. The "just desert" and its apportionment are a delicate matter of beliefs in what is just, what works, and what comes spontaneously, all touching on the profoundest bases of human relationships guided by religion and ethics.

For instance, some superegos are based on the slave driver's model: every transgression elicits a prompt demand for sanctions through an inner whiplash, an angry shout, an expected privilege forfeited, with never a word of praise or an encouraging glance when the person is staying in line and doing well. In such cases, good behavior is taken for granted and not deemed worthy of any attention. The ego has no friend in the superego —only a bullying overseer, who upholds the belief that what counts is the performing of duties. Other superegos are based on the model of the prodigal son's father: transgressions are left to yield their own sorry aftermath in practical life, without shouting or retribution, and with lavish forgiveness when there are signs of a change of heart. The friend outweighs the taskmaster, not only in the rules he lays down for conduct but also in the response he makes to moral failure. He acts on the belief that love is greater than justice, that love is more powerful than hate, and that spontaneous repentance is more effective than the rubbing in of sin in producing changes of behavior. Moreover, the father need not have been conscious of those beliefs he held; it is likely that he was the sort of fellow who was quick to embrace and give his blessing, to forgive and forget. Like some parents, there are superegos which demand no special retribution for misbehavior but only a solemn promise for betterment: "Try again—next time should be better!" At the root of this attitude lies a humanistic belief in the essential goodness of man and his penchant for self-improvement.

A third way in which beliefs enter the divided self consists of the techniques which the ego has learned to use in rehabilitating itself before the superego—that is, its habitual methods of placation. Normally, moral instruction involves not only the inculcation of rules and the imposition of sanctions, but also the modeling of ways of atoning for transgressions and relieving guilt feelings. It is a poor educator indeed who does not suggest to his child or pupil how he may come to terms with his guilt feelings and rehabilitate himself so as to gain positive self-esteem after misdeeds. Such techniques of placation are taught, and they tend to be part of a distinct set of beliefs. I remember a patient suffering from involutional melancholia who tried to atone for a bad deed first by simple restitution: he paid back what he had taken. But soon he felt the need to make an additional sevenfold restitution, and when even this failed to relieve his guilt feelings he played with the thought of making up seventy times sevenfold. This sacred arithmetic was taken directly from the New Testament, and its application was an expression of the fundamentalistic belief with which he approached the Biblical passage.

Indeed, how shall one placate for moral transgressions? Are sanctions to be taken concretely—an eye for an eye and a tooth for a tooth? Or can they be taken abstractly—do something very good, but with freedom of choice, to make restitution for something bad? Can one make inventions of one's own and show some initiative in making restitution or paying fines, including the possibility of not paying a fine but showing a change of heart? Can one use symbols, like buying a nice present for someone he has offended, or doing tedious chores for mother after having hurt her feelings? All these choices seem embedded in beliefs: for instance, the belief that among people who love each other tit-for-tat exchanges are inferior to spontaneous and inventive manifestations of betterment, or the converse belief that atonement involves, in addition to restitution, some shouldering of pain, sadistically imposed.

And so one learns to interpret the superego's sanctions and to deal with the fluctuations in self-esteem that vary with obedience and disobedience to the superego's rules, all the while testing and expressing certain beliefs and sometimes experimenting with new beliefs. In fact, the degree to which one will tolerate a divided self produced by wide discrepancies between superego demands and ego accomplishments or strive to heal promptly such division appears to be a matter of belief. Freud put his finger on this point in *The Future of an Illusion* when he noted the latitude which certain Christians give themselves, with priestly toleration, in sinning against the divine commands they profess to uphold:

> God's kindness must lay a restraining hand upon his justice. One sinned, and then one made oblation or did penance, and then one was free to sin anew. Russian mysticism has come to the sublime conclusion that sin is indispensable for the full enjoyment of the

blessings of divine grace, and therefore, fundamentally, it is pleasing to God. It is well known that the priests could only keep the masses submissive to religion by making these great concessions to human instincts.[13]

Freud the moralist, the puritan, was also shocked by the apparent ease with which Dostoevsky kept pursuing the pleasure principle in his gambling and other activities while claiming to promote the highest moral standards. Freud commented: "A moral man is one who reacts to temptation as soon as he feels it in his heart, without yielding to it."[14] Obviously, such moral promptness keeps the self unified. But Dostoevsky could live with great divisiveness within the self, assuming that this is possible and true for all people who believe that personal conflict is only a mirroring of large-scale cosmic conflict in which even the deity is divided within itself.

A fourth form of the divided self has been pointed out by Bertram Lewin.[15] It hinges on the differences between what one believes and what one knows. One can know without believing and believe without knowing. On the surface, this would seem to be a cognitive distinction within the ego between two types of certainty, each pertaining to a special class of information. But the distinction goes deeper than this, and can in some cases lead to a divided self. For Lewin feels that many beliefs are internally justified only by a historical premise: "I believe thus and so because I have *always* believed it." Such beliefs are part of one's being and intrapsychically self-validating, no matter how odd they may be from the reality standpoint. In contrast, many bits of valid knowledge offered by reality are approached with an "I will take it or leave it at my pleasure" attitude, with great selectivity. Lewin concludes on the basis of his case material that beliefs have much to do with feelings of infantile omniscience and omnipotence. "In a sense, belief is a partial omniscience," and in this way different from ordinary knowledge that can be judged coolly for its worth.

Some beliefs are rooted in emotional convictions about their truth stemming from early childhood, when they were given narcissistic sanction ("It is good or pleasurable for me to think this way") and were intertwined with magical acts which enhanced their trustworthiness ("If I pray when it thunders, lightning will not hit me or my house"). Much of the debate between religion and science (which of these is true and which one false) finally hinges on this distinction between the roots of several types of conviction. Ordinarily, the distinctions between religion and science as well as the overlap between them can be dealt with through a myriad of rationalizations and all sorts of logical tightrope walking, and in most cases will not produce a painfully divided self. One way to forgo division is precisely to maintain the distinctions between believing and knowing which Lewin emphasized, to realize the differences in validation procedures and the different orders of "Truth," and to enjoy the cognitive pluralism. Another way is to elevate one realm of truth to absolute or ultimate certainty and denigrate the other. But trouble comes for some souls who take both forms of cognition seriously, who want to believe knowingly and to know believingly, combining infantile trust and logical certainty into one state of conviction. Apparently, this is a difficult feat to accomplish, and serious efforts toward that goal are often accompanied by much torment at seeing its failure. An excellent historical example of the self so divided, and tormented by its division, is Augustine's *Confessions*, a book of most ambiguous form, being prayer, dialogue, systematic philosophy and theology, and a kind of principles of psychology all rolled into one, with different orders of conviction now separated, now combined. Because it is the story of a search and a case history of a divided self, it is a tortuous book, but the fact that it has stood the test of time suggests that the problems it tackles have been experiential ones for millions of readers. The dynamics of this kind of divided self and its reunification play a role in those worthy books which famous scientists are wont to write in their golden years, when they publicly come to terms with their religious beliefs or seek to explain the roots of their faith and the grounds of their convictions.

Finally, there is a divided self submerged in great tragedy and with rifts that go very, very deep. Certain persons grow up feeling from early childhood a profound insecurity. The feeling of being unquestionably alive and real, which directly vitalizes and innervates most of us, and forms the basis of our certainties (I am, therefore I feel, think, perceive others, and so on), fails to develop. Instead, a keen awareness of disunity within the person develops; depending on how well it is masked, it may be noted by others and evaluated as odd or eccentric. The word "schizoid" has come to be applied to such disunified persons, implying that if the division within the self becomes very severe and the psychic defenses against it break down completely, abject madness is the outcome. Much modern psychiatric literature is devoted to this kind of personality organization and the ensuing psychiatric syndromes. It is pointed out that splitting is the basic dynamic process in such cases and that it often eventuates in fragmentation of not only basic psychic processes but of the very personality structure. In some crucial dimensions, personality fails to achieve the unity which in normal development is taken for granted. For instance, mind and body may be experienced as disjointed, the self as it were "holing up" in the mind and relegating the body to the status of a thing, like other objects "out there" from which it feels divorced. Or, as Laing[16] has described so well, a "true," highly private, and secret self is nourished through fantasy, as opposed to a "false" public self which merely plays a role, going through the motions of conforming to certain social expectations. The true self may feel hollow, but it is also filled with a sense of omnipotence which is the product of imagination that cannot be verified through overt acts providing realistic feedback of the person's assumed secret powers. Or again, the self is divided in such a way that outsiders (others) are experienced as being inside (me), and that inside things (for example, my feelings) are experienced as coming to me from the outside in the form of other people's aims or intentions ("they are after me").

For those who think in terms of an existentialist frame of reference, as Laing does, the word "alienation" suggests itself almost automatically as a description of such people's lives. The true self is alienated from other aspects of the self; the person feels alienated from other persons, being shy and uncomfortable with them and often missing their intentions or feeling offended by their *joie de vivre;* fantasy and reality shade too easily into each other, and a sense of futility and meaningless-ness prevails.* As many clinical observers have pointed out, the large element of destructiveness in such persons sets the stage for feeling that they live in a dangerous world which requires their constant vigilance, or else leads to self-destructive acts and fantasies. It is a bleak inner world; empty, forlorn, without spon-taneity or trust.

This kind of divided self has of course many gradations of severity. Camus[17] has vividly described one form of it in *The Stranger.* Many of Kafka's heroes find themselves in an environ-ment that forces them, by systematically undermining their basic certainties, to develop such a personality structure if they do not already have it. Much of Kierkegaard's work is a shrewd dialogue based on extraordinarily lucid internal perceptions of true self with false self, with much hopelessness about mankind at large. Had Kierkegaard not had a deep belief in Christian ultimates the split in his personality would have been an un-breachable gap, but some healing of the divided self occurred precisely through his religious beliefs.

Beliefs can be the public *mise en scène* for such divided selves. The splitting of mind from body, in a far-fetched consis-tent dissociation, lies at the heart of some venerable metaphysi-cal or religious systems: Platonism, Neoplatonism, and Gnosti-cism. While it is one thing to merely verbalize a metaphysical scheme, it is another thing to live it and arrange one's whole being around the conviction that the body is only a tomb for the precious soul, which should be set free as quickly as possible. Quite a few bodies have been starved, parched, flogged, cas-trated, burned, frozen, poisoned, or neglected to death by their proud possessors "to the glory of God," in the hope that some pure essence of spirit would reunite with its alleged source, as if creation with its earth and matter and bodies were one huge

*In a review of *Mary Barnes: Two Accounts of a Journey through Madness,* by Mary Barnes and Joseph Berke (New York: Harcourt Brace Jovanovich, 1972), Joel Kovel tellingly says: "And thus Mary 'went down'—gave vent to her madness, exchanging her ordinary alienation for a more acutely suffering au-thenticity" (*New York Times Book Review,* July 2, 1972, p. 13).

mistake. Typically, such belief-induced self-destructions have been preceded by total avoidance of any commerce with people through withdrawal into the desert, a mountain wilderness, or onto the top of a pillar. Eccentricity? Yes, but also devotion and sainthood in some cases. And sometimes with small bands of followers who holed up in their own cells or private caves.

Laing speaks of "ontological insecurity." I think he means "ontic" rather than ontological, for the insecurity he describes does not stem from taking college courses in ontology. He cites the case of patient A who argues with patient B. B argues for sport, as it were, whereas A argues desperately and out of desperation, from torment, in order to preserve his very existence. Patient A's lucid self-awareness gives us the clue that any very frantic, overly verbose, and terribly zealous adherence to beliefs is likely to stem from last-ditch efforts to heal a divided self of the kind we are considering here. The world has always had its Elmer Gantrys, and the evangelists' circuits are full of eccentric characters with bleak personal histories, who are as divided personally as they are divisive socially. Dostoevsky has portrayed an aristocratic, ecclesiastical form of this divided self in his picture of the Grand Inquisitor,[18] who cannot come to terms with the spontaneity and forgiving attitudes of the Jesus he interviews.

On the other hand, the divided self of schizoid makeup and the divided self that has turned cynical from the persistence and magnitude of the world's woes are not prone to embrace commonly held religious beliefs. For embracing anything is precisely their main problem; nothing is trustworthy, everything is felt as a sham or a dangerous, evil intrusion. The self, what precious little there is of it behind the mask of conformity, cannot be risked to display its nothingness in any furtive attempt to give it over to a reciprocal object relationship.

Making Easy and Felicitous What in Any Case Is Necessary

"At bottom," said James, "the whole concern of both morality and religion is with the manner of our acceptance of the universe."[8, p. 41] No matter how we may sputter and wriggle, we are in the end dependent on cosmic givens and arrangements. An important function of any ideology, any -ism, philosophy, or religion, is thus to modulate the basic feeling tone that will prevail in life. From this point of view, our options are not merely between one formal truth and another, between winning or losing certain stakes, or between conformity and idiosyncratic self-assertion. There is another option that has to do with our mood, and hence with our spontaneity, our feeling of freedom, our "bounce," and our sense of well-being. If we can never be radically autonomous, if we must bow before some ultimate facts that leave no exits, will we do so with a grudge, a frown, stone-faced, or with grace, if not assent? Can we manage a smile or two? The issue is one of pain or pleasure. It is, strictly speaking, not a live option between the reality principle and the pleasure principle, for those who take the cosmic facts realistically will still have their pleasures or sorrows with them, unless they are such radical Stoics that they have managed to be devoid of all feelings.

James's thesis is that most religious beliefs are at least realistic enough to contain the assertion that man is dependent on the universe; from that point on, however, the question of pain or pleasure in accepting that dependency is of great pragmatic significance. There is value in being heartily involved and finding some modicum of happiness in one's lot, for in reality the only viable alternative to happiness is unhappiness. Life as lived always has a "temperature," and the thermometer always measures heat or cold—it has no neutral zone. All arguments as to whether heat is the absence of cold or vice versa are spurious; they are only logical conundrums.

One of the main differences between the religious and the philosophical world views lies in the mood with which assent to either is given. Philosophy may be convincing, persuasive, beautiful, and even binding, but it rarely produces the *love* of the ultimate reality it poses as religions do. Its propositions remain abstract because philosophy perceives reality in an abstract way. It deals with Process and Reality, Creative Evolution, Critique of Pure Reason, Philosophical Investigations, to cite but a few classical titles.* It is hard to love the "stuff" of philosophy or the philosophical "stuff" of the universe with the same abandon, thrill, or zeal with which one can love people. In philosophy, the universe cannot easily become a *Thou* as it does in most religions which endow ultimate reality with personal characteristics.

Here then lies a very basic option. Shall one embrace a religious view and allow a large range of affects into his relations with the universe, or shall one "cool it" a little by adopting a philosophical stance? Both options entail profound beliefs which can capture truth, promote a better life, and stimulate the sense of beauty. Both choices can ennoble life, enrich it, and guide it. The difference is largely stylistic. Philosophy may describe and formulate with admirable clarity and certainty what is necessary, but religion, according to James, "makes easy and felicitous what in any case is necessary."[8, p. 51] The question is how it manages to do so.

Rather than repeating the old assertion that gods, the objects of religion, are staged as persons or made in the image of man, I would venture the assertion that religion is a unique approach to reality which allows maximal transference of experienced human object relations to one's dealings with the world at large, in the conviction that such object relations are the deepest, truest, and most abiding experience we can ever have. The universe can be a Thou to the extent that we have come to cherish the experience with other Thous in our lives. This assertion is simpler as well as richer than the traditional one because it allows for gods which, like the Hebrew Yahweh or the Islamic Allah, may not be portrayed, as well as the Hindu symbol deities which have no human attributes. Not all gods are personal in the sense of having human traits or features. What is important about gods is that they are held to be sacred, just as the deepest and most basic

*Nietzsche's *Die Fröhliche Wissenschaft* is not quite *The Gay Science* as the official translation has it—its ring is much closer to Good Tidings, the *Euangelion* that lies behind gospel. Like *Thus Spoke Zarathustra*, which suggests revelations by somebody, such phrases are quite exceptional in philosophy. Small wonder, then, that Nietzsche's work has often been approached as if it were a religion. It appeals to feelings, and much of it works directly on such an elementary feeling as self-esteem.

human relations are felt to be sacred, and gods may be portrayed or not, imagined in lavish forms or held to be formless, merged with the tribal ancestry or placed outside human genealogy. The diversity of religious objects is enormous, even including atheistic conceptions, but all such objects allow an attitudinal transference which makes the approach to ultimate reality as easy and felicitous as our most meaningful human encounters.

The importance of attitudinal transference to preserving the value of spontaneity is beautifully illustrated in one of the letters of writer James Agee to his older friend Father Flye. Catching himself in the act of writing "God bless you" to his friend, he writes on: "But will you please tell me: are you in any way offended that I, who don't even know, most of the time, whether I believe in God, should say that? I realize my lack of right to, but I believe in obeying a thing which is spontaneous."[19] To such acts of spontaneity we can also relegate all swearing, which betrays a momentary vestige of belief symptomatically, even though the ego may have abandoned the belief system that would warrant the use of such elementary theological language. One could at this point paraphrase James's celebrated definition of religion: ". . . the feelings, acts and experiences of individual men in their solitude . . ."[8, p. 31] into "what one does with his spontaneity."

The religious option is the evocative and expressive option. It allows the transference of feelings of admiration, exaltation, warmth, and tenderness to accompany our approach to reality. It allows the transference of action propensities such as embracing, clasping, contending, or surrendering. It allows the transference of complex sentiments and affect states such as hope, love, fear, or remorse to enter into our relations with the universe. It allows indeed the act of speaking in declarative, evocative, or plaintive sentences such as "I love you," "Bestow your grace upon me," "Lord, Thou hast been our dwelling place in all generations," or Job's cry: "Though he slay me, yet will I trust in him!" *

---

*James, who did not know object relations theory, looked at it from the other side, and came close to saying the same thing. In a note on the manuscript of his *Varieties* he wrote: "Remember that the whole point lies in really believing

Psychoanalytic object relations theory assumes that there is isomorphism between person-to-person relations as experienced and the relations that any person maintains with the farther reaches of reality: his social world, his Mother Earth, his heavens, and his Ground of Being. If this is a plausible assumption, it holds a clue to the reasons why some people would prefer the philosophical to the religious option. If object relations have been experienced as "too hot" or not quite gratifying, solace may be found in a more detached, contemplative, and rational engagement with the universe. One may wish to hold back before approaching or embracing. One may wish to proceed analytically rather than spontaneously or expressively. One may wish first to transpose everything to a cooler and more abstract level by logical or mathematical modalities. One may wish to assert nothing but hypotheses, and let experience test them out. *Le style c'est l'homme.* It is possible, as Jaspers[21] has proven, to produce a psychology of *Weltanschauungen.*

Allowance should be made, of course, for combining the two basic options. One can buy both the religious and the philosophical option at once—provided his accumulated capital of experienced object relations is large enough to afford it. Many cases are mixed: Plato, Thomas Aquinas, Spinoza, and Nietzsche come to mind. In fact, mixing per se is a live option that can produce intriguingly complex systems of belief and unbelief which also affect the modes of thought and the literary forms in which these are expressed. Plato taught by myth, dialogue, and logical demonstration. Nietzsche used poetic verse. Spinoza used mathematical formulations. Others have used poignant aphorisms. Aquinas equated the Judeo-Christian God with the philosophical *ens realissimum* and the *summum bonum.* Whiteheadians approach God as Process and Reality. Many an existentialist theologian waxes warm, if not ecstatic, when he approaches the Ontological Mystery. And Tillich bestowed considerable affect on his Ground of Being—as much as

that through a certain point or part in you you coalesce and are identical with the Eternal. This seems to be the saving belief both in Christianity and in Vedantism. . . . It *comes home* to one only at particular times."[20]

British Presbyterians used to invest in their royally robed deity enthroned in heaven.

More

"More!" is the cry of the hungry toddler and the lament of the child who is told stories at bedtime. It is the watchword of the expanding economy which wants an ever growing gross national product. "More" is part of a prevailing Western ideology, as Looft[22] has pointed out.

The Jamesian *more* is of a different order. It is not the signal of demandingness. It is tied in with self-discovery and curiosity about the universe. It is a way station of thought—a tentative term which we use in our gropings about reality. Starting from his observations about religious conversion, James took his informants seriously when they testified to having been transformed from a former divided self into a unified self, from a callous self into a gentle self, from a bad self into a better self, or from a lower self into a higher self. The variations are endless, but the gist of them is that people can and many persons do have an awareness of a higher self, not now realized, that can be potentiated and become manifest. Many people know that there is *more* to them than meets the eye, even their own eye, and that that *more* has value. Call it the transcendent self, if you wish. The point is that it sets up strivings which enrich the self, enlarge mankind, and ennoble the universe.

James also thought that we are so constituted as to assume that our larger, higher selves are attuned to a *more* of the same quality that exists in the universe—that is, the essential truth and the ultimate reality of the universe. Does such a cosmic *more* really exist?

Theologians will say yes and identify the *more* as deity or creator or ground of being. Mystics will also reply affirmatively and identify the *more* as that with which they have occasional contact in an expanded or altered state of consciousness. Some philosophers will say yes and describe the *more* as ideal or principle which undergirds the world. And practically all those who affirm the reality of the *more* see it in dynamic terms. They believe that it acts, that it has energy and power. This is the great and consistent theme of Teilhard de Chardin's writings. Magical minds are concerned with harnessing and obtaining that power; religious minds are concerned about aligning with it, but not for selfish exploits.

Obviously, these are all speculative thoughts—but not necessarily wild speculations, according to James. For the *more* that we find ourselves speculating about has an empirical, experiential root in the dynamic unconscious. We are all like icebergs whose depth into the dark waters is not known. Nor do we know what lies beyond the waters, what contains them. The *more* has a hither and a farther side; the hither side is our own *more* presenting itself to us as the unconscious part of our being. We know from experience that our unconscious self is dynamic. It produces dreams, it presents us with embarrassing symptoms or mistakes, and it comes to our aid in creative work. Kekule first "saw" the arrangement of the benzene ring in a dream. The unconscious produces symbols or makes us see ordinary things as symbols. Could it not be, thought James, that all these activities of our unconscious self provide us with intimations about an unseen reality? We may not know its essence rationally, but we have as little doubt about its existence as we do about the reality of our own unconscious. Maybe our unconscious is only the hither side of that Reality of the Unseen, that cosmic MORE, of whose farther side we get glimpses as through a doorway that is slightly ajar.

James coined a word, "over-belief," for the way we interpret the glimpses we get when we step through the doorway.[8, lect. xx] Over-beliefs are usually proclaimed as if they were firm knowledge: the prophets speak as if they know the divine message exactly, the mystics claim to know that there is a cosmic Self with which their own little self was united for a moment, the convert insists that he was touched and transformed by a divine hand or cleansed by heavenly water. The trouble with such over-beliefs is that their truth is subjective, not compelling or persuasive for those who have not had analogous experiences or whose speculative bent results in different images or assumptions. Some persons who have had glimpses of the farther side of the *more* hesitate to transform them into certainties, not necessarily because their glimpse was a blur but because they experienced no more than a glimpse. Hence, they might prefer an agnostic position, and they disbelieve the over-beliefs of their fellowmen.

Between the rather clear-cut positions of the theist on one side and the atheist on the other side, the agnostic holds a fascinating place. Assuming for a moment that both theism and atheism are over-beliefs, since they contain assertions that lie beyond empirical validation (apart from the plain fact that they are often made in doctrinaire ways), one could ask whether agnosticism is also a form of over-belief or whether it is the ideal belief: "I believe because I do not know for sure." The answer will vary according to the types of agnosticism that can be recognized.

Some very tolerant agnostics may never have had a glimpse at the doorway but know that others, whom they deem reliable, have apparently had glimpses. And so they remain open to that possibility for themselves, with a calm temper, willing to say for the moment no more than: "I don't know." A second group of agnostics may have had a blurred, confusing glimpse of a sort, enough to be intriguing but not enough to produce any light. Their "I don't know" includes a "could be" but with the proviso "I am very unclear about it." A third form of agnosticism is based on having had glimpses of some clarity which raised more questions than answers. Their "I don't know" has a ring of "I must do some thinking about it" and "Yes, there seems to be something there, if I only knew what." A fourth group of agnostics may be apt at speculation and may have entertained a number of interpretations, but opting for any particular interpretation or settling on any distinct over-belief seems whimsical to them. Their "don't know" entails an acknowledgment that the possibilities may be tremendous but that it is better to keep things open-ended rather than foreclosing them by a rash decision: "Why commit yourself now? The risk of error is too great, and I don't seem to be losing anything by postponing a decision."

I think there is a fifth group of agnostics who are somewhat paradoxical. They may have had more than a glimpse at the door. Besides, they may have had considerable instruction in over-beliefs that both channels and inhibits their speculative potential. They may have been instructed in the idea that gods, by definition, are always hidden and that man is bound to be entrapped in idolatry when he gives free reign to his speculative bent. Lots of over-beliefs there that can be buttressed by chapter-and-verse quotations from scriptures! So they may come to an "I don't know" which has the meaning of "If I claimed I knew, I would probably falsify the objects of my surmises." Or, with greater input from the superego: "I should not pretend to know, for my pretensions may obscure what is really there." Clearly, such agnosticism can be labeled Jewish agnosticism, Christian agnosticism, and so on. Cases of agnostic over-belief or, if one wills, of believing agnosticism are very paradoxical, very sophisticated, and very intriguing. They demonstrate the subtleties of the will to believe and the immense complexity of coming to terms with options.

CHAPTER VII

Coming to Terms with Providence

A psychiatric patient I have known, a single woman in middle life, had a penchant for experiencing and operating at two levels of reality at once. She came from a cultured family whose members had significant accomplishments to their name. Father was a refined intellectual, given to lofty ideas and idealistic talk, but prone to extramarital affairs. Mother was a proper socialite outwardly, but quite disorganized privately, and disorderly at home. The several siblings as they grew up went through considerable turmoil, for the parents seemed to do everything passionately. They confided their emotional woes to their children at an early age, and the children were exposed to striking polarities in the parents' overt behavior which made their world highly ambiguous: periods of strict sobriety alternated with periods of heavy drinking; times of marital fidelity and tenderness alternated with periods of extramarital affairs; periods of productive and creative work were interspersed by stretches of intellectual emptiness and emotional flatness.

Well read and talented, and with a sustained interest in religion (in which she seemed very well instructed), my patient repeated the feelings and attitudes she experienced with her family members on a supernatural plane with the divine personalia. Anglican rites attracted her for their pomp and aesthetic richness, parallel with her plush home which seemed decorous and bohemian at once. She loved the Old Testament prophets for their ardor and impassioned single-mindedness, though they had their eccentric features. She had a hard time with God: How steady and reliable was he really? He seemed graceful one moment and forbidding the next. Was his alleged grace in fact some kind of weakness? She had conveniently split herself into a body and a soul, in which the former got all the beatings she felt it needed (including a suicide attempt) while the latter was kept attuned to purely spiritual things such as church symbols, Neoplatonic scripture selections from the New Testament, and various hyperintellectualistic discourses with friends.

All the fierce ambivalences toward parents and siblings and her own self were reenacted toward the members of the Christian Trinity symbol, toward the church, toward clergymen, and toward members of congregations she was exposed to. She saw herself as very special, claiming extraordinary attention and care both from her family figures and from the divine figures which formed her spiritual household. She held herself untouchable in her sufferings, which in turn were aestheticized into a form of literary art so that her problems seemed to gratify her sense of beauty. Much too dependent on her physical father and at the same time terribly angry at him and her mother over that continued dependency, she repeated the same conflict in relation to her heavenly Father and the church. Much of this conflict centered on the question of her acceptability "as she was" and forgiveness for her weakness and waywardness— again both from her father in the flesh and her Father in heaven. At times she held herself unforgiven and unforgivable in God's eyes, insisting that her self-derogatory evaluation of her own person was a final, ultimate, and cosmic judgment. She felt she was refractory to grace, proudly insisting that she knew better; and she appeared to be testy with clergymen. Despite weeping and handwringing she held fast to such judgments, particularly in moments when the clinician saw occurrences of blatant regression to infantile megalomanic fantasies.

This case powerfully illustrates an exceedingly common and

almost trite theme in the psychology of religion. It is the theme
of the two families: one on earth, the other in heaven. Though
Ernest Jones did not invent the concept, he formulated it rather
starkly, single-mindedly, and with almost uncouth reductionism: every image that furnishes our spiritual realm stands *in
loco parentis*.

In his article "The Psychology of Religion" Jones wrote:
". . . the religious life represents a dramatization on a cosmic
plane of the emotions, fears and longings which arose in the
child's relation to his parents."[1] In a more specific article on
Christianity he stated:

> When our parents' limitations and imperfections begin to become
> evident, it is no wonder that those who are unable to sustain life
> without help and who are still dependent on an outside source,
> should seek for an all-powerful and all-loving Person who should
> stand above all the vexations of this earth and who should never fail
> one. Never, that is to say, as long as one's relation to Him was
> satisfactory, one of dutiful love and obedience.[2]

The indication is that the role of one family begins where the
other leaves off, on the basis of a principle of scarcity. The
theistic family, which is conceived to have greater power,
greater wisdom, greater love, and greater durability and con-
stancy, does what the natural family fails to do for the individual. But from family living to cosmic dramatization the needs
of the individual remain the same: help, love, nurturance, guidance in coping with the problems of life, and sustenance of hope
for a good eventual outcome after death. The individual's contributions also remain the same: dutiful love and obedience.

One should not assume from the triteness of this observation
that it is false or of no use. On the contrary, it is one of the most
pertinent themes in religion, one which most ordinary believers will uphold without further ado, which many theologians
feel constrained to qualify, and which many unbelievers consider so utterly childish that it is their primary reason for dis-
missing religion altogether. Jones gave it a firm psychological
twist by observing that ". . . what one really wants to know
about the Divine Purpose is its intention *toward oneself,* how

to discover the way to be well treated in the next world."[2] In
other words, belief in personalistic deities is not ultimately the
holding of an imaginative conception of an abstract and distant
reality "out there," but a need-fulfilling system of meanings in
which the believing individual himself is one of the major
dramatis personae. His experience, needs, and wants are what
count; they condition his curiosity about the ultimate nature of
things. The believer is not concerned with the abstract
generalities but with his own lot, now and hereafter, and the
issues are for him a matter of life or death.

One could sketch the two-family model as follows:

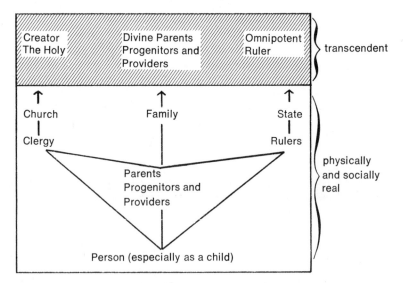

Despite the inadequacy of spatial diagrams for conveying
ideas, the sketch indicates the typically religious reduplication
on a cosmic or transcendent level of realities that are experienced at the mundane level. Three major institutions,
family, state, and church, have their religious analogues, each
with a special nomenclature to designate its particular principle. The sketch also tries to convey that the person who takes
recourse to religion for the reasons which Jones advanced does
not have to produce the transcendent analogues *de novo*,

through his own creative imagination. He is getting constant references to the transcendent in and through the institutions in which he participates; in fact he is likely to get several clusters of ideas, for these are all carefully and purposely transmitted to him by his culture. Whether these ideas are to be classed as fact or fiction, they are culturally real—not only in the form of transmitted beliefs, but also in the form of authorities, buildings, taboos, organizations, fiscal allocations, and power plays.

I am emphasizing the transmission of religious ideas and their cultural visibility because the genre of psychoanalytic writings on religion which Jones exemplifies seems at times peculiarly blind to them. An exclusively intrapsychic point of view runs the risk of encapsulating the individual and making him responsible for fantasies regarded as private, if not neurotic, which are in cultural analysis not only widespread and shared, but adaptive. They are culturally real, with textual formulations, artistic elaborations, institutional symbolizations, and in some eras and places enforced by the police! Moreover, in pluralistic societies various transmitted beliefs are publicly scrutinized for their worth or pitted against each other. And in some totalitarian lands certain beliefs are forced underground or into the privacy of a person's head, while other beliefs are played to the hilt and grafted onto a person's outward conduct. All these instances add a note of social reality and of demands for adaptation to the so-called whimsies of the imagination.

The theological word that presses itself upon us when we consider Jones's observations is Providence. In fact, Jones himself used it fondly, as did Freud, in describing the essence of the religious object relation to the deity, with special reference to Christianity. Providence is not merely the attribute of a god who provides in general; it is the description of a particular relation to a god, seen as heavenly Father, who provides for *my* needs and wants, who nurtures *me*, and with whom *I* must be on good terms.

Articulate theologies of Providence seem to wax and wane with the times.[3] In the seventeenth and eighteenth centuries Providence held a central position among theological topics. Since the middle of the nineteenth century until our own time there has been a marked decline of interest in it. I can see two main reasons for such a decline. One is that the classical post-Reformation formulations of Providence fell into disuse because they appeared dated—their conceptual models were too closely bound to culture and time to hold true for later generations. The other reason is that with the increased splendor of scientific and industrial accomplishments man has undergone a marked increase in his feelings of competence to ward off some of life's risks and to gain tokens of well-being for himself.

The classical formulation of Providence was influenced by the social model of the enlightened monarch and the then nascent scientific model of the competent thinker, economist, and engineer, all of whom would take a hand in making this the "best possible world." The enlightened monarch was no despot: he took a fatherly benevolent interest in his subjects' well-being. Under his wise government wealth and taxes would be apportioned (with favoritism to be sure), and in the long run this arrangement would work toward the best for all people. Privileged status existed socially because it was also considered to exist naturally—in the unequal equipment of the species, the unequal hospitality of climates, and the (now no longer so obvious) unequal endowments among men. And thus, heavenly Providence provided for each creature according to his needs. The scientific model added other features to the meaning of Providence. Like a good engineer, God maintained his creative contraption in excellent working order. Like a learned scientist, he knew everything about making things and how things work, with keen awareness of causes and effects and with fine distinctions between primary and secondary causes. Like a good statistician he knew how to predict; with masses of data before him he could foretell what kind of groupings would shape up. Even Newton acknowledged that the laws of nature were nothing but the discoverable side of the rules of God. And so we have a model of Providence in which God gets a whole series of humanly derived epithets: Sustainer, Provider, Omnipotent, Omniscient, Prescient, Father, King, with unsearchable wisdom and infinite goodness. Let me quote just one sentence from a classical doctrinal formulation:

God, the great Creator of all things, does uphold, direct, dispose, and govern all creatures, actions, and things, from the greatest even to the least, by his most wise and holy providence, according to his infallible foreknowledge, and the free and immutable counsel of his own will, to the praise of the glory of his wisdom, power, justice, goodness and mercy.[4]

Functionally, such a statement served purposes other than those of describing the divine roles I have mentioned. Back of it lay a doctrinal concern with safeguarding the freedom of God and his spontaneity toward his creatures. Providence was linked with the idea of divine predestination and election, which in turn were attempts to come to grips with the mystery of grace.

But the whole idea of Providence has fallen into discredit,[5] perhaps because today few of us can recognize our own fathers in the classic doctrinal sketch, few of us can recognize our own wordly rulers in a predemocratic image, and few of us would uphold omniscience as the scientific ideal. The doctrine got eroded because our situation has grossly changed from that of our forebears. If Mitscherlich's analysis is correct, we now live in a "society without the father."[6] Feudal lords, benevolent monarchs, captains of industry to whom one owes strict allegiance, and dominant fathers exist no longer, although some people are still making bungling attempts at playing such atavistic roles. This is the age of the child—not of the father. It is the age of the self-conscious woman—not of the husband who owns his wife as chattel. It is the age of trade unions, participatory management, broad democracy, and voting rights for young people.

It is therefore somewhat anachronistic to hear the early psychoanalytic students of religion describe God almost exclusively as Providence. Or is it? There is a considerable difference between the production and revisions of doctrinal statements and the feelingful beliefs of the man in the street. Theology is responsible and knowledgeable inquiry; religious belief is closer to the primary process of wishful and need-determined gropings for help in a precarious situation. The waning of an articulate, modern theology of Providence is obviously not matched by a waning of interest in heavenly providers. How the governance of the world may proceed is one thing, but what *I* can expect from *my* heavenly *love object* is another thing. And so Jones pinpointed, perhaps unwittingly, an important psychological truth: we all have to come to grips with the idea of Providence, in one way or another. What personally helpful force can we count on? Is any benevolence anywhere directed toward us? Dependency, autonomy, mystery, choices—all these are important dimensions of life, but we want something more: benevolent attention. We want a right and correct universe in which we can assume our place, but we want more: a considerate cosmos in which we can be happy.

The patient whose case I cited in the beginning of this chapter was not primarily interested in philosophical truth. She was desperately concerned with her well-being within the two families she knew: the family of her birth and the symbolic, transcendent family of a cohesive creation. It's all in the family, she may have thought, correctly. But she had failed to reach happiness in either family, for the two seemed too much alike.

Disbelief in Providence

Experiences like those of the patient I have described may lead to simplifying life by discarding the religious reduplication of the family. There are only real fathers and mothers and siblings, and one has to learn to take them for what they are: neither angels nor beasts, neither gods nor devils. What modicum of happiness life has in store for us is to be reaped in the families into which we are born and in those we establish. Compensations or amplifications occur only in real flesh-and-blood object relations and in such activities as work and play. The rest is illusory. Religion is wrong precisely in that it detracts from the task of making our day-by-day relations with our families, our friends, and the "family of man" maximally rewarding. Why chase after illusions when there is so much to be done here and now? Let our belief be in man, in his capacity to love, and his potential for improvement. Every man should be his own providence, or else we should be provident toward each other.

No doubt such a soberly humanistic belief works for some people. Moreover, it has the noble ring of voluntary abstinence from childish demandingness and quick wish fulfillment, as Freud would put it. Whatever Providence exists, it should be found through self-control and all those renunciations that enable us to get along with our fellowmen in a civilized way. Providence boils down to prudence: the prudence to nurture what happiness there is and the prudence of not asking for too much. Such a humanistic belief sounds like a reasonable objection to religious belief in a divine Providence, but it presumes a condition of feeling happy enough to sustain it. It presumes that one is happy with what happiness is coming one's way. It presumes a state of relative contentment, either by keeping one's sight modestly low or by finding that one is comparatively well off.

Before we praise this noble and reasonable position too highly we should take hold of one of its psychodynamic strands. Contentment with little and modesty of demands are immensely gratifying attitudes for those who emulate them as exquisitely human values, and their practice secures pleasant nods of approval from the superego and ego ideal. Somebody loves us for our sobriety and abstinence: father or mother, cherished friends, admired philosophers, or some half-personified ideal of mankind at large. As Rieff[7] has pointed out, being sober and abstaining in one's claims on happiness is a pointedly moral attitude, and in being as moral as one should, one reaps built-in psychic rewards, for that is the function of conscience. In addition, direct narcissistic gratifications can be had when one elevates himself in his virtue of abstinence a notch above his driven fellowmen who chase after illusions. And one has satisfaction of aggressive urges by engaging in polemics against the masses who seem to seek more, more, always more!

Disbelief in divine Providence does not necessarily or typically imply denial of belief in benevolence. On the contrary, psychiatric observations would suggest that renunciation of demandingness necessarily involves a good deal of benevolence, some basic happiness, and some trust in a "good object." Benevolence lies at the heart of Erikson's concept of basic trust

—both are the developmental enablers of virtuous and moral attitudes. In Winnicott's terms, both presume a "good-enough" mother, who stimulated the capacity for finding satisfactions in transitional objects and elaborating the play sphere.

In Winnicott's view, as noted earlier, the transitional sphere provides the first practice of illusion. Unlike psychiatric hallucination and delusion, illusion can be regarded as a good thing inasmuch as it enriches the natural world by all those niceties we call culture: art, literature, drama, music, religious ideas, metaphysical speculations, and ethical propositions. Why would anyone abstain from such fruits of benevolence? The answer is that almost everybody is quick to pluck some of these fruits of benevolence, but that there are particular tastes. Some like music (illusory noise) but do not like metaphysical speculation (illusory thoughts). Some like sculpture (iconic illusions) but avoid religion (illusory imagery). Beliefs, like tastes, are taught and acquired, and there are constitutional differences in the selective sensitivity of taste buds. Sometimes we have faith in somebody else's faith, said James; and so we may acquire taste in someone else's taste. I put it this way in order to suggest that it would be truly civilized if arguments for and against certain beliefs could be handled more playfully, like matters of taste, and without ponderous dissertations about the ultimate nature of reality about which we know so little! We should feel entitled to play freely with all the rich and interesting things that culture offers—that is, if life's enrichment is the function of culture.*

Objections to the idea of divine Providence are not always so reasonable as the one just described. One may scorn the notion because of flagrantly contrary personal experiences. One's life may have been beset by malevolence from many sides: born without a silver spoon in one's mouth, harassed or rejected by parents, picked on in school, discriminated against in the neighborhood or in the job market, out of luck in finding a supportive

*Not everyone agrees that enrichment is the primary function of culture. Some would hold that culture's primary function is control: control of unruly passions so as to minimize friction and maintain the peace. But that is a typical abstainer's view, opting for order at the price of playfulness.

mate, left naked or ruined by war, injured in body, or emotionally crippled for life. Clinicians in public hospitals know that
there are lives like this, and prison wardens would know it if
they bothered to interview their charges. Trust and benevolence do depend on experience, even when the first experience
comes late in life, as in Victor Hugo's moving episode in *Les
Misérables* when Jean Valjean is sheltered in the house of the
priest. And as in Jean Valjean's case, trust may remain very
brittle.

In such cases, everybody is a bad object, including the subject
himself. Bad people, bad self—nobody can be trusted. What
sense does it make to speak to such people of benevolence, what
sense to direct their gaze to a heavenly provider? In psychiatric
practice (and I would hold in evangelistic endeavors as well)
such approaches make no sense at all. The best one can do is to
begin providing, patiently and assiduously, so that the person
may start experiencing some demonstrations of benevolence
and develop some sense of trust. Or as Bertolt Brecht said in
The Beggar's Opera: "Erst kommt das Fressen und dann
kommt die Moral." Psychiatrists would give credence to the
Marxist thesis that consciousness is determined by life's circumstances, at least to a large extent.

It is evident, then, that on the basis of grossly malevolent
experiences in life, the very idea of benevolence, let alone any
notion of divine Providence, can be rejected. Irrelevant at best,
Providence is a teasing confrontation at worst. The rejection of
well-intended, noble, and humane thoughts has been dramatically demonstrated in the efforts in the last decade to inject
hope in poverty areas. Many "antipoverty" programs have
foundered when workers were confronted with profound suspiciousness in the would-be recipients of their help, and it was
learned that middle-class talk and beliefs simply do not fit the
so-called culture of poverty, in which the struggle for survival
demands entirely different coping styles.

But most lives are not as starkly and persistently beset by
malevolence as these. Most cases are mixed: benevolent as well
as malevolent forces are experienced, entailing attitudes that
lie somewhere between trust and distrust, between belief and

disbelief. The patient I cited had, despite her better than average religious instruction and her openness to religious ideas, great difficulty with the notion of divine Providence. She knew the classical doctrine of Providence fairly well, intellectually, but it was no living reality for her in terms of her experience. Too much of the faltering father and the distant mother was projected onto her image of God. Though she could have nice moments with God, she could not believe in any consistent benevolence on his part. Distance, rejection, perhaps damnation, always lurked in the background of their relation. While she could hardly trust herself either, she so manipulated her good self and bad self that in the end she wound up with the verdict that she was "no good." This judgment, whether true or not, took precedence over any judgment by others. Beyond the ordinary social amenities with which she could deal in good grace and even with some charm, she would systematically defeat staff attitudes which conveyed to her that she was worth saving, that she could be helped, that she could be liked, and possibly cured.

Attitudes like these illustrate an important psychological (and theological) dynamic. Despite the net of dependencies in which our patient was caught and despite the attentions bestowed on her by her family and friends, she had managed to encapsulate her inner self so well that she thought, felt, and acted with peculiar self-sufficiency. All psychological processes are by definition our own, but most of us are open to and even desirous of outside influences and corrections. We know that our feelings about anything can be wrong, our ideas warped or slanted, our perceptions distorted, our actions impulsive, and so we welcome comparisons with others from which we may profit. We have a need for exchange because our self is limited. We know that we thrive on embeddedness in larger patterns with others, if only to enlarge the scope of our vision, notably the vision of our selves. Competence does not mean utter self-sufficiency in the sense of the encapsulatedness of our patient, who demonstrates the dynamics of narcissism.

Rejection of the idea of divine Providence may proceed from excessive narcissism. "So you seem to think that I am in need of provident care? Who do you think I am? Providence is for weaklings. The *Sklavenmoral* was long ago buried by Nietzsche." It is no accident that Jones, who was so astute in saying that "what one really wants to know about the Divine Purpose is its intention *toward oneself,*" also wrote a paper on the God complex.[8] Concern with the divine intention toward oneself may in some characters lead to a takeover of the divine role through an identification of the self with God. Such a megalomanic fantasy of being God is usually grafted on earlier fantasies of being identical with one's greatly beloved and admired father, who is yet so much hated and envied that one also wants to displace him. But still-earlier fantasies of infantile omnipotence, uncorrected by normal growth experiences that set limits to the scope and demands of the self, may nurture the bloated, narcissistic self. The narcissist may acknowledge certain social or physical limitations, but in privacy he can easily become religious in a special sense: he begins to think and feel cosmically, he assumes divine prerogatives, and he is at home in heaven or hell.

We all know the blatant cases which are "crazy" because they are imprudent enough to act out their fantasies. Some psychiatric patients who claim to be God or Jesus or the Virgin Mary (and thus seem to engage in a plethora of religious language) are as a rule also atheists, for the very idea that there may be other gods is intolerable to them. They illustrate the cogency of Sidney Mead's statement, quoted before, that the functional meaning of "God" is to let man know that he is not it. Most cases are not so blatant. Clinical wisdom tells us that many God complexes remain private, and that they often go masked behind a very modest and unobtrusive outward mien. What they have in common with the more severe cases is great loneliness, a peculiar solitariness which becomes occasionally manifest in an eccentric judgment, shy manners in company, and lack of empathy for other people's misfortunes.

Disbelief in divine Providence, then, may be based on the narcissistic assumption that one already is God, capable of influencing one's own fate and that of the world by magical manipulations. In more attenuated cases, disbelief in Providence may be so close to omnipotence that no cosmic assistance is necessary. Clinical acumen warns us, however, that the delusion of being God is rarely as straight and uncomplicated as thus far presented. The delusion of being God is usually mixed with the delusion of being the devil. In the modern world, "God" is a shorthand expression for both cosmic good and cosmic evil, and the magical mind likes the euphemism as much as do many ordinary believers. This was not always so: in times that had official room for devils as well as gods it was not uncommon for a person to labor under the delusional idea that he was the devil. I am not referring to any and all forms of demon possession (such as those that led to priestly exorcism), for in many cases the idea of being the devil was an ego-alien experience which the helpless victim wished to get rid of just as much as did the officialdom of the church. The case of the Bavarian painter Christoph Haitzmann, on which Freud commented,[9] is one in which the poor subject finds himself helpless in his regret over having sold his soul to the devil, which was more like being victimized by extortion than an act of identification on his part. The internalization of object relations in the primitive megalomaniac position usually includes the good as well as the bad object, particularly when the important object is felt to be overwhelmingly powerful. It is good *and* bad father, good *and* bad mother, and finally good *and* bad self that become projected to a cosmic plane and identified as deity. Good and bad are insufficiently separated, with the result that cosmic good and evil are rolled into one, which receives the epithet "God." Undoubtedly, a culture that does not recognize the devil as a separate entity influences such euphemistic nomenclature.

And that is why Satanism and witchcraft, in the modern age, are such hapless fads and truly atavistic. There is something psychologically unreal about playing to be the devil or his helpmeets. Considerable awe of God is necessary for anyone to play the devil. Cosmic evil requires cosmic good, and vice versa. I am arguing this not on metaphysical grounds (although the thesis has a venerable metaphysical history) but on psychological grounds. No "bad object" is solely a bad object; it is only the reverse side of a "good object." Splitting between good and bad objects is rarely done so neatly that the two realms are cleanly separated. Splitting is only an attempt to deal with ambivalence, so that traces of the opposite feeling always attach to the cosmic projection. The delusional gods with whom the megalomanic identifies himself are never pure benevolence; the delusional devils with which the demoniac (just as megalomanic) identifies himself are never unmitigated malevolence. All are mixtures of good and evil, good and bad objects, love and hate, God and Satan, good self and bad self. Their similarity consists only in the person's megalomanic self-expansion and his magical mode of thought.

From a social point of view, however, preoccupations with the occult that lead to ceremonial magic with all the liturgical trimmings of priests and priestesses and a "church of Satan" are, of course, also a protest against the prevalence of rationalism or the emotional flatness of much modern life. They extol the primary process: the wish-fulfilling thought, the influencing of other people across a distance, the casting of spells, the easy substitution for people of animals which seem united in their obscenity (goats, snakes, and so forth). In an age of easily obtainable credit cards for anything and wide-open and undemanding church membership, the mere initiation rites into an arcane clique can give a starving soul a boost. Occultism conjures up mystery for anyone who has lost fascination with the secondary process. And it may well be that for millions of people in industrialized and commercialized societies the secondary process is insufficiently stimulated, perhaps even hardly demanded, in mechanical jobs and bureaucratic routines. If life has become utterly trite, some "kicks" can be had from arcane pursuits, all the more when they are innocuous and do not demand a profound attitudinal change.

An entirely different objection to belief in divine Providence, or a denial of one's need for it, stems from tested and more or less realistic feelings of competence, which stem from respect for the secondary process. The first Russian astronauts, upon their return to earth, tantalizingly stated something to the effect that they had not seen God in the dark blue yonder. Though it sounds a little abrupt and provocative, the statement has a basis in fact and reflects a deserved feeling of human self-sufficiency. Who can deny that technology has come a long way in opening up and conquering spaces formerly held to be the secret hiding places of the gods? In many ways, the realm of the sacred, as a territory or domain, has shrunk. Next to technological progress, medicine has managed to bring some old scourges of mankind under control and can work "miracles" in individual cases of suffering which formerly spelled certain doom. Some floods and famines have been forestalled by appropriate technical planning and action. Two most important biological events, formerly entirely ascribed to the gods, are coming more and more under human regulation; birth and death can be increasingly manipulated.

Thus, one of the former *functions* of the idea of divine Providence, which accounted in the popular mind for special blessings as well as special calamities, has shrunk in significance. Something has happened, realistically, to the proportion of human success in the old adage: Man proposes, God disposes. We may and should think, on good grounds, that twentieth-century man feels greater overall competence vis-à-vis nature than did his seventeenth-century counterpart who needed a secular Lord Protector, an ecclesiastical Papa (in Rome, Augsburg, Geneva, or elsewhere), and a divine Provider. Chemical fertilizers and insecticides alone have effectively eroded the relevance of Providence.

But what has been eroded is an old and badly vulgarized concept of Providence. Thoughtful people would object that belief in that kind of Providence was no better than belief in any *deus ex machina,* and Providence rightly conceived can never be in competition with science and technology. More thoughtful people might add that the conquest of nature, which has indeed made a triumphant march, has singularly ignored (perhaps even handicapped) much needed progress in the conquest of *human* nature—that is, man's inner nature. Are we now really more competent than our forebears were in arranging our inner affairs and our social relations? Do we have anything to boast of in these respects? Have cruelty, violence, deceit, and selfishness diminished?

We should indeed no longer project the old, and now unsuitable, images of kings, rulers, caretakers, insurance brokers, or heads of households onto our gods. As Mitscherlich suggests, we live in a kind of "fatherless" era. Few people today have the live experience of a strong, all-knowing, all-powerful, all-providing father. Fathers (and to some extent their various analogues—bosses, supervisors, clergymen, heads of state, and administrators) have changed. As advisers, consultants, or friends, their "care" is of a different order from that of the old tribal fathers and feudal lords. Their providence is no longer a matter of protecting children against the elements, shielding them from famines or wars, and feeding their mouths (in affluent societies). So what can be a realistic "fatherhood of God" today, at least for those who do wish to maintain the theme of the "two families"? Is a modern definition of Providence possible, based not on old doctrinal formulations but on today's experiences in living? Such questions lead us back to benevolence. But first we must attempt some discussion of its opposite: malevolence.

Coping with Malevolence

We have seen that belief in cosmic benevolence is a tenuous thing. Not everyone has it. It is curious that belief in cosmic malevolence is even more tenuous. What seems to some people the most obvious feature of the universe in its intention to themselves has been for others the starting point of whole belief systems whose purpose is to deny it. The three little monkeys' taboo on evil is that it should not be heard, seen, or spoken, so that it will not "be." The Christian Scientist deals with evil by denying it the status of real existence—it is only a false perception that makes things "look" evil. Better perceiving and straight thinking demonstrate that only goodness exists. The optimist insists that good will come even from evil. The instrumentalist holds that evil is a prod or spur that helps us keep our eyes on the good. Romantic socialists, such as Rousseau, see evil as a product of urban circumstances which have spoiled rustic goodness and turned the noble savage into an ignoble citizen. And so there is ample evidence that people tend to tinker with the reality status of unpleasant things. Attempts have been made to reduce malevolence (literally: wishing to do ill or evil) to ignorance, dumbness, error, mental blindness—all rather mild conditions that can be forgiven. *Tout comprendre c'est tout pardonner.* Malevolence has also been ascribed to characterological sadism. It has been seen as a reaction to stress and as the manifestation of an instinct of aggression. It has been seen as "the animal in man"—nature red in tooth and claw. Such anthropological beliefs are supplemented by metaphysical and religious concepts about malevolence based on the origin and status of special malevolent gods or demigods: fallen angels from Lucifer to Mephistopheles, antichrists and anticreations. And one can play verbal or logical tricks with unpleasant realities: what we call evil is only the absence of good; what we call malevolence is really only the absence of benevolence.

To all such efforts at interpreting the unpleasant, raw experience says: Pain hurts! Evil is evil, pain is pain, death is death, and don't you deny it! There is no neutral zone between benevolence and malevolence. The important things are either pleasant or unpleasant. The slaughter of the innocents at Bethlehem, the Nazi atrocities, the Stalinist terror, the napalming of Vietnam citizens as well as the birth of a malformed and defective child and the persistence of racial hatred among men—they all come to mankind as malevolent assaults. They spell Malevolence with a capital M which is all too real.

And so there is a difference between experiencing malevolence and learning to cope with it. Many religious, metaphysical, and moral beliefs are reasoned attempts at coping with malevolence in the world by locating its source, attributing it to various agents, describing its essence, alerting people to its presence in diverse forms, investigating who or what is accountable for it, and seeking ways of alleviating its impact. If one also believes in an all-good God who made a good creation, there is the difficult question which any theodicy faces: How can the goodness and justice of such a God be vindicated without either denying the reality of evil or holding him responsible for its presence? And if one in addition believes that God is a heavenly Father who provides for his children, and is curious about "the divine purpose in its intention toward oneself," theodicy is no longer an abstract business but a very personal quest for integrating the good objects and bad objects in one's life and assessing their respective powers.

That quest will be lifelong. I do not know how one comes to an integrated and realistic view of good and evil, but observations of normal (or optimal) psychological development give some pointers about the way we integrate the benevolent and malevolent experiences in our lives. One step in this integration consists of trimming our important human objects gradually down to realistic size: father and mother are neither gods nor demons. They are sometimes benevolent, sometimes malevolent; they love and they hate. They are only human. They are frail and faltering beings, mixtures of love and hate, as their parents and grandparents were before them. And so am I: I'm neither a god nor a demon, neither all benevolence nor all malevolence.

A second step toward integration is to know that love is longer than hate,[10] that love seems to have the edge over hate in energy and potency, so that, by way of speaking, an ounce of love may thoroughly dilute a pound of hate. Freud boldly formulates[11] that erotic drives not only fuse with the death instinct but have the capacity of neutralizing it. Menninger[12] holds that, under the aegis of love, aggressive and destructive impulses can be put to constructive use.

A third long step toward integrating benevolent and malevolent experiences in one's life consists of what Jung[13] calls individuation—a slow process of self-scrutiny in which one discovers that much that passed for love in one's own past actions was tainted with hate, and that the "better self" is still to be cultivated through proper remorse and more genuine forms of caring.

Add to this the old ethical precept that means must be commensurate with ends. One of the best pedagogical formulations I know is Berdyaev's,[14] to the effect that an all too exclusive focusing on evil gives evil an aura and makes a man paranoid, and that fighting evil by evil means puts one into the camp of evil. Such warnings have a sobering effect, for they make us see how close each of us is to malevolent impulses, thoughts, and actions. If that awareness makes us more ready to forgive others for their malevolence, we let love win over hate.

An intriguing relation between belief systems and coping with malevolence has recently been described by Sims and Baumann,[15] a psychiatrist and a geographer respectively. They studied how people cope with the threat of tornados, starting from the observation that of three major tornado belts on the United States mainland (the central Midwest, the Great Lakes area and New England, and the deep South) the highest tornado death index (equating for area, population, and number and severity of tornados) is in Alabama. This is not due to poorer warning systems, more fragile homes, and similar "reasonable" causes. A careful study of attitudes toward first hearing the warning signals showed that in the Alabama region, by and large, people "emphasize their belief in a future controlled by an external force"[15] (directly or indirectly from God). Along with this belief they have "less confidence in their own ability to have an impact on reality."[15] They "confront a tornado in a manner that is consistent with their attitudes. They place less trust in man's communal knowledge and control systems; they await the fated onslaught, watchful but passive."[15] There is a penchant here for letting malevolence have its way, if it must, or else for embedding it in an ulterior, unfathomable divine benevolence. The latter maneuver is one of hope, or wishful thinking, that some good may come out of evil if all the pieces of the puzzle are in their final place.

But malevolence can be so repetitive and omnipresent that it leads to despair or stupefaction. The suffering of innocent little children is the great stumbling block to many of Dostoevsky's sensitive people. It has been put succinctly by Camus: " . . . I shall not . . . try to pass myself off as a Christian in your presence. I share with you the same revulsion from evil. But I do not share your hope, and I continue to struggle against this universe in which children suffer and die."[16] In such a world, the sensitive person can find no use for Providence. Camus can find in it no ground for hope. Is hoping, in the face of such brutal facts, only a case of what James called "making easy and felicitous what in any case is necessary?" Is it self-deceit?

Care and Hope as Aspects of Providence

It has been said of the Christian doctrine of Providence that it tries to spell out how God is constantly related to his creation. With Ernest Jones's emphasis on the individual case this general theme becomes: How is God involved in *my* life at all times? The particular individual of Jones raises both a psychological and a theological question: he is interested in the Divine Purpose *for himself.* And he assumes something like a two-way street between himself and his god: If God is to care for me, what must I do to be a working part of such a caring relationship? Any formulation of Providence must take human freedom, human initiative, and human activity into account, or else it would be a doctrine about marionettes, who are not known for having any interest in why and how their strings are pulled.

The nearest analogue to a caring God is, of course, a caring parent and his child. There are other analogues, but more remote: the teacher and his pupil, the artist and his artwork, the boy and his pet dog. Since we all begin as children, the parent-and-child model of caring is primary in our experience. Caring holds clues about Providence, but caring can assume many different forms, depending on the growth of the person cared for and the personality of the person cared for and the personality of the person who cares. For instance, the care received in infancy consists of many tangible gifts and ministrations: food, warmth, blankets, bed; being cleaned and groomed, cuddled, spoken to, and laughed with; being provided with sights, sounds, touches, tastes, smells, and opportunities for motor activities. All these things have their intangible aspects as well, but the media are largely tangible and concrete, and most of the initiative in the specific instances of caring is parental. In childhood, the patterns of caring are different: the child will take much more initiative in providing for his own wants and with the aid of free locomotion will explore his world to seek the stimuli that are fit for him, by his own choice. Still, many basic things such as food, shelter, and consistent access to his parents and others must be made available to him, since they go beyond his powers to arrange them for himself.

As time goes on, the caring parents will increasingly become aware that they are not to hover over their child or mold him into a preset form, but that they are to help their child grow according to his own destiny and timetables and "essence." Their care of him now includes eliciting in him the desire and capacity to care for himself and to care for others, according to his abilities. He is to assume responsibility for himself and others, and give up some of the old dependencies. His freedom is to be exercised; he is to have a chance to make mistakes and learn from them. And while continuing to care for their growing child, the parents are also to gain in their freedom and exercise it in new ways, liberated from their earlier urge to express their care in food, shelter, clothing, and specific behavioral directions.

According to Mayeroff,[17] who wrote a beautiful essay on caring which does not contain one pious word, the giving, receiving, and reciprocating of care are intimately associated with autonomy and freedom. Caring, for anybody or anything (for one can also care for an idea or a principle or "cause"), becomes a way of life which actualizes and fulfills the self while it actualizes and fulfills others. It gives a delicately poised certainty, a place in reality, a sense of wonder for the unfathomable mystery of existence. A life in which caring is the central dynamic factor is enough in itself. It satisfies.

If our experiences, from infancy through childhood and adolescence into adulthood and possibly parenthood, have been favorable, caring is by its very nature personalistic. We have received care from persons, and we have given care as persons. Organizations, bureaucracies, states, or associations do not care —at best they may facilitate the ways in which one person may care for another. They are equipped to administer or manage, but they themselves cannot care. In fact, many of their habits and procedures militate against the essence of caring: they often perceive needs falsely; they often fail to grant autonomy or respect freedom; they rarely see any person as "the other" in his full integrity and with his own growth program. Not only are they more distant from us than the persons we meet in our life—their distant existence is so overwhelming and molding that they thwart the essence of caring. I am not echoing in these statements an anarchistic critique of institutions or establishments; I am merely saying that caring is such a personal process that we need other words for describing what institutions do. Certainly they render services and provide facilities and do so at a price, but caring is of an altogether different order.

In psychoanalytic psychology of religion, the theme of the two families, one in heaven duplicating the one of earth, has always emphasized the need of the child to be cared for. That need can be so great and can be so frustrated within the earthly family that the child gladly latches on to religious ideas which proclaim another, mightier family or parent in heaven. When speaking of religious adults, the two-family theme in psychoanalysis has stressed the continued childishness of such adults which forces them to seek superior care and protection from a heavenly Father. I think this emphasis is correct—at least it seems substantiated by many observations. Moreover, the theme and its interpretive emphasis were in circulation long before psychoanalysis took root.

It has been sadly overlooked, however, that projections of a divine carer who relates benevolently to his creatures can also emerge from rather mature, autonomous, and active human beings who have found the meaning of life in caring for others! They give care and know caring as the highest human value. They know how personal it is, and therefore all other patterns of caring assume a personalistic character for them. Their perception of the universe is suffused with emotional, person-derived features, and they speak about it in a language of caring which alone can convey the meaning of life which they have empirically found. They strive for consistency between self-view and world view. Such a projection of a fatherhood of God can be quite conscious, although it will undoubtedly have many unconscious determinants also, including the wishes of the "child in the man."

To such persons, disbelief in divine Providence is tantamount to the assertion that the universe is cold and uncaring toward its inhabitants. It would have neither benevolence nor malevolence; its governance—if indeed that term is appropriate at all

—would consist of the automatisms of its own natural laws or the statistical rules of chance. And while such a world view may be respectable or sophisticated enough, it ignores the fact that man who is part of that universe experiences benevolence and malevolence. Should that experience be relegated to mystery or written off as delusion, or should it rather be made the starting point from which conceptions of the universe may be elaborated?

Much has been written about children's fears, and the accounts of childhood phobias suggest that malevolence is a substantial part of early human experience, against which they seek protection by clinging to their loved ones. But as Winnicott has pointed out, children also develop the capacity and the wish to be alone, seemingly unprotected. Being cared for does not mean being constantly surrounded by caretakers. The child with the "good-enough" mother, even the infant, at times accepts and enjoys being by himself. What makes this possible? It depends, says Winnicott, on having a good internal object—a rich, pleasurable, and peace-producing image of the mother present in the psychic reality of the child. The child feels related to the mother even when she is absent. And this is an ego relationship, for it helps in the self-government of the child, even to the extent of aiding in the control of id impulses which would demand her presence here and now.

Such an appreciation of the continued existence of a caring, loving person in one's life makes solitude not only possible but enjoyable. Beyond the years of childhood the positive experience of solitude may recur after the intimate closeness of satisfying sexual intercourse, and in strong men and women who have lost their spouses but still feel loved by them. That ability to be alone is obviously an offshoot of caring and being cared for.

From the experience of the self as caring and cared-for object, as well as the other as caring and cared-for object, stem our cognitive gropings about the rest of reality, our metaphysical speculations, our creative imaginations, our leading thoughts, and our religious ideas. That is the thesis of this book. Our beliefs and disbeliefs do not hang in thin air way above our heads, but they emerge from how we experience self and others in the bowels, the heart, and the liver, to put it Biblically. The intellectual content of over-beliefs is not a matter of chance or whimsical choosing. As James put it, the self-reflecting person who knows of his own benevolence and malevolence

> . . . becomes conscious that this higher part is conterminous and continuous with a MORE of the same quality, which is operative in the universe outside of him, and which he can keep in working touch with, and in a fashion get on board of and save himself when all his lower being has gone to pieces in the wreck.[18]

The speculative idea of a *more* which first emerges from experience gradually serves to produce the new insight that any benevolence on my part is only the greater benevolence of the *more* mediated by me. For when benevolence is narcissistically appropriated, it stops being benevolence and becomes calculated self-interest. If there is no transcendent reference to benevolence we have only a euphemistic word without substance. That is why poets and lovers intuitively capitalize the word Love when they start writing about it. Love is always larger than the person experiencing it—such is the phenomenology of the person in love, beloved or loving.

Caring, then, can be seen as an aspect of the *more*, maybe its essence, by people who care. While they may feel at times the need to be cared for, they are autonomous enough to take care of themselves for their daily wants and many special needs. They have energies enough to invest in the care of others. And so they can think of a divine Providence without being passive or childish or helpless, and without passing the buck to a heavenly agency. They have found an identity that permits them to recognize their limits and to ask at times for help. Help from others, help from a god, help from a heavenly Father—it does not matter too much how you phrase it, for in the end, the care received from other human beings is seen as mediated care whose fountain is in a cosmic *more*. There is no magic in that thought.

A second aspect of Providence is clarified by hope. As caring arises from benevolence, it may be said that hoping arises from malevolence in the sense that hoping presupposes a tragic life situation, a captivity or an oppression, from which liberation is sought. If everything goes well with us and if we face no calamity there is not much reason to hope. We may *wish* our happiness to continue unabated, but that is just wishing, not hoping.

Hoping and wishing are different things. Gabriel Marcel[19] has given a useful rule of thumb for distinguishing between these two. Realizing that the word "hoping" is frequently used as a euphemism for all kinds of desires, he finds the phrase "I hope that . . ." suspect. The more one emphasizes and specifies the "that" the more likely it is that one is only wishing. The farmer hopes for rain, the investor hopes for a good return on his investments, the vacationer hopes to have a sunny time in the Rockies. These are plain wishes, directly instigated by the pleasure principle. Hoping, according to Marcel, requires a far more diffuse and global content than wishing. One hopes for freedom when one is in bondage, one hopes for liberation, salvation, life. When one is seriously ill, one hopes for betterment. When one is bereft, one may hope for reconciliation with one's lot.

These psychological differences between wishing and hoping can be clarified very nicely by the theological ideas of apocalypse and eschatology.[20] Apocalyptic writings, including some of the Old Testament prophetic books and the New Testament book of Revelation, are replete with wish-fulfilling fantasies derived from the writers' concrete worlds and their plight in it. Divine revenge on the enemies in a time to come and a reversal of fate are major themes in apocalyptic thought. Trumpets will sound, the gates of heaven and hell will be opened, whores sitting on beasts dramatize the wicked, trumpets of revenge will be heard, and the seals of the scrolls of judgment and destiny will be broken. The world will be "set straight" according to the writers' ideas of straightness. Along with such visions as pearly gates leading to heavenly cities in which the saved will be welcomed, all these themes suggest that today's bad situations are compensated by fantasies of the opposite which the heavenly father or ruler will provide. What a letdown if any of these fantasies will not be fulfilled! The wishes are quite fervent, and quite specific; they are derived from concrete earthly situations from which some extrapolations are made. In distinction to these "primary process' imaginations, eschatology entails an entirely different style of thought. Eschatology abhors specific details, for the simple reason that it distrusts man's penchant for prescribing to Providence what it should deliver. Eschatologists know all too well that if man's wishes are allowed to go unbridled, man will wish for the moon, and seize another opportunity to displace God. Therefore, they keep things undefined, for belief in Providence primarily involves letting God be God and trusting in his good will. Thus, the apostle Paul speaks modestly: "For now we see in a glass darkly, but then we will see face to face." He does not say *what* he will see, for he knows that concrete fantasies and specific speculations are mere wishing, with the added sin of in effect telling God what to do for him, Paul.

If hoping is dominated by the reality principle, as I hold, we should be clear about the ways reality is perceived in hoping. Reality has a time dimension, and hoping draws on a special time perspective. For instance, when a man truly hopes, say, for survival despite a diagnosis of terminal illness, I cannot fruitfully protest against his hopefulness by citing the grim statistics of cases like his. He will remain unconvinced by my statistical arguments (in fact, he may share these himself), for the point is that he hopes where I would not hope. He knows that in my "unhope" I draw exclusively on past experience (medical statistics, knowledge of pathology, and all the rational inferences one is entitled to draw from such data), and he realizes that such knowledge, however impressive, is limited. It is based on the past and today, and whatever one can extrapolate from these. The man who hopes takes the future into account and lives toward it. He assumes that the world's process is still moving so forcefully that all that has happened and is now occurring has not yet been coded. He believes that the *more* is indeed surpassing. He will see my presumed expertise as limited because it draws too exclusively on the past and does not take the dynamic "thickness" of the present and the potential novelty of the future adequately into account. And so, while testing reality, but seeing it in slightly different time perspective, the man who hopes takes experience as *experience in formation* and time as *not yet finished*, reckoning with the possibility that novelty may occur. By definition, novelty is a characteristic of the *more*. For people who are alert and alive and who subscribe to some sort of practical process philosophy (whether or not they have ever heard of Whitehead), hoping can be a feature of good reality testing.

Second, hoping is not mere optimism. Optimism and pessimism are moody perceptions which skew, slant, or warp reality. Optimists and pessimists will never agree on the import of reality, for reality appears to either in a very different light. Moreover, both stand pat on keeping a certain distance from reality so that certain obstacles which have been insurmountable now seem attenuated or, conversely, a path which has been clear now seems beset with obstacles. Marcel feels that optimists as well as pessimists accentuate aggressively the importance of the self and its opinionated views. The optimist reasons: "If you could only see things as clearly as I do . . ." or "If you could only accept my viewpoint. . . ." The pessimist also stresses the uniqueness of his view. The hoping person, on the contrary, tries to remain part of the scheme of things without narcissistic distantiation and without argumentativeness. His attitude toward reality is far more humble and modest than that of the optimist or pessimist.

Third, an intriguing developmental-dynamic sequence in the situation of the dependent infant throws light on hoping, elaborated by psychoanalyst W.C.M. Scott.[21] He notes that when an infant's activities do not lead to immediate satisfaction of his basic wishes a series may arise of: (1) waiting; (2) anticipating; (3) pining; (4) hoping. When there is a strong wish but the gratifying object is absent, hallucinations will occur—and the infant now waits for the hallucinatory image to be transformed into actual sensation. Hallucinated food is not real food. In anticipating, the infant goes beyond mere waiting for the taste and smell of food: he waits for the sensory satisfaction to be obtained. Hallucinated satisfaction is not real satisfaction. In pining, the infant wishes his situation to undergo change, that food will come, that sensory satisfaction will be obtained, and that there will be an object that satisfies. The hallucinated mother is not the real, actually present mother. Finally, in hoping there is the added belief that an object will be forthcoming which has itself the desire to satisfy the longing infant. The mother is not the same as the good mother. The infant who has learned to hope for the satisfying life has vested his hope not in food or taste or smell or the sound of his mother's steps as she walks to him, and certainly not in hallucinations of all these, but in the mother herself as the good object who desires the infant as much as he desires her. Hoping requires trust in benevolence as an actual trait of another human being or as a quality of the universe.

So, hoping can be clearly delineated from wishing and the primary process. Hoping can be firmly embedded in reality and guided by the reality principle, but it takes reality in a deep sense, as we all do when we face important issues which affect us personally. It takes reality as animated reality, as a reality suffused with purpose and meaning and feeling. This is not animism which populates the earth and sky with ghosts, nor is it magic which tries to appropriate power from the universe. Animism and magic can be clearly present in wishing—they are antithetical to hoping.

Hoping, then, defines one important aspect of Providence. Whatever Providence may be, hoping is an approach to it. From the human proclivity to hope a vision arises that benevolence itself has the desire, so to speak, of showing its benevolence. Benevolence is seen as an urge. In Scott's paradigm, the hoping infant knows that his mother is so constituted that she wants to satisfy him. To the hoping person the cosmic *more* is benevolence and is so constituted that it wants to respond to the person's longing. And if, as we saw, caring always tends to be perceived in the personal mode, then whatever is caring and benevolent in the universe will tend to be fashioned personalistically. Providence will be a Person. An analogous phrase says it well: "Sin is only a word—forgiveness is a person."

Now, persons make promises to each other, and reportedly, gods make promises to man. Hoping also consists in taking a person by his promise, and in seeing a promise in certain situations. For those who believe in a divine Providence, what are its promises?

Here we come upon a plethora of beliefs and, by implication, reasons for specific disbeliefs. Some believe that upon their demise they will be lodged in a special mansion that is part of a heavenly palace. Some believe that they will turn into angels, and rejoin their already angelicized relatives. Some believe that on the musical circuit above they will encounter only friends, for all their enemies will have been pent up elsewhere. These are some crass examples of what the promises of Providence are held to be—"for the Bible says so!" Providence is held to be the dispenser of specific, almost labeled goods which are to be delivered without fault. Others believe that Providence will eventually deliver them from their bodies and turn them into the pure spirits they were always meant to be in the first place. Still others believe in the resurrection of the body, then to be immortal. Some believe in another life coming—another life to be lived through, perhaps in several successions of reincarnation, until the higher life will have been completed and one is liberated from all individuality. Of note in all these beliefs is how specific they are and how concretely they take any divine promise. Of further note is how strongly they are centered on the question of immortality.

Just as one should distinguish between wishing and hoping, taking these as evidence of the primary and secondary processes respectively, one should distinguish between primary and secondary process varieties of promising. Schlesinger[22, 23] has elaborated this distinction. In primary process promising the person makes his promise more or less in the manner of writing a blank check, oblivious of how he can ever live up to the implications of his act. Some promises extorted from young children by parents are of this order: "I will never get my clothes so dirty again!" says the child "willingly," under pressure, unable to foresee what new situations for dirtying his clothes will arise. Or when an adolescent in a gesture of good will promises his mother that he will give her an annual $25,000 pension in her old age, he does not and cannot know what control he has over the fulfillment of such a promise. He engages in a momentary fancy, which may be endearing enough, but his promise has the status of a wish. Secondary process promising demands commitment and some reasonable measure of control and foresight, so that the promise can be delivered. Precisely, therefore, secondary promises may have to be somewhat global, harnessing a good intention. For instance, if the adolescent would promise his mother that he will do his very best to take care of her in her old age, there is a reasonable chance that such a promise can be fulfilled and the son can adequately deal with the tension system which the promise has set up in his psychological household.

Those who believe in a divine Providence and those who disbelieve in it must be clear about what they take the divine promises to be. Does Providence engage in primary process promising? Do we hope that Providence will deliver specific goods, "as promised," so that we have a case against God if there is any reneging on the promise?[24] Obviously, that is not hoping but wishing. Or do we see Providence predominantly as Benevolence, whose benevolent intention will come through even in incalculable events and unforeseeable forms? That is hoping—and believing that the divine promise is of the secondary process kind. Eschatological (contrary to apocalyptic) believers take any divine promise as a global promise: God promises to deliver them, to be with them in trouble, to be present in their hours of agony, to bring them their salvation. There are no golden mountains here, no magical cures for cancer, no miraculous healings, no angels sent forth to break open prison doors, no horns of plenty for those in poverty, no postponements of the hour of death.

Providence provides no goods and renders no services. Providence cares and is benevolent and is a ground for hope, and in being so it can hardly be seen in other than personalistic terms. When Jones notes that "what one really wants to know about the Divine Purpose is its intention towards oneself," the foremost discovery to be made is that one must come to terms with benevolence. Without benevolence no caring, no hoping, no Providence.

CHAPTER VIII

Coming to Terms with Fantasy

In the corridor of a psychiatric hospital I overheard a middle-aged woman patient say: "Chaplain, I want to thank you for the sermon you gave. I have never felt so close to God as when I heard you preach." That utterance is all I know about this patient, and it continues to puzzle me.

What did she mean by "feeling close to God"? Is it just one of those cute religious clichés, one of those pious verbal routines, which believers exchange when they are entre nous? Did she merely want to be nice to the chaplain and express her sentiment in words she thought he would particularly appreciate? Was her expression metaphorical in the sense that she really liked the chaplain and felt close to him but dared not say so? Or was she subtly indicating that she did not care for the chaplain at all, but felt close only to God, her real lover? Was she in love with God—or with the chaplain? Was her phrase symbolic in the sense that God had appeared to her in the image of the chaplain, or that the chaplain's words had sounded to her as the word of God? Was "closeness to God" a product of her own unbridled imagination, or was it a sample of those mass fantasies which are stimulated by religious instruction and religious language? Had she failed to maintain the difference between the world of fantasy and the world of reality? And how different are these two worlds anyway?

A whole genre of critiques declares religious belief to be fantasy and therefore dismisses it as "fantastic," childish, primitive, whimsical, illusory, unreal. This genre of critiques also finds religious language bombastic, and its logic utterly faulty or at best strained. Such critiques make the most of the ordinary distinction between fantasy and reality but proceed to augment this distinction by notions of truth which identify truth and reality, more precisely the immediate reality of sense data. Those notions of truth imply a denigration of fantasy.

Although I have tried to show elsewhere[1] that Freud devoted considerable time and energy to the study of religion and analyzed it with great acumen, making well-considered and refined statements about it, in the last analysis his rejection of religion (for himself and those to whom he appealed) derived from his seeing it as fantasy, *pure* fantasy, *mere* fantasy. This is somewhat baffling when one remembers that Freud was also the man who contributed so much toward the understanding of fantasy by his analysis of imaginative processes, uncovering some of their laws and showing their enormous role in human life. Of his own books, he liked *The Interpretation of Dreams*[2] best, until the end of his days. He saw the analysis of dreams as the "royal road to the unconscious." He formulated the pleasure principle and the reality principle, putting these concepts in close connection with the primary process and secondary process respectively. He defined the primary process as a kind of feelingful thought which in dreams and reverie is largely pictorial, and in contrast with rational thought is replete with displacements, condensations, and symbolizations. It is close to, and significantly determined by, the deep stratum of vital urges and dearest wishes of the heart. Freud felt that the primary process was native to man: early infancy is under its sway until the reality-testing functions of the ego develop and promote the control of the head over the stirrings of the heart. With so much awareness of the actuality, omnipresence, and vitality of fantasy in human life, why did Freud commend its abrogation by deprecating religion while accepting the role of fantasy in art? Or, to use his own words, why did he accept the "narcotization" which the arts provide, while rejecting the "illusion" which religion creates?[3]

The answer is complex, for Freud was a complex thinker. I would venture to say that he essentially saw art as embellishment and religion as falsification of reality. He also knew that historically art does not seem to have led to aggression and bloodshed, whereas religion has precipitated wars and oppression. Art is innocuous, and its pleasures are peaceful; religion has an immensely powerful hold over the minds of man and can lead to dangerous fanaticism, brutal thought control, and flagrant reality distortion. Art does not claim to be ultimate truth; religion does. In the name of truth, religion has produced holy wars—the Inquisition, anti-Semitism, and the tearing out of live human hearts as sacrifice to deities. And so, as a reasonable man, as a scientist, and as a positivist, Freud vested all his hope in rationality, rejecting the irrationality of religion and most metaphysics. He lived by high moral standards which he thought to have developed from reason, and he bore his pains stoically. He knew more about religion than he is generally given credit for, and he had enduringly warm feelings toward his clerical friend, the Swiss pastor and psychoanalyst Oskar Pfister.[4] But he spoke with derogation of the "clerical phantasy" which produced witchcraft trials,[5] and he struggled throughout his professional life with the question whence the belief in a divine being which the ancient Jews had acquired "obtained its immense power which overwhelms 'reason and science.' "[6] For as a sober reality tester he knew that religion has power, and he never minimized it. In fact, I think it is fair to say that he stood in awe of its power, as he stood in awe of the vast scope of the irrational anywhere in life.

The woman who "felt so close to God" illustrates the presence of fantasy fragments and symbols in the stream of thought during the waking state. An adult who communicates with another waking adult, both at that moment in good contact with reality, she seems to assume that her communication makes sense, as if the fantasy were shared and quite natural. She employs the common "God-talk" which believers use among one another. Apparently, she and the chaplain divide reality and fantasy in ways different from what other people do. At any rate they do not pit reality and fantasy against each other. Or else, in the context of this brief conversation, they make no forced choice between fantasy and reality. Some questions emerge: Should anyone make a forced choice between fantasy and reality, denigrating the one and extolling the other? Is it not possible for the human mind to have loyalty both to the pleasure principle and to the reality principle, to exercise both fantasy and reality testing, and to engage appropriately in the primary as well as the secondary process? Such questions lie at the heart of psychoanalytic ego psychology and the theory of object relations. Our human task is as much to come to terms with fantasy as with reality.

Functions of Fantasy

In general, psychoanalysis has ascribed to fantasy two major functions, both abundantly observed in everyday life and in clinical situations. In Waelder's[7] formulation, fantasy provides gratification for instinctual urges and mediates in the assimilation of unpleasant experiences. Both functions occur in dreams and can be witnessed in children's play. When reality does not offer satisfaction of our urges and wishes, a modicum of satisfaction can be had by imagining a gratifying situation in which wishes are fulfilled. If the mind is overwhelmed by pain, some relief may be found in reveries of pleasure or in remembering an earlier time of well-being. I recall the case of a patient who was suffering from third-degree burns over his entire body: his pains were unmanageable until he was led under hypnosis to let his mind dwell on pleasant and relaxed episodes in his youth; while he was quieted, his wounds could be dressed and his recovery was speeded up. And every parent knows that children, after a painful or fearful visit to the dentist, may reenact the episode at home in their play, thus coming to terms with the unpleasantness which takes time—remembering, mulling over, and reenactment—to master. In our dreams, we may come to terms with pleasures missed as well as with pains experienced or feared. After an insult our fantasy allows us to retaliate mentally by subvocal diatribes against the offender.

The latter example also suggests that fantasy is a kind of experimental action. Freud was well aware of this; he always held that *all* thought, whether the free play of the imagination or goal-directed reasoning, is a substitute for action, a trial action, or an anticipation of action. If acting is final and risky, so much the better if one can think first, or think instead of acting. But within the category of thought, the distinction between fantasy and reasoning is paramount. Fantasy belongs to the primary process—it is instigated by concerns which stem from drives and wishes. Reasoning is part of the secondary process—it derives from concerns with adaptation to the demands and opportunities of reality.

Freud's distinction between primary process and secondary process thought has parallels in other psychologies. Aristotle and the British empiricists differentiated voluntary from involuntary thought, and directed thought from spontaneous thought. Philosophers are wont to speak of disciplined thinking which abides by canons of logic and reasoning as contrasted with everyday thought charged by emotions. McKellar[8] speaks of A-thinking (for autistic thought, derived from Bleuler's[9] observations of schizophrenic patients) and R-thinking (for reality-oriented thought), and conceives of these two as the ends of a continuum, allowing for mixed forms in various A/R and R/A ratios. But Freud added two important factors to the descriptive differences. The primary process belongs to the system Unconscious. It is exempt from the logical principle of noncontradiction; it does not abide by the linearity of time arrangements; it replaces external by psychic reality, and it has mobile energy charges. Urges with contrary aims exist side by side in the unconscious, and therefore the primary process can coalesce contraries by condensation, displacement, and symbolization. The second factor Freud added is that the primary process is present at birth but the secondary process arises only after development of the ego. Primary here means "developmentally first," and secondary means "acquired later." And since Freud postulated the infant to be egoless, and the ego in turn to be the product of the cumulative impact of the outer world and culture, the primary process is essentially something primitive that is eventually to be renounced. The point here is not whether the primary process *can* be totally renounced as one grows up (for Freud well knew its persistent power, even in very mature and rational men), but that it *should* be renounced and replaced by the secondary process. This normative or moral prescription embedded in Freud's developmental view is importantly related to his evaluation of fantasy in general and of religion in particular.

Holt[10] has convincingly argued that psychoanalytic ego psychology demands an adjustment of Freud's view of the primary process. Ego psychology postulates an "undifferentiated phase" in infancy, not an id to which later an ego is added. Though the infant is not as highly structured, differentiated, and specialized as the adult, he comes into the world with many structures ready to function. While the neonate may not have structures deserving the names id and ego, he is equipped with possibilities for both primary and secondary process activity. I think one could speak of the infantile proto-id and proto-ego, along with which one can recognize proto-primary process thought and proto-secondary process thought.

In adopting this ego-psychological viewpoint, one can fully endorse Freud's statement that the primary process is germane to the unconscious and a sign of its activity, without having to feel that it should be overcome at all cost by the secondary process. No categorical moral indignation over the use of fantasy, imagination, myth, or symbolism is necessary. And there should be, in addition, some awareness of the possibility that an exclusive advocacy of reason may in turn harbor a myth: the myth of rational man who confines his world to facts, figures, and logical operations. My point here is a faint echo of the celebrated controversy between Bultmann and Jaspers.[11] When Bultmann the theologian sought to demythologize New Testament materials in order to find their purely formal message, culture-free and cleansed from their metaphysical and mythological trimmings, a point was reached when Jaspers, philosopher and psychiatrist, raised the question whether myths are not indispensable to man. Jaspers, being far from naïve about human nature, held out for mythopoesis as a legitimate human activity—in its place and at its time, to be sure. A world without myths would be an impoverished, inhuman world. Fantasy, myths, the imagination, symbols, art, and religion will have to be evaluated not by comparison with something else, but by standards that evolve from within each of these activities. There are good and poor fantasies, fine and mediocre myths, sublime and poor art, primitive and sophisticated religion; and many mergers are possible between the primary and the secondary process.

Object relations theory (although some of its adherents reject far too much of drive psychology for my taste) also entails an upgrading of the value of fantasy vis-à-vis the obvious virtues of reality testing. It holds that every wish leads to the formulation of an ideal, and that the world of internal object images is in constant interaction with the world of external objects. In this interaction, the one series is checked against the other, with the eventual result that the ideal object, including the ideal self as an object, becomes an important motive for behavior. In fact, children as well as adults respond to the idealizations that others have made of them by seeking correspondence to these ideals in their actual behavior.

Schafer[12] has addressed himself to the finer points of these processes in the formation of the ego ideal and the ideal self, and Jacobson's[13] work in particular stresses the potential of early wishful fantasies for "all future types of identification," without losing sight of the important distinction between progressive and regressive use of fantasy. Guntrip, in describing Melanie Klein's ideas, refers to the "ruthless inner drama" of the infant's struggle with contrary instinctual impulses, which "then becomes projected onto the outer world, as the infant's brain and sensory organs develop the capacity to discern external objects."[14] This statement signals the Kleinian option as having the opposite danger of Freud's option: it runs the risk of playing down the enormous importance of the outside world and seems to put genuine, real object relationships on a loose footing. Fantasy is here not merely "primary" in the sense of being developmentally early; it is primary because it has almost overruling impact during the rest of life. In fact, those dramatic fantasies between Eros and Thanatos were clinically observed not in infants but in developed children of two and three years who had already gone through some stages of sensory-motor development known from Piaget's[15] work, but apparently with insufficient corrective influence. While ego psychologists would hold that these fantasies are a product of gradual differentiation, in Klein's view they are primordial and exert a very long, almost lasting, influence on years to come.

Briefly, then, my thesis is that we do not have to make a forced choice between the values and virtues of the primary and the secondary processes. Both are human; both are useful and appropriate for certain purposes. Both are adaptive: if we did not dream, our lives would be haunted by unmanageable tensions. Or, as Kris[16] would have it, if the primary process could not be marshaled by the goal-directed ego, there would be little creativity in human thought and action. Lovers need poetry. World views are prone to demand metaphysical speculation. The transmission of wisdom is apt to require myths and allegorical narratives. Moral teachings demand critical incidents for teaching purposes and memory aids. Thinking about the essence of personhood and human relations eventually becomes so encompassing that it requires metaphors and analogues of a family of man, cosmic consciousness, creators, ways of pilgrimage; or ideal men, men of God, or God-men. And there is enough historical evidence to show that such ways of thought can occur with good overall results in the same brains that achieve respectable expertise in physics, astronomy, social science, horticulture, or engineering.

Such a positive attitude toward fantasy does not in any sense abrogate the clinical truisms about the dangers of excessive fantasy indulgence, of regressive fixations to fantasy when reality becomes unbearable, of defensive retreats into fantasy, of autistic forms of thought in mental disorders and the role of the primary process in symptom formation and regression. It is true that primitive thought is dominated by the primary process and mature thought is dominated by the secondary process and the reality principle. But a new, fine discrimination is to be brought into the classical psychoanalytic discussion, away from positivism and scientism in the direction of the values of fantasy and imaginative thought. This new appreciation of fantasy comes from several fronts: the work of Kris[16] and Gombrich[17, 18] on art, the work of Erikson on Luther's religion[19] and Gandhi's ethics,[20] and the enormous shift that seems to be taking place in anthropology between, say, Lévy-Brühl's[21] *Primitive Mentality*, which made so-called primitive societies look almost like mental hospitals for their alleged autism, and the new structural anthropology of a Lévi-Strauss,[22, 23] who sees astute reasoning and conceptual schemes in the myths of tribal societies. Lévi-Strauss's *Savage Mind* is far from savage!

Living with Illusions

In the furious debate about Freud's *The Future of an Illusion*, it has generally been overlooked that its author, in addition to making an assessment of religion, also made a prediction. Like Marx, who analyzed the socioeconomic situation of his time and then forecast the coming proletarian revolution, Freud was bold enough to forecast the eventual victory of reason over illusion. Or so he hoped in 1927 when the book was published. Nearly fifty years later, we cannot say that Freud's hope has been fulfilled or that his forecast has become more plausible. On the contrary, the religious illusion and many other illusions besides seem today very strong and widely held. Since I have always been partial to Freud's thoughts on religion, I make this observation with some chagrin, not with glee. It would have been nice if religion had shed some of its crasser illusory features and moved in the direction of greater rationality and ethical pertinence. Tillich's work seemed to move into that direction. The theology of the death of god seemed a step on that road. Bultmann's demythologizing was of great help. Robinson's *Honest to God* made the trend almost seem popular. Secularization, attrition of church membership, and the increased expressions of alienation from traditional beliefs by the young and the old seemed to augur the slow death of once entrenched illusions, particularly those of a Father in heaven, a Godman who wandered on earth, and an infallible vicar in Rome.

But then came the countertrend. Large numbers of people wanted to pray in the public schools. The American president took an evangelist into the White House. The armed services stepped up their chaplaincy programs commensurate with the expansion of the Vietnam war. Staid religious mainliners broke out in glossolalia, even in such a rational place as Yale University. Many young people began to dabble in Eastern religions and mystery cults. Old evangelical groups modernized their looks somewhat and proved to have a strong hold on their children, who now parade their beliefs in well-organized and well-financed campus crusades. Fringe groups abound everywhere, representing various syncretisms of older traditions, old heresies in new forms, imported cults, arcane wisdom selections, and latter-day medieval obsessions. In mainline Christian churches as well as in Jewish congregations the old particularism which extols historical precedents and roots is gaining new strength. Pope John XXIII's *aggiornamento* drive was not only brought to a grinding halt but overtaken by an authoritarian reaction under Pope Paul VI. Even bumper stickers are marshaled to proclaim the old transcendent truths and to tout the cause of the old gods. The very things which Freud had described as illusions seem to have gained new life.

In addition, the allegedly secular world which does not declare itself religious nevertheless abounds in pietism in creed and cult. The Human Potential movement, the so-called Encounter culture, and various marathon groups that promote the experience of intimacy have adopted transcendental jargon and procedural liturgies strongly reminiscent of sawdust trails in nineteenth-century camp meetings and revivalist tents.[24] Messianic language is again quite respectable in today's urban world. Free universities give courses in astrology, meditational techniques, the cabala, and the *I Ching*. "Meditational Tarot" and "Ceremonial Magic and Witchcraft" feature next to "Dream Analysis and the Psychology of Jung" in one prospectus of "alternative education" in the San Francisco area. Downtown in many a metropolitan hub, young men and women stand mumbling prayers in the streets, at the very corners formerly occupied by the Salvation Army.

Enough to indicate that the fantasy will not be smothered, and that the voice of reason is, as before, only a still, small voice asking for a hearing in the tumult of illusions. In a somewhat gloomy mood but with admirable realism, Freud called that voice persistent: "it does not rest till it has gained a hearing"[25, p. 53] He hoped he would hear it loud and clear, but he knew that he could count only on its persistence. But then, maybe Freud was too severe in his anti-illusionism. By this I do not mean to ask indulgence for the clamor of the masses for bread and games, as in Rome under the emperors, but to suggest that Freud may have had too dim a view of illusion and separated it too radically from reason and the secondary process.

Winnicott's views of transitional phenomena seem more penetrating into the original, irreducible, and *sui generis* character of illusion and play. The transitional sphere belongs neither to inner reality nor to outer reality solely. The child and his parents engage in a contract, as it were, not to challenge the origins, belongingness, or propriety of transitional objects and activities. They play, and let illusions emerge, in the shared knowledge that this is not only essentially human, but a good thing for both emotional and cognitive development. The transitional sphere sets bounds to the primary process and brings it under cultural norms, and it also gives impetus to reality testing. In a word, the transitional sphere deals with *symbols,* in perception, action, and thought. Symbols are neither purely autistic fantasms nor ordinary things in the natural world. Therefore, Winnicott can say that "this intermediate area of experience . . . constitutes the greater part of the infant's experience and throughout life is retained in the intense experiencing that belongs to the arts and to religion and to imaginative living, and to creative scientific work."[26] To put it concretely: did the woman who "felt so close to God" during a sermon experience her God as a transitional object in Winnicott's sense? Was God *her* God in the sense that the toddler's security blanket is *his* special blanket—not merely a figment of his imagination or one

sample of all the blankets in his household, but something special and uncontested that *he*, with the consent and shared understanding of his family, may consider his own, sacred thing,
endowed with many surplus values? Knowing that such an object is *always* around and that he can at times be close to it is
important to both the toddler and his family. *Closeness* is what
the transitional object offers, and this closeness transcends both
the extreme interiority of the imagination and the extreme
exteriority of ordinary objects. Strands of such childhood experiences may well have been present in the woman's closeness
to God.

But there is more to the transitional object than the possibility of closeness to it and its uncontested status and origin. Transitional objects are also stepping stones in the process of ideali-
zation. Schafer states in a strategic article:

> Inherent in human thought is a tendency to create ideal images,
> to stabilize and elaborate them however vaguely and unstably, to
> search the environment for their counterparts, and to perceive and
> assess the environment (and the self) in terms of its correspondence
> to these ideal images. In this conception, *every wish creates an ideal.*
> Perhaps it is more precise to say that the ideal inheres in the wish,
> or in the fantasy or expectation that expresses the wish.[27]

This statement has a large bearing on the nature of beliefs.
Inasmuch as belief is commitment to an ideal, belief is apt to
include references to an ideal object as well as an ideal self, and
neither of these is purely internal or purely external. Both are
part of the confluence of primary process (fantasy, wish fulfillment) and secondary process (naturalistic observation, reality
testing). Ideals are part of the play sphere, both as Winnicott has
described it in children and as Huizinga has described it in
adults as an essential element of culture. Ideals are also close to
symbols—perhaps they are symbols—and Schafer's formulation
allows us now to discover in such symbols two strands: one
referring to the self, one referring to the outer world. In addition, these strands are so interwoven that the self and the object
appear engaged in "an ideal wish-fulfilling relationship." These
words are Schafer's, and I think they form a very good word

picture of what Freud had in mind when he described religious thought as an illusion. Freud was careful to differentiate illusion from the psychiatric delusion or hallucination, on the one hand, and from observable reality, on the other hand. Said Freud:

> These [religious ideas which profess to be dogmas] . . . are illusions, fulfillments of the oldest, strongest and most urgent wishes of mankind. The secret of their strength lies in the strength of those wishes. . . . An illusion is not the same thing as an error; nor is it necessarily an error. . . .

> . . . it was an illusion of Columbus's that he had discovered a new sea-route to the Indies.[28, p. 30]

> In the case of delusions, we emphasize as essential their being in contradiction with reality. Illusions need not necessarily be false, that is to say, unrealizable or in contradiction to reality.[28, p. 31]

To return to the woman who felt close to God, can we now entertain the thought that she might have spoken of an ideal she upheld, "God" being to her a symbol which was a condensation of her ideal object as well as her ideal self, something immanent as compared with objects and transcendent as compared with self? We could speculate then that closeness to this symbol might mean several things at once: (1) that she experienced a closer approximation during the sermon of her experienced self to her ideal self; (2) that she felt herself in a gratifying way related to the transitional object "God," which had phenomenological qualities of nearness and closeness not inherent in other objects; (3) that she felt herself in a gratifying relationship to the real object "chaplain," who mediated the first two experiences by his words, gestures, zeal, testimony, or appealing personality; (4) that she experienced a similarity of wishes and attitudes between herself and other worshipers which may have convinced her that her fantasies were shared —not solipsistic or autistic flights of her private imagination.

The fourth inference emerges from the fact that certain fantasies are corporate within a given culture or tradition, and have to that extent a certain kind and degree of objectivity. They attain this special kind of objectivity through symbolism which is transpersonal. There is something in any ideal self and any ideal object that amounts to a recognizable "common humanity"—a common value of excellence or completeness that attains special form in the symbols which are alive in a culture, whether in symbolic words, symbolic objects, or symbolic rites. To hold a belief and to be a believer mean sharing common strivings, having common ideals, holding shared views of certain paths toward attaining these ideals. Ideals, and thus beliefs, imply directionality. And in the practice of life, directionality demands orientation and at times guidance. Whether one believes in supernatural ideas, in theistic tenets, or in humanism, one will have to find in culture or tradition certain symbols which wrap up these ideals and the paths along which one wants to move toward them. Some of these symbols are "God," "Savior," "nirvana"; others are "universal compassion," "righteousness," or "Zen"; still others are "man," "selfhood," "rational man," "human dignity." There is ample choice to allow for individual differences, but all of these symbols have in common that they are neither completely autistic fantasms nor concrete sensory reality. They are elaborations of the transitional sphere. They are concrescences of the ideas of self and others. They fulfill some wishes while at the same time showing how far actual reality is from consummate or final satisfaction. They act as a goad toward betterment. Inasmuch as illusions are ideals, they are not *merely* wish fulfillments but also attempts at holding up mirrors which reflect actual shortcomings. In that sense they transcend the wish, and to that extent they do not satisfy. Rather, they impose a new demand by setting as yet unachieved goals. And the interesting thing is that such new demands are not imposed merely by external reality (although there is usually plenty of external reinforcement) but are also elicited by the dearest personal wish.

Winnicott's description of the transitional sphere and the transitional object implies that illusions are embedded in trust and arise from trusting relations. Trust has become an Eriksonian concept, but it is, of course, a tacitly implied factor in all humanistic psychologies and therapeutic work. The transitional sphere arises in a trusting relationship, in which parents (and older siblings and other caretakers) benevolently trust that the child's nascent illusion formation is good and normal for him, that it will help him grow comprehensively and richly, and that it will contribute to his full humanity. Whenever they play together or use symbol language together, the child learns that his illusions (for which he does not use this technical term, of course) are trustworthy inasmuch as he finds that the parents actually respond to his illusional moves, not merely with indulgence but with the kind of seriousness that attaches to all symbolism, ritual, art, religion, and other "goods" that are the earmarks of Culture (with a capital C) and cultured activities. Culture contains a large element of play, and such play has its own seriousness.

The classical case showing the dynamics of trust in illusion is capsuled in the book of Job, one of the most moving and perennially appealing parts of Biblical literature. When Job, after having been declared by God as well as the devil to be an upright man and a faithful believer, finds himself successively bereft of nearly all gratifying relations and objects, he is engaged in lengthy debates with friends. They moralize with him and exhort him and try to tax the viability of his illusion—that is, his belief in a just God. But Job's faith remains unshaken, despite the obvious signals from reality which should convince him that his faith has little empirical ground. The deity is not nice to him. His actual condition is one of gravest adversity. But Job bursts forth with the phrase: "Even though he slay me, yet shall I trust in him!" What defines and maintains Job's belief is his trust that there is more to God than he has thus far encountered. In the terminology of James, the *more* must be multifaceted, or else it would not be a *more*.

Elaborating on Winnicott's ideas, I would say that both the bad object and the good object are part of a whole real object whose sum is larger than its parts and whose essence is yet to be discovered, but to which we have access by three channels: through private fantasy on the basis of wishes; through reality testing on the basis of consensually validated facts; through activities in the transitional sphere, that is, through symbols which elicit play and enlist creative imagination that can be shared through cultural media.

We have seen thus far that illusions are immensely complex products of mentation. Because of the complexity of their origins and structure, and the "intense experiencing" (Winnicott) with which they are invested, illusions are beset by two contrary dangers, autism and reality. If autism prevails, illusion is no more than a daydream, an unproductive reverie without cultural benefit and hardly an enrichment to the dreamy person, except perhaps for a slight immediate satisfaction (but no enduring one) and a partial drive discharge. It does not promote growth. In fact, it fosters stagnation. The unbridled fantasy is likely to deteriorate quickly into hallucination and delusion, both of which are by definition utter falsifications of reality. Undoubtedly many belief systems and fragments of belief—religious or otherwise—are quite crazy in this sense. Hallucinations of winged angels or horned devils, fears of a wandering golem, visions of a witches' Sabbath on a bald mountain, and allowing one's life decisions to be guided by numerology are plain cases in point. Judge Schreber's[29] fantasies about the divine plan that would transform him into a woman were completely autistic, even in his own judgment after he had somewhat recovered from this mental aberration. In his case we can be sure, moreover, that his childhood lacked the trust which forms the basis for learning to elaborate the transitional sphere. The same thing can be said of Boisen's[30, 31] accounts of his various episodes of mental illness, which were often full of religious ideation. Tying in with my observations in the previous chapter about the differences between hoping and wishing, I would venture to say: the more concrete, detailed, and fixed the imagery of wishful elements in belief is, the closer it is to autistic dominance.

But there is also a danger from the other side: the sphere of reality. If reality is too narrowly regarded as containing only things, countable or measurable items, matter subject only to mechanical laws, or otherwise approached by what Whitehead called a "finger and thumb philosophy," illusions will be largely regarded as mistakes, errors, and distortions. Extreme or exclusive reality regard in the positivistic sense has no use for symbols.* Moreover, in the determination to flee from all illusions in the name of radical rationality one is wont to overlook the possibility that an ideal of rationality is an illusion in its own right. This danger besets those forms of militant humanism which have arisen in reaction to the more superstitious, degrading, or dehumanizing aspects of religion. Faced with the evidence of ancient, cruel rituals of the Aztecs, or of child sacrifices in the Near East, as well as the more modern cruelties, stupidities, and silliness of, say, Jewish and Christian religion, the humanist proposes of course a valuable and proper correction. He is right, selectively, and as far as it goes. But as Pannikkar[32] has recently suggested, today's secular world led by social engineering and humanistic ideologies can hardly be called a significant improvement on the order of presumably more religious eras.

At any rate, we see large-scale dehumanization and alienation occur in our secular age, spearheaded by bureaucracies and technocracies, and aided by computers and other triumphs of applied science. Many thoughtful humanists will themselves rail against such a world, and I am not insinuating that humanists must carry the blame for misfiring reasoning and misfiring engineering. But in the name of what will they rail against these unforeseen and unwanted encrustations that are now obstacles to becoming fully and richly human? Are they not in need of an illusion in turn, a better illusion, a more progressive illusion, a more refined illusion if you will, but an illusion nevertheless that may improve a bad situation?

The point is that some old illusions have been fulfilled or are on the brink of fulfillment and we do not find them to our liking. The effects of pest control have become a new scourge on earth. In the biomedical field the possibilities are rich, from transplants to interventions in human gene structures. And as Jonas[33] has recently pointed out, our old ethical maxims and norms no longer suffice to help us make wise decisions among these possibilities. Traditional ethics, says Jonas, evolved from an ethics of neighbors in small communities, fit for proximate

---

*It may use plenty of arbitrary signs in its endeavor at mathematical formulation, but signs or emblems are to be distinguished from symbols which, according to Tillich, participate in the power to which they point.

goals and proximate means, adapted to small scales of space and time. While man's weak powers for intervention in the scheme of nature (and other men's lives) in the past demanded humility as a key virtue, he now needs humility over his excessive powers! There is need for a new bioethics adapted to the vast scale of man's powers of intervention, to the vast consequences in space and time of his drastic acts. Such an ethics cannot be developed merely from a world of observable, cold facts, nor can it be left to the private moral fantasies of a handful of individuals whose own wishes may abound in sadism. It demands searching in that transitional, mediating sphere in which ideals and illusions are born. Already voices are asking: Will man have a future? If the answer is no, we can let things ride. But if the answer is yes, we will have to create the illusion of a future for man, and give it content. That will require lots of beliefs, lots of ideals, lots of creative and productive fantasies, to be carefully checked against one another—plus a double check against our wishes on the one hand and the external facts on the other.

Appeal and Affront of Ritual

Belief, disbelief, and unbelief are cognitive words. They describe a state of mind, a knowledge or conviction of truth, an intellectual assent or dissent. This should not lead us to think, however, that beliefs are divorced from action. Typically, the relation between belief and action is seen as follows: belief (knowledge) is prior and subsequently leads to action (practice). The possibility of the opposite relation in which action is prior and affects belief is largely ignored. But in religion, it is folly to ignore the impact of action on belief. Religious belief is embedded in religious practices; creed is grafted onto cult. In the development of mankind worship existed before articles of faith or a theology. Even the priests in ancient times were first and foremost doers: they officiated at altars, robed themselves in ceremonial costumes, and danced or chanted. And so it is in the development of individuals, even to this day: one can hardly inculcate verbal statements of belief in young children, but one can engage them in celebrations, take them to church or temple, pray with them, and expose them to rituals. The act of circumcision precedes by many years the literacy of Hebrew school. Let theologians make the most of this for their purposes and extol worship as the be-all and end-all of religion! My purpose is merely to point out that in religion, creed and cult are a twosome and that a large part of religious belief becomes visible in ritual, not only as its expression but also as its source.

In psychoanalytic writings on religion much attention has been paid to demanding, energy and time-consuming rituals having to do with feelings of guilt and their expiation. Reik's[34] book *Ritual* has been a classic for years. Freud wrote a foreword to it and then went on in his clinical papers to describe the private rituals which some of his patients invented to ward off anxieties or to atone for their guilt feelings. Since these patients suffered from obsessive-compulsive symptoms a theme gradually shaped up in psychoanalytic literature which tended to equate rituals with compulsions and obsessions. In other words, rituals were largely seen as being in the service of psychic defense, particularly in conflicts between the ego and the superego. I have no desire to make light of this construction or to deny the validity of the clinical observations on which it is based. Nor do I doubt the value, as far as it goes, of Freud's famous aphorism that the obsessional neurosis is a private religious system and that religion is a universal obsessional neurosis.[35] The history of religion and the themes of religion—Judaism and Christianity not excepted—are full of bloodshed or reminiscences of crimes, full of revenge and retribution, full of sin and guilt; and even when these are gradually mitigated by the alternatives of forgiveness and love, the themes are still there to exert a dynamic influence. But the pairing of rituals with compulsions and obsessions gives ritual short shrift—it fails to do justice to those many other rituals which we may call celebrations and which call for joyous spontaneity rather than laboriously upheld defenses.

Winnicott's "facilitating environment" contains rituals of a much greater variety than those described by Reik. As already noted, the toddler's transitional object is in the true sense of the word a ritual object. Both child and parents consider it sacred, and it is put under certain taboos. Call it a fetish if you wish; at any rate, it is loaded with protonuminous qualities. The mother knows intuitively that the child's special object should not be routinely washed with the rest of the laundry, and the child knows that he may tote it around, finger it, stroke it, stick it into his mouth, and take it to be with him in ways and at times not tolerated in his dealings with ordinary objects. The transitional object is a ceremonial focus of the whole family, surrounded by laughing and crying, holding and sharing, taking and receiving. The transitional object is a center of ceremonial engagement conveying some basic beliefs, including: "everybody needs succor," "some things are sacred," "one must venerate something," or "life must have its moments of play." In more sophisticated language: There is something *between* (Buber) subjectivity and objectivity, or between your subjectivity and mine.

Guided by the positive outlook of the facilitating environment on ritual, we can see right away that ritual is a multiform activity that cannot be tied to one particular psychological type, let alone one form of psychopathology. Ritual comprises such contrasting activities as feasting and fasting. Some rituals proceed from abundance in the outer world. (such as harvests, the coming of spring, affluence) as well as the inner world (such as love bubbling over, availability of free energy); others proceed from scarcity or imposed deprivations (such as abstinences, avoidances, sacrifices, and taboos). The theater knows comedy as well as tragedy. Many fertility rites with their symbolic enactments of coitus are essentially pleasurable and stimulating, as are celebrations of "togetherness" on joyous occasions. In contrast, the reenactment of frightening or painful experiences, such as children "playing doctor" after a visit to the dentist, is driven by repetition compulsion in the service of mastering the original anxiety. It involves defense mechanisms such as identification with the aggressor, denial, or intellectualization.

Briefly, then, rituals may deal with grace (and its derivatives: graciousness, gracefulness, gratefulness, geniality, cordiality, and affability) as well as the threat of damnation (and its deriva-

tives: condemnation, dooming, cursing). Beliefs, when grafted
on rituals, thus partake of one or the other quality in various
proportions. It is often overlooked that the new or revised beliefs of the Protestant Reformation emerged largely from considerations of ritual, particularly the rituals of grace. The underlying and agonizing question was: How can we or should we
celebrate the meanings hitherto dramatized in the Eucharist?
The answers were not merely verbal—they were given in action by very diverse arrangements for celebration, which in
time came to define the new churches and sects.

Today, rituals are again at stake. Certain objections to belief
are primarily objections to rituals: some liturgies are considered
stuffy, dull, demanding, excruciating, guilt-imposing, or just not
participatory enough. It seems to me that the sharp decline in
church attendance in west European countries since the half-
way mark of the century is to a significant degree a form of
disbelief first in traditional rituals, and in some cases only sec-
ondarily in the correlated cognitive beliefs. In countries with
empty churches people may still continue to think theologi-
cally. On a lesser scale, the same may be true for the American
religious scene. In both cases we can see, moreover, that attempts are being made among the unchurched to reritualize
life according to certain convictions. Political protest gladly
takes recourse to processions, bearing of standards and placards, and the chanting of litanies. The Soviet Union has its
wedding temples. Many young people in the West avoid the
status-oriented diversity of clothes of yesterday in favor of a
humble, standard uniform of workers' clothes which testify to
an egalitarian ethic. The preferred jewelry is inexpensive,
made of natural or very simple materials such as beads, seeds
and nuts, and leatherwork, again testifying to a sense of brotherhood and sisterhood of all people. In other words, the so-called
new beliefs (which may be basically very old beliefs approached
with new freshness and honesty) are as much embedded in
ritual action and ceremonies (including the smoking of various
substances) as the traditional beliefs of the churchly crowd have
always been. The same coupling of belief and ritual leads other
groups to feel attracted to evangelistic mass meetings with in-

stantaneous conversions and public pledging or witnessing. Stark polarities of right and wrong, grace and damnation, and being for or against God are accentuated in the styles of conflict and the pairs of emotions that the liturgy of such mass meetings stimulates: crying and laughing, self-accusations and desire for betterment, pent-up feelings and release, guilt feelings and atonement.

At a certain point in the engagement in rituals the purpose of it all may be sharply questioned. Rituals may become hollow exercises and the attending beliefs phony. This at least is the observation of many ethicists. Led by the great Hebrew prophets, or by modern social reformers or revolutionaries, the cry may go out through the land: "To what purpose is the multitude of your sacrifices?" (Isa. 1:11) "We . . . look for new heavens and a new earth, wherein dwells righteousness" (2 Peter 3:13). Ritual may become an outrage or an affront when it absorbs too much precious energy or hallows a dubious status quo. The ethicist (who, ironically, may have obsessive-compulsive traits) is apt to see through pious rituals and unmask them for their pretense or hypocrisy, perhaps chicanery. Starting to reject the rituals, he may also come to reject the attendant beliefs and in that sense become a disenchanted disbeliever; or else he may uphold the beliefs but draw from them different conclusions for action, action of a pragmatic rather than ceremonial kind.

The popular Anglican distinction between High Church and Low Church denotes various degrees of emphasis on ritual as well as degrees of pomp and circumstance within ritual. Churches, sects, and congregations differ widely in the place and form they give to ritual, and on account of these differences they have friends and foes. But there is almost always some ritual, some stylized, decorous, or symbolic action. Unitarians are outspokenly nonliturgical and very cerebral; in their meetings they come as close as possible to discussion groups and studious lecture sessions, but even so, they start with moments of listening to some recorded music or to a recitation of poetry or wisdom literature. Quakers sit in pensive, but nonetheless ritual, silence in their meetinghouses. Man, it seems, cannot do without liturgical or ritual action of some kind, at least periodically. Winnicott's transitional sphere may be large or small, elaborately or miserly appointed, but its existence and necessity seem beyond question for most people.

The finest psychological appreciation of ritual I know is Erikson's.[36] The first occurrence of ritual, which is quite spontaneous according to Erikson's observations, is in the nursery between mother and infant, who greet each other with playful gestures, smiles, and noises after a short time of separation. Such activities are charismatic. Each person conveys a sense of hallowed presence to the other, which is mutually felt as a numinous, sacred experience that stands apart from the various practical ministrations mother gives. Note the joyful, pleasure-laden, spontaneous nature of Erikson's account. There is nothing defensive or obsessive-compulsive in these greeting rituals. Thus prepared, the infant is on his journey into Winnicott's transitional sphere and indeed into the whole world of Huizinga's *homo ludens*—man, the player. In his reflections on that great ethicist and practical sage Gandhi, Erikson remarks that he was an inveterate ritualizer who knew the power of ritual in mobilizing the workers to seek their best interests.

The growing child will come to terms with ritual, and through ritual will come to terms with life's problems, whenever he moves forward. After the ritualized mutuality of recognition in infancy, the period of early childhood poses the problem of discriminating the good from the bad and the enlistment of the child's will in doing and being good. Approval and disapproval, shame and guilt, are ritualized in the various styles of "upbringing." The child is presented with quasi-sacred norms and sanctions through which he attains the rudiments of identity, both in a positive and in a negative sense. He must want to be "good" (however defined), and he must also want not to be "bad" (however defined). He comes up against judgments, ceremoniously pronounced, and he is asked to internalize such judgments and their attending sacredness.

In the play age the child will engage with his peers in games and role playing which tend to have a coherent plot, dramatic turns and a climactic conclusion. He assumes some of his future roles, with all the ritual trappings he has thus far seen in his elders plus new ritualizations which he may invent on the spot, individually or in concert with his peers. Erikson sees in this engagement a forerunner of the role of the theater and the dramatic in adult life, as he sees the concern with right and wrong in early childhood as an anticipation of the judicial element in adulthood, and the nursery rituals as the beginning of all numinous concerns.

School age introduces the rituals of perfect performance. Today no one needs to be told how ritualistic schools are—Ivan Illich's[37] radical proposal for deschooling society is only one sign of that awareness. Erikson is open to the thought that children's "readiness for school" can also mean the children's readiness to engage in just such rituals of performance as educational systems demand. At any rate, exposure to rules of performance prepares the child for dealing with the Formal as a special category in life, with its attending risks of overformalization.

Adolescence combines the Ideological and the Generational in all those rituals whereby a solidarity of conviction is established. These rituals may be improvised by the adolescent himself or with his peers, or they may be more or less official in the sense of a planned progress of confirmations.

Throughout this epigenetic list Erikson makes clear that the growing person is not only caught up in and confronted by the ritualizations that his culture has adopted (some of which may themselves be in transition), but is likely to proceed with new rituals of his own, invented by himself and his peer group. Thus, ritualization is seen as native to man. In fact, it can be observed in the animal world also, which increases the likelihood of its having adaptive value. Its value does not lie merely in socializing the individual, despite the fact that cultures put it to such use. Ritualization is identity building in that special Eriksonian sense which treats neither the culture nor the individual as isolates.

In the context of this book on belief and unbelief I have of course stressed the numinous element in ritual, but with full awareness of its concomitance with judicial, dramatic, formal, and ideological shades of meaning. Some religious believers object to the formal element in ritual, wanting to have their numinosity in privacy and in silence. Protestants have a long tradition of disdaining the dramatic in worship, being more concerned with judicial and ideological perspectives in addition to the numinous values. So there is much diversity in the mix of values. As a child of my time and culture, I inherited the profoundly biased view that certain faith groups and denominations—not my own, of course—held out for veritable Punch and Judy shows in their celebrations, and I was supposed to despise their attending beliefs. This established my negative identity, a very important feature for growing up in a pluralistic society. Positively or negatively, and with all the diversity of inherent values, one has to come to terms with rituals. Those who claim to despise all ritualization may have many rituals of their own of which they are unaware.

When we reconsider the woman who felt close to God during a sermon, we may now wonder whether her experience was not in some measure induced by the ritualization of the setting in which that feeling occurred. It was a worship service—I do not know where, how large or small, or in what religious tradition. I do not know whether there were any benevolent symbolic greetings, any outstretched arms to receive her, any statue of the Virgin smiling on her, any dramatization of a scheme of salvation, any gesture of solidarity of conviction with others, any declaration of her goodness or sinfulness. But I surmise that she was caught up with others in a meditative hour, hearing and speaking stylized words, seeing and making stylized movements, hearing music or making song, and all of this in a place set apart for just those things. The group she worshiped with probably called the place a "house of God." If I make myself vividly aware of the phenomenology of this total setting it no longer puzzles me that she felt "close to God." The experience is not so different from that of an advanced psychoanalytic candidate who in a particularly brilliant meeting of his local society may end up feeling close to the spirit of Freud—and discovering in that feeling an element of grace. It is not so different from attending a great tragedy in a theater and noticing that tears roll down one's cheeks from the intensity of identification with the tragic hero—and indeed with all humanity at its best and its worst.

Even the antiritualist who despises all formality, all dramatization, all ideology in order to be just himself, as he says, will sooner or later find himself asserting that unusual self ritualistically. And his beliefs too will be co-determined by the practices in which he engages. If Winnicott's observations are correct, the antiritualist may never have learned to play. If Erikson's ideas pertain, such a person has by and large only a negative identity. In Freud's metapsychological view, he might be an epigone of the Enlightenment, an arch rationalist—but I am sure that Freud the clinician would have grave doubts about his mental health.

Enjoyment of Myth

In a previous book on the psychology of religion I had the audacity to end a section with the phrase: Without stories no religion. The section was part of a chapter dealing with the varieties of thought organization that can be found in religion, comprising clear concepts, functional modes of thought, concretism, syncretism, symbolism, and fabulation. The phrase captured the propensity of religious traditions to present their tenets, among other thought forms, by way of stories. In addition to codifying their beliefs in articles of faith or building their case on philosophical declarations, religious systems abound in narratives which comprise the lore of the group. Religious educators tell or read stories, congregations listen to and ponder stories, sacred texts contain stories, and sacred rites reenact some of these stories in symbolic form or justify their perpetuation by recourse to stories which explain how they were instituted.

I have used the common English word "story" to stress the special quality of this kind of thinking. Unlike conceptual thought, which creates order by grouping things and ideas according to similarities and differences and by abstracting from concrete items and appearances, narration creates order by letting an event or a plot unfold in a span of time, by portraying happenings brought about by certain actors. In the bewildering manifold of things that bombard our senses and crowd our minds, conceptual thinking creates order by taking hold of a "slice" or cross section of reality and classifying it, using various levels of abstraction. Narration, in contrast, makes arrangements of events in time, with particular emphasis on acts and experiences of animated beings: human, animal, divine, or cosmic. Stories that are relevant to beliefs tend to be preoccupied with the question of origins and destinies, with genealogies and the life crises of heroic figures whose experiences, properly dramatized, have exemplary meanings for other people within a tradition, if not for all people.

Stories related to beliefs are technically called *myths* by social scientists and students of comparative religion. Mircea Eliade offers the following definition:

> Myth narrates a sacred history; it relates an event that took place in primordial Time, the fabled time of the "beginnings." In other words, myth tells how, through the deeds of Supernatural Beings, a reality came into existence, be it the whole of reality, the Cosmos, or only a fragment of reality—an island, a species of plant, a particular kind of human behavior, an institution. Myth, then, is always an account of a "creation"; it relates how something was produced, began to *be*.[38]

Thus defined, myth meets at one of its borders *history,* which reconstructs the past within the natural coordinates of time and space, and at the other border *fiction, fabulation,* or *gratuitous stories* which are not bound to any time and space frame. Mythographers who collect the narrations of certain cultures know all too well that the members even of primitive societies relating their myths make distinctions of this order. Their accounts of the tribe's recent history are quite factual, and they know the difference between "true" and "false" stories. The false stories are mere flights of fancy used for entertainment. The true stories, however, are the myths which deal with the more remote histories and the more transcendant aspects of experience. Myths have a numinous message which reveals some cosmic arrangement of lasting significance. They belong to the sphere of the sacred as well as the sphere of beauty, for myths notably tend to be finely crafted by poets and dramatists.

Thus, profound beliefs take recourse to narration to demonstrate their viability and to portray, through myths, some abiding and existential truth which would pale or flatten in conceptual language. The language of myth is *convictional* language, as Zuurdeeg[39] would call it.

In addition to their great myths of creation and flood, the ancient Hebrews told the myth of the "death" of the prophet Elijah, who at the Jordan River, in the plain view of fifty followers, was taken up by a "chariot of fire, and horses of fire . . . and went up by a whirlwind into heaven" (2 Kings 2:11). The modern Negro spiritual "Swing Low, Sweet Chariot" perpetuates that myth. The Greeks told their story of Oedipus, who was doomed to marry his mother and kill his father; Sophocles the dramatist only gave the extant myth the most moving form we know today. And Freud seized upon the Oedipus myth to explain an essential quality of family life. Certain Jews of the Hellenistic period, later called Christians, told the story of the resurrection of a fellowman Jesus who had died on a cross a few days earlier. And the Christian church has repeated the story ever since. Muslims tell the story of Muhammad's splitting the moon.[40] The period of the Crusades gave rise to the myth of the Holy Grail. The myth of a lost Atlantis is perhaps more alive today among archaeologists than in previous centuries. Many peoples on earth have their myth of a Golden Age. Many social thinkers since Rousseau have held to the myth of the Noble Savage. Rosenberg, Hitler's philosopher, formulated a myth of the twentieth century based on racism. These examples sufficiently indicate that mythological thought belongs to all ages and cultures and that it cannot be written off as a quaint archaism which mankind has outgrown.*One could consider myths, particularly those meant to explain or give cohesiveness to cus-

*Classifications of myths come up with enormous topical diversity. One list contains the following groups, purporting to explain: (1) periodic natural changes and seasons; (2) natural objects; (3) extraordinary or irregular natural phenomena; (4) origin of the universe; (5) origin of gods; (6) origin of animals and mankind; (7) transformations (e.g., Ovid's *Metamorphosis*); (8) heroes, families, and nations; (9) social institutions and inventions (e.g., fire); (10) existence after death and places of the dead; (11) demons and monsters; (12) historical events (e.g., Troy, Alexander, Charlemagne). From E. A. Gardner, "Mythology," in *Encyclopaedia of Religion and Ethics,* ed. by James Hastings, IX (New York: Charles Scribner's Sons, 1955), 117–121.

toms and convictions, the *regnant fantasies* of a culture in any period of time.

Since it belongs to the definition of myth that it is widely held by the members of a culture it would seem that a myth does not spring full-blown from a private mind but accrues from material that lies dormant in the minds of many persons, ready to be awakened. Jungians attribute mythical themes to inherited archetypes, which, like a template in the mind, elicit symbolic surplus meanings in things perceived in the real world. Freudians attribute myths to the pervasive commonality of mankind's unconscious, plus the impact of their cultural transmission on an individual's consciousness, plus the dynamic traces of repression, distortion, and other attempts at conflict resolution prevailing in an individual's preconscious. Structuralists like Lévi-Strauss see myth as the intersection of several lines of logical classifications and inferences, the mythopoetic mind being so constructed as to produce emphatic statements of multilevel meanings, combined into one aesthetic form, like polyphonic music. Chomsky's linguistic theory[41] postulates that man, the languagemaking creature, is naturally gifted with syntactical abilities and a system of grammar which allows him to understand and make sentences, independent of the particular words he acquires through learning. In some such fashion one might say that man has a native talent for combining partial observations and contingent truths into one narrative whole which holds his conviction, that is, a larger and deeper truth that is no longer contingent but constitutive. Such a truth is not individually unique—it finds a prompt response in others of the same culture. The mythical theme is widely shared and worked over by generations, allowing for variations which, as in music, only reinforce the theme's sonority.

Myths are thus clearly in the category of James's over-beliefs. They proclaim a belief behind beliefs. And inasmuch as they have narrative form which lets truth *evolve* rather than *be*, they acknowledge in a unique way the process character of reality. Myths show not what reality *is*, but how certain realities came into being by their own unfolding. This kind of thought, which the Greeks called mythopoesis, is remarkably adapted and germane to the mind of the young human being according to the accounts of psychoanalytic ego psychology. It is the mind in transition from an undifferentiated stage to various stages of differentiation. It is the mind that learns to discern between the primary and the secondary processes, between inside and outside, between privacy and the public world, between the subjective and the objective. In the beginning of life, none of these distinctions is pat—they evolve slowly and in incessant interaction of the terms in each comparison.

Here again, Winnicott's transitional sphere and the orbit of play offer themselves as a helpful model. Primary process and secondary process, autism and pure objectivity, are not the exclusive options. There is a third, transcendent sphere, a special level of thought and action which combines strands of premises and meanings into a kind of experience that has its own validity, *and its own consensual validation.* A story becomes a myth only when it is widely accepted and given the status of ultimate wisdom or sacred knowledge.

Anchoring mythopoetic thought in the transitional sphere and finding its origins in the differentiating phase of early childhood does not imply that mythological thought is childish. Because anthropologists collect myths of primitive peoples and other scholars collect myths of archaic civilizations it does not follow that mythological thought is primitive or archaic. Endless tomes have made innuendos about primitivity, but such denigrating inferences about myth stem from comparing mythical thought with rational or scientific thought, not from considering mythical thought in its own integrity and measuring it by its own standards. We are beginning to see that mythmaking is an original human activity that can be exercised at high levels of civilization and with a great deal of sophistication.

Let me divulge a personal experience. Being an admirer of Martin Luther King I seized the opportunity, exactly one year after his death, to see a film of his life from the first stirrings of the civil rights movement to his tragic end. I saw realistic episodes assembled from tape recordings and documentary filmstrips: his preaching in churches, the bus boycott, the march from Selma to Montgomery, the great "I have a dream . . ."

speech in Washington, the march through Cicero, where he
and his companions were spat upon by angry bystanders as they
protested the segregated housing codes, the motel in Memphis
where he was fatally shot, and finally his great funeral, all with
mercifully little commentary. It was a raw, sober, factual por-
trayal. We all knew that King was dead, irrevocably dead.
Deeply moved by what I saw, I had the following fantasy. I
imagined myself at that moment, together with his nearest
friends and followers, saying: "But he lives!" None of us denied
his death, but all of us affirmed that King's stature was in some
way transcendent because of the sincerity and greatness of his
ideas and the ultimate sacrifice he had made for them. "He
lives!" I thought, because his impact lasts. And I suddenly
flashed back to a life that King himself knew all too well. Was
this affirmation "But he lives!" perhaps the original, and now
quite understandable, conviction of the small band of followers
of Jesus of Nazareth upon his undeniable and irrevocable
death? And was the notion of the resurrection with its specific
three-day timetable and the presence of an angel perhaps only
a priestly elaboration of that basic conviction of his followers
that Jesus' impact was lasting and transcended his factual
death? If so, the resurrection story was a clear case of myth, and
my appreciation of King's exemplary influence, if widely
shared, could be the beginning of a new religion or a new cult.

And so I felt free to demythologize the elaborate mythical
trappings of the accounts of Jesus' demise. But I also felt free to
mythologize, through an artful form of thinking attuned to existential meanings, the life and death of King. None of these
strands in my thought merged either with any private autism
on my part or with my capacity for upholding canons of public
rationality. Neither the "primary process' nor the "secondary
process' thought captured the essence of these speculations.
Involved was a third mode of thought, so to speak, that is playful, inventive, and insightful and that has its own form of consensual validation. It has to do with a belief behind beliefs, from
which vantage point certain concrete beliefs can be modified or
given up altogether, or new beliefs developed.

I think this episode of fantasy also helps us see that it is difficult, if not altogether impossible, to assume an attitude of disbelief in all myths if one is to remain a cultured person in touch with the arts, poetry, and all liberal learning. The scientist will properly eliminate myth from his scientific enterprise, but should he or can he eliminate it from his life? The dedicated rationalist and proud son of the Enlightenment may wish to excise mythical explanation and replace it wherever possible by logical explanation, but in this attempt the phenomena to be explained undergo alterations. The theologian may wish to demythologize the Biblical narrative in order to get at the pure *kerygma*, but how radical can he be in this endeavor? Bultmann's own work suggests that cutting out the old myths proceeds by introducing new myths, in his case the myth of Heidegger's existentialist hero.

Somewhere in the crannies of consciousness or in the public domain, myth remains despite efforts at its elimination. Rationalist that he was, and was proud to be, Freud did not shun using myth when he wanted to foster a deep understanding of knotty empirical problems or when he sought to set forth his deepest convictions. The Sophoclean version of the Oedipus myth became for him an explanatory principle. He liked to half-personify his concepts by giving them the names of Greek deities: Eros, Anangke, Thanatos. He obviously enjoyed mythological thought and wove it cannily through his scientific writing, even while he was providing a rational analysis of the contents of other myths. He knew the power of myth and realized that it was indispensable when the aim of communication is richness. And so he obtained the Goethe prize, well deserved.

The title of this section is "Enjoyment of Myth." Myths, like everything evolving from the transitional sphere, provide pleasure, the pleasure of play, inventiveness, creativity, and novelty of perspective. The so-called cultural goods are indeed *goods* to be enjoyed. Renaissance man came into his own when he discovered that joy can exist in many cultural activities; he strove to be a good lover, a good poet, a good warrior, a good amateur scientist, a good politician, a good churchman, a good connoisseur of art, and a good accumulator of wealth all at once. The Renaissance myth was, apparently, the myth of the multifaceted, multicompetent, multipleased, and zestful man. Later ages developed their special myths of man. The Enlightenment believed in the myth of rational man. Romantics believed in the myth of the noble savage and the myth of the homeless soul. Technology believes in the myth of man the specialist who should concentrate on small bits of reality by sticking to a narrow and precise mode of thought. Some existentialists believe in the myth of the disillusioned solitary individual with the stiff upper lip who will not be fooled by any appearance, including the false fronts he unwittingly creates for himself. Some modern men uphold the myth of the disengaged seeker after transcendent truth, to be found in meditations that will produce enlightenment for the private soul. Others believe in the myth that salvation is to come from groups engaging in incessant encounters that allegedly promote human potentialities.

Belief in Myths

These are all myths, and it seems that for every old myth renounced a new myth arises. Disbelief in one myth means belief in another myth. James, in calling such key beliefs overbeliefs, realized that they were speculations about the nature of the *more.* Knowing one's over-beliefs, that is, one's myths, allows a person at times to disavow particular beliefs he once held, or which are persuasively presented or imposed by others. The opening line of this book signals such a situation: Einstein's phrase "I am a deeply religious unbeliever" upholds a belief— a strong over-belief, one might say—which induces him to renounce certain smaller beliefs deriving from a special tradition that had its own mythology. In his statement he did not turn his back on myth, but revised his own mythology. Some old myths fell by the wayside as "false stories" but only because he had discovered a new "true story."

And the woman cited at the beginning of this chapter, who said that she "felt so close to God," may simply have used mythological language to express her conviction. I guess the chaplain understood her.

CHAPTER **IX**

Coming to Terms with Reality

In an ordinary skirmish between a religious believer and an unbeliever, a point inevitably occurs when both recognize that the believer holds certains things for real which the unbeliever considers unreal. The issue is not only the celebrated question of whether God exists; it is likely to entail smaller points or consequences, such as whether holy books are inspired and inerrant, whether prayer is efficacious, whether the pope is infallible in doctrinal matters, or whether ancient dietary laws which once had hygienic usefulness should still be binding for modern man. The debating parties will find themselves in different realms, not only of discourse, but of assumptions about the nature and span of reality. The unbeliever may point out the fictitiousness of the believer's ideas; the believer may question the unbeliever's dry and narrow factualness which leaves no room for any reality of the unseen. In Dostoevsky's *The Brothers Karamazov* Ivan says: "I understand nothing. I don't want to understand anything now. I want to stick to the fact. I made up my mind long ago not to understand. If I try to understand anything, I shall be false to the fact; and I have determined to stick to the fact."[1] And so the one will ask: What's the point in all your pious musings when you allow children to be maimed or go hungry in this world? And the other may ask: Is your life entirely a matter of fate or luck, one damned thing after another, to which you react opportunistically?

But when Ivan Karamazov tells his brother the story of the Grand Inquisitor and the gruesome tales of cruelty to children which he has collected from newspaper clippings,[2] the two are no longer arguing as believer and unbeliever. Now they are two believers, but with a difference. Ivan does not wish to question the existence of God. In fact, he has a lofty conception of him. But he denies that man is to be seen as God's creature. For the cruelty of man in torturing children and animals springs so directly from an evil human mind that God should not be viewed as its author. No God would torture a living being. No animal would. Only man does. And if the problem of evil lies hidden in a divine mystery that will eventually be disclosed, Ivan would rather reject the mystery altogether, because the price for its discovery is too high. But Alyosha picks up another motif which he finds more gruesome: If God is dead, everything will be permitted. More cruelty! Obviously, these are two believers in dialogue: one impressed by the reality of good and puzzled about evil, the other impressed by the reality of evil and puzzled about the good. The experiential, subjective reality is different in each case, and the wider inferred reality also differs in each case as a consequence.

Reality is thus not one single undisputed thing to which all people have equal access. Phenomenologically, reality *presents* itself selectively to people, and each person in turn *takes* reality to be thus and so. The result is many different realities. There is an external environment to which we have access by the senses; despite large commonality in perceiving, the senses differ functionally from person to person, and each person is exposed to a different chunk of the outside world. There is also an internal environment, private to each of us though also with some commonality, but differing widely in body feelings, memories, emotions, and fantasies. Murphy and Spohn[3] distinguish between two realities: with one we *have* contact, and we cope with it for survival; in a reality of a larger kind we *seek* contact out of curiosity and for self-fulfillment. Thus all reality, whatever we find or imagine it to be, has a self-reference, and the intensity of reality experience co-varies with the intensity of self-experience; in cases of depersonalization one also finds evidence of derealization. All these are empirical realities. Undoubtedly, each person's experience of reality includes something like a more or less dim vision of total reality, or a more or less vague guess about reality-as-a-whole which stems from his explorations and guides him.

From these empirical realities to the philosophical question of the "really real" is a large step. Each philosophical school offers its own hypothesis about ultimate reality or makes its own declaration. Most such declarations have been written up and circulated in the culture: they are taught in some fashion, by persuasion, exposition, innuendo, or inference. Thus, the world is full of ideas about what the world *is*, and these ideas often serve as a framework into which the bits and pieces of our empirical reality contacts are made to fit. Such large ideas are special beliefs, what James called over-beliefs; others term them ontological beliefs or ontologies. They vary in clarity from dimly held notions and surmises to articulate credos. Some people are interested in spelling out ultimate beliefs to themselves and others, but many people have only a crypto-ontology, a tacit or hidden ontological position which remains submerged in lower-order beliefs.

Dealing with Ontological Options

I have dwelt on the diversity of reality views at some length in order to make a special psychological point: ontologies, whether overt or covert, are not merely philosophical feats or intellectual exercises. There is every indication that choices between one ontology and another are not made on purely intellectual grounds but have much to do with the basic feeling for life and the emotional appreciation of the self and the world that each person acquires from his personal experiences. It is possible to write a psychology of philosophical systems and styles. No matter how objective a philosopher may strive to be, his thoughts are *his*, determined by his personality, his culture, his teachers, his era, and his *Sitz im Leben*—his life situation.

And so it is for the reality picture each philosopher paints. Karl Jaspers[4] was well suited to writing such a psychology of *Weltanschauungen*, for he was both a psychiatrist and a philosopher.

I am prone to emphasize, more than Jaspers did, the special psychodynamic qualities that characterize philosophical positions. For instance, there are the profound pessimism and the misogyny of Schopenhauer's work, which stresses the role of the will in human life and the cosmos. The proverbial orderliness and meticulousness of Kant were paired with a predominantly aesthetic and ethical outlook on all things. Spinoza's deep emotional glow and great sense of righteousness needed to be contained by mathematical devices that foster reason and clarity. Why should anyone (like Plato and the idealists) want to make a distinction between the obvious world of appearances, calling it shiftless and unreliable, and a hidden world of ideas, to be called stable and reliable, unless he really does not feel at home in the sensory world? Why do some people see ultimate reality as a stable structure, strong and obstinate as rock, while others see it as process, fluid and forever changing, if not because they find personal comfort in the one picture and discomfort in the other?

Jaspers once called the world as a whole "the encompassing" *(das Umgreifende)*,[5] which I find a nice term. I would be inclined to be slightly more metaphorical and warm about it, by calling it "the embracing." But others might give it the meaning of a viselike grip that holds man against his will, or as a dull situation from which there is no exit. Pascal was frightened by the "eternal silence of the fathomless vastness."[6] To some, the universe appears as a friendly abode, to others as a horrible, bleak space into which they find themselves "thrown," in Heidegger's[7] telling phrase.

Some people are bored by the sameness of things and may seek an exciting, dynamic ultimate reality; others are upset by the changeability of their world and seek a stable, fixed frame for their ultimate reality. Some people are frightened by the richness of the universe and seek a neat, simplified reality model. Others love the richness and the vastness and do not mind living with resulting world views containing certain unresolved contradictions and incompatibilities. The "really real" obviously has very deep emotional meanings that are highly idiosyncratic.

These considerations of the concept of reality are also necessary to highlight a knotty problem that is inherent in Freud's writings about religious belief.[8] It involves the ideas of development and sublimation. Freud always took a developmental view of things. He looked forward and backward between child and adult, and between primitive and developed societies. Growth, maturation, fixation, and regression are key words in his *oeuvre*. He saw the pleasure principle, regnant in infancy, giving way to the reality principle as development proceeds. He saw the infantile omnipotence of thought giving way to the reality-testing function of the mature ego. He saw cultures in historical progression and saw cultural activities in a developmental series: in the first, animistic phase, people accept their infantile omnipotence of thought and use it to influence nature and society in their favor by magical manipulations. In the second, religious stage, people cede part of their omnipotence to their gods, but retain a portion of it for themselves by which to influence divine action in their favor. In the final, scientific stage, man gives up his omnipotence and permits himself to be guided exclusively by reality, except for that trace of omnipotence which continues in his belief that he can know and perhaps influence reality by scientific means.

The outstanding feature of this thought pattern is that development is at times equated with successive emancipations. Everything is in transition and gives way to something else—life is full of qualitative changes, in which the old is left behind in favor of something novel. In this vein, Freud saw religion as archaic, primitive, or childish, and science as advanced. His hope was that people would outgrow the reality views (that is, reality distortions) of religion and move toward the kind of reality appreciation that science stands for. The mature person is an emancipated person who leaves religious belief behind in favor of faith in scientific reasoning.

Freud's persistence in advocating this emancipatory view of development is tested by what he made of sublimation in relation to religion. Granted that sublimation was and is a rather vague concept in psychoanalysis, Freud saw sublimation at work in the activities of creative artists and scientists.[9] Curiosity, penetrating inquiry, and manipulation of materials and ideas may have had their beginnings in the sexual and aggressive watchings and doings of childhood, but under favorable circumstances the original aims of the sexual and aggressive drives become inhibited. The drive energies shift toward intellectual, aesthetic, or other cultural aims, with continuity of drive satisfaction for the individual, but also with cultural approval and benefit. In sublimation an instinctual tendency or impulse is discharged through noninstinctual channels, on noninstinctual objects, with culturally defined aims, and in culturally useful forms.

Can religion be seen as sublimation of infantile wishes or childish drive aims? Freud occasionally acknowledged that sexual dynamics can be transposed to the highest ethical and religious interests. In the case of the "wolf man"[10] he felt that the patient's Bible knowledge allowed him to sublimate his sadomasochistic attitudes—but also that this religious sublimation eventually came to impair the patient's former intellectual acumen. Strangely enough, *The Future of an Illusion* mentions sublimation only once, to reject it. It is brought up by the imaginary interlocutor who suggests that religion allows "of a refinement and sublimation of ideas"[11, p. 52] by which the infantile traces are left behind. But Freud is quick to reply that in his opinion the religious person is too impatient, too demanding, too self-seeking in the gratification of his wishes for a nurturant Father in heaven. Religion does not ask enough renunciation of infantile wishes! It consoles directly, in the here and now, and indirectly by promises for the hereafter. It gratifies too much! On these grounds, Freud holds that religion tinkers too much with reality under the impetus of fantasy and therefore is not a sublimation. Freud insists on renunciation of instinctual wishes, and he feels that such renunciation is lacking in religion. In true sublimations, renunciation comes first—then come the transposed, more subtle, more refined, and considerably toned-down satisfactions which the new activity offers. The infantile omnipotence must be given up. Religion, Freud feels, holds on to omnipotence, and by that token is in a class by itself. It is a way of coping distinct from scientific work or the creative arts.

There are other reasons why Freud denied that religion is a sublimation. Religion is a mass phenomenon, a popular thought form and activity. Sublimation, however, is a rather rare process, confined to the happy few who have talent and favorable life situations. Religion also tends to constrict the range of thought, or at least of permissible hypotheses. Freud was impressed by what he called the "ban on thought" that religions tend to impose. In sublimation, however, curiosity is an important feature. So, religion turns out for Freud to be a special mode of problem solving, in which omnipotent wishes for safety, security, help, and alignment with great cosmic powers are not given up but maintained.

If, nevertheless, sublimation is grudgingly entertained as a possibility in religion, a fascinating problem presents itself. Is it possible to distinguish between childish religion and mature religion, or between primitive and sophisticated or highly developed religion? Or is religion doomed to give way to something else if the individual or social group develops to high levels of maturity? In other words, is there a point at which religion becomes developmentally transformed into an ethics, a philosophy, or a *Weltanschauung?* Such a progression is, to be sure, desirable to Freud, for it is linked with his notion of development as emancipation. But in such a transition what would happen to beliefs?

In raising these questions we come back full circle to the idea of secularization with which this book started. Freud's reality view was positivistic. It allowed him to see as a social observer that there is a secular drift, away from religion to rational preoccupations with scientific thought and social engineering. Freud's view of religion was jaundiced: he focused on its seamy side and exposed its enormous childishness. Biased as this view is, I do think we badly need to hear it, for religion's seamy side is very large and again today very strong. Many religious beliefs are exceedingly childish, drive-determined, and self-seeking. And many religious people seem to nurture just this childishness in their beliefs, whitewashing it with Biblical quotations that hold out for the pristine innocence and trust of little children. But these two views of Freud, when combined, did not allow him to see a second kind of secularization: the developed religious mind's willful turning to the world, not to promote a secularization of drift, but to increase the secularization of religious purpose. Though developed strata of religion may show grave ethical concerns, they do not thereby become merely ethical world views. Though they may advocate or even pioneer in social reform, they do not thereby become political systems. Though they may push for a revaluation of values, they do not thereby become philosophies of life. They remain religions. Freud did not see what Parsons[12] saw, that societies may move toward a closer approximation to religious values and to answering some persistent religious questions.

Noting how close some religious beliefs remain to the pleasure principle, Freud seriously questioned religion's capacity to be loyal to the reality principle also. He found religion wanting on that score, and therefore, in line with his special view of development and his positivistic ontology, he saw religion as something to be emancipated from. If religion could develop along the lines he felt desirable, it would become something else: a philosophy or an ethic. This view is far less tenable than it may have been in the twenties and thirties, when *The Future of an Illusion* and *Civilization and Its Discontents* were written. Both religious beliefs and nonreligious beliefs are so immensely varied that all of them can be placed on a scale between childish and mature, primitive and developed, pleasure principle and reality principle. Primitive and developed religion are as prevalent as primitive and developed art, politics, philosophy, ethics, or marital relations. Winnicott would allow for distinctions between primitive and mature play. Modern scholars in the history of ideas distinguish between primitive and developed science. Man does not outgrow or relinquish functions that are germane to the human mind and expressions of his human nature. We have seen how fallacious it is to regard mythopoesis an archaic activity confined to ancient civilizations. The modern world is full of it. And we are now seeing that

COMING TO TERMS WITH REALITY   229

science, of a sort, has been practiced in the most "primitive" cultures, if not from the dawn of mankind. *Homo* is many things beside being *sapiens*—he is *faber, ludens, religiosus, economicus, politicus, amans.* He is also a sensuous, aesthetic being. And he is all these things in more or less mature ways, with higher or lower degrees of development, and with greater or lesser dedication to the pleasure and reality principles. Such is the human reality—and these are the aspects of reality, if not realities, with which man has or seeks contact.

Nevertheless, Freud's point on emancipation has been and is being heeded by many thoughtful persons. Einstein's personal reflections seem to match it at many points.[13] For instance, Einstein felt that the doctrine of a personal god should be given up because it maintains man's childish fears and hopes, and has in the past placed far too much power in the hands of priests. On the other hand he insisted that the aspiration toward truth and understanding, which is a *sine qua non* in scientific work, springs from the sphere of religion. And he placed much emphasis on "that humble attitude of mind towards the grandeur of reason incarnate in existence" which comes after one has emancipated from the "shackles of personal hopes and desires." But then, and this is a very important qualification, Einstein considered this emancipated attitude "to be religious, in the highest sense of the word." Such emancipation is not *from* religion, but *within* religion. Freud identified religion with the idea of a personal God portrayed in the simplest terms of a heavenly Provider of childish needs. For Einstein, religion has a much broader sweep and allows for a range from primitive to sophisticated attitudes.

Emancipation implies qualitative change, but it does not mean transition from one genus of activity to another. I would hold that, looking backward, religion comes from religion, as art comes from art and science comes from science. And looking forward, religion gives rise to religion, as art gives rise to art and science to science.

I also take a broader view of sublimation than Freud did. Sublimation is a *sine qua non* for engagement in any and all cultural activities. Sublimation is what makes a person cultured in the first place. Sublimation is what distinguishes cultured man from an uninhibited brute. This means that traces of libidinal and aggressive impulses can be found in all cultural activities, but that the aims or objects have shifted. It also means that traces of childhood conflict can be found in almost all cultural activities, but with significant transpositions to new planes of operation, new styles of problem solving, and novel ways of coping with tension. Sublimation entails a widening of the world, a broadened view of reality, the discovery of rich and interesting avenues of self-expression, and the gaining of many permissible satisfactions. It does not necessitate giving up any of the ways of looking at and dealing with reality that man has found germane to himself in the course of his slow emergence as a cultured person, except the raw and uninhibited expression of those instinctual promptings which would shackle him to animality.

The Outer and the Inner Tremendum

We have earlier encountered Otto's idea of the *mysterium tremendum,* that pattern of experiences based on contact with the holy or the numinous. Whatever is holy in a person's life presents itself to him with a peculiar forcefulness and tends to hold the person in its grip. He stands in awe before it, spellbound. Spellbound indeed, for the tremendum is also a *fascinosum:* it repels and it attracts. It is awesome as well as blissful. It overpowers, but it also fascinates.

As Otto described it, the *tremendum* appears to be largely external to the person. Noah perceived the flood coming on. Lot witnessed the destruction of Sodom and Gomorrah. Moses stood before the burning bush. Modern man sees his UFO's in the sky. The *tremendum* is the cosmos, the mysterious power of nature, gods, or demons—all of which are felt to reside "out there" beyond man himself. Perhaps the externality of the *tremendum* is an understandable assumption made on the basis of its overwhelming power: if the individual feels weak and shy in relation to it he is likely to regard it as outside himself, transcendent to himself.

But does the *tremendum* lie exclusively outside man? Could

it not also be inside him? It was Goodenough who refined and broadened Otto's idea of the numinous by pointing out that there is also a *tremendum* within man, to which he reacts with the same feelings of shuddering and fascination that pertain to the gods outside. It is the id, as defined by Freud. Says Goodenough:

> The id is with all of us always. . . . This personality within us seems never to be socialized. It may be repressed, guided, thwarted, but continues in every person as a quite irresponsible craving for direct gratification of purely selfish urges. In itself, it contemplates murder, rape, robbery, or any chicanery with complete indifference. But it is the *élan vital* within one. A man without a powerful id is a psychological eunuch, colorless and spiritually flabby.[14, p. 66]

Rightly, man is afraid of his id. He cannot deny its power, which he carries within himself. It is mysterious to him, and it holds him so tightly that he cannot escape from it by walking away. It constantly lures him while its power also repels him. He loves it and shuns it. Its élan is too strong and too raw for him, but Eros and Thanatos are nevertheless immensely attractive.

After calling attention to the internal *tremendum*, in addition to the external one, Goodenough offered a creative synthesis. With fine insight, he noticed that people shield themselves from direct contact with the *tremendum*. They seek something by which to protect themselves from its power, lest they be overwhelmed. But they feel constantly drawn to that shield, for what lies behind it exerts a powerful attraction. Combining two great images, the old religious notion of the veil that hides the deity and Freud's psychological concept of repression, Goodenough suggested:

> Man throws curtains between himself and the tremendum, and on them he projects accounts of how the world came into existence, pictures of divine or superhuman forces or beings that control the universe and us, as well as codes of ethics, behavior, and ritual which will bring him favor instead of catastrophe. So has man everywhere protected himself by religion.[14, p. 8]

Call it what one wills: curtains, veils, screens, the blanket of repression, the threshold of awareness—the essential feature of Goodenough's proposition is that the *tremendum* is put at some distance from the beholder, for direct contact with it is too dangerous. Otto had already remarked that religious imagery contains many hints that people need a covering of some sort when approaching the holy. They put their hands before their face. So man seeks to cover the *tremendum:* he puts a protective blanket over it to hide its powerful and possibly explosive content, and on that cover he scribbles images, ciphers, hieroglyphs, words, and various symbols to suggest what might be under the cover. The cover conceals, the scribbles reveal, but the knowledge of the content is never complete.

The concept of the dynamic unconscious[15] is, of course, an ontological construct. Schopenhauer built a whole metaphysical system on it. As described by Groddeck[16] and articulated by Freud, the dynamic unconscious is not merely an appendage of consciousness containing memories, but a fountainhead of energy, a "seething cauldron of forces" which sets life on its course and brings it eventually to an end. It is "really real" by its potency. For Freud, it is the psychobiological matrix out of which all other psychic structures arise as a result of its interaction with the outer world. It has power. It is timeless. It defies logic. It transcends the neat space-time coordinates of the conscious mind and the canons of reason. It presents itself to awareness so unobtrusively that one must echo James's phrase: "There's something there!"[17] Such an acknowledgment may be a long way off from defining it, but it is the crucial ontological leap, for it affirms the id's existence as something in its own right, to be reckoned with. And when the dynamic unconscious is repressed, denied, or otherwise tinkered with, such maneuvers only testify that we consider its existence substantial enough to seek ways of coping with it.

Two *tremendums,* then, are presented to consciousness, two substantial and dynamic realities which elicit our reactions. Even if we wished to deny the external *tremendum* and eliminate the idea of the holy from our mind, we would still have to cope with the internal *tremendum.* One may not wish to consider it holy, but is it anything less than numinous? Is it anything less than mysterious? If it is not divine, might it be seen as demonic? Or an ambiguous mixture of both, in that awkward but inevitable combination of gods and demons and good and evil which every mythology seems to produce from ancient times until today?

The frail mortal beings who inhabit Plato's cave can see only the shadows of the world's doings on their wall—if the sun is in the right direction. From their very limited vision of things they draw inferences and speculate about the really real. They know there is "something there" but cannot fully grasp it. It is never in plain view.

In Goodenough's image of the painted curtains, modern man is in somewhat the same position as Plato's cave dwellers, but with a significant difference. He has inherited the painted curtains whose pictograms and symbols represent the accumulated wisdom of the ages about that aspect of reality which is the *tremendum*. The curtains contain a cultural record: they are scribbled full of guesses and intimations, inferences and conclusions which millions of people have made about the "really real" that lies hidden behind the curtains. The curtains are densely covered with a bewildering panoply of signs, pictures, words, codes, and symbols. One can imagine in one corner of the curtain the word "Beware!" Elsewhere is an Ankh sign. Yonder is a triangle containing the all-seeing eye of God. Here are the Ten Commandments—there is a cartouche with falcon-headed Horus. In Arabic script someone has written: "Muhammad is his Prophet." At the bottom edge one can discern the two arms of Demeter pulling the maidenly figure of Persephone back into the underworld. In seventeenth-century French characters it says "Take a bet!" Crosses of all forms cover the surface. Here and there one sees a pigeon, and sun rays. Angels are flying across. Vipers curve around trees. A few German letters spell "Opium." The finger of God touches a Neanderthaler. A witch rides on a broomstick. Mandalas and other archetypical symbols are all around. The word Sex is written in many languages. A splendid montage pictures an emaciated Dominican friar leading a flaming auto-da-fé in Sevilla. Latin, Greek, and Hebrew are strewn between pictures of altars and shepherds' staffs. Actually, the picture is a collage, for pieces of scroll seem to be glued onto it. Among the graffiti one can spot in modern English the word "Hogwash!" And in French: "Godot was here."

All these scribbles are beliefs, and disbeliefs, piled up through the ages. There is no space any more for new scribbles—one has to draw the new pictures over the old ones, or change figure and ground. Standing before the painted curtains the visitor is hardly in a position to make up his own mind about the content on the other side. The record of the beliefs and disbeliefs of the past and of other people keeps storming at him. The putative content of the mysterious something behind the curtain has already been labeled a million times over by the beliefs and disbeliefs of previous graffiti artists.

Whatever may lie behind the curtains, those paintings on the curtains themselves are all too real. Much of daily life and many of the social institutions anywhere are organized so as to instruct individuals and groups in the correct interpretation of all this pictorial tumult. One learns to ignore or overlook certain pictograms systematically, in favor of others which must come to stand out. Instead of coming to terms with the outer and inner *tremendums,* exhaustive efforts are being spent on coming to terms with the painted curtains. How do the pictures stack up against each other? Which picture do you like most? Whole educational systems are devoted to the task of sorting out. Belief is pitched against belief, and your belief is my disbelief. Belief hardens into doctrine, and a battle of doctrines is on. The radical who wrote "Hogwash!" on the curtain has his point—as long as he is not doctrinaire about his gutsy reaction.

Commonsense Reality: How Plain Is It?

Apart from any ultimate reality and any *tremendum,* there is, of course, the immediate reality of the outside world, our bodies and the accessible portions of mind which are given to us in sensory perception and as objects of action. This reality is so patently "there" that it seems to present itself to us by its own momentum and force of existence. To deny it entails grave risks. To tinker with its existence is dangerous. If the word "adaptation" means anything, it encompasses that obvious world of our environment which comprises geology, nature, things, bodies, people, technology, houses, implements, books, money, medicines, political parties, schools, churches, stores, mores, collections, files of information, and means of communication. One can make nice distinctions, such as outer and inner environment, physical and cultural things, or *Umwelt, Eigenwelt,* and *Mitwelt,*[18] but the first rule of living with the outer world is to acknowledge its existence and never to doubt its obviousness. For our environment has a thickness and resistance which would victimize us if we were to be cavalier with it. Breach of contact with it and failure to acknowledge it mean psychosis or autism—madness. The person who thinks that he can walk through a tree will hurt himself. The patient who thinks that all doorknobs are poisoned or contaminated will become immobilized and starve to death, or else exhaust himself in ludicrous avoidance rituals. For this reason, psychiatrists have to assume in their practical clinical work with seriously disorganized patients a simple, nonphilosophical view of the world which takes its focus on the here and now of ordinary sensory reality. Similarly, the businessman has to take a direct and simple view of this world—he stands to lose money if he approaches it with philosophical subtleties. The cook must serve food, not ideas. The worker must perform, not dream. The house must be built on solid ground, not in the air. You cannot cross a busy highway if you want to stay alive. You cannot call yourself Jesus if you are only Albert Nobodaddy.

This ordinary quotidian world has been held for a long time to be the most evident reality. Reality principle, reality contact, reality sense, reality testing—all these psychological terms pertain in the first place to this kind of reality. It has long seemed an assumptionless and self-explanatory reality which is beyond belief or disbelief. But the conviction has been growing that a naïve acceptance of our accounts of this reality is too simplistic. While there has always been some criticism of this naïveté by speculative or critical philosophers, in our century a new kind of criticism has come from the side of empirical observers. Reich,[19] whom I cite mostly for the recency and popularity of his book and not from agreement with all his ideas, has tried to demonstrate how much of this ordinary reality is skewed by the state of consciousness of the person who is seeking some degree of well-being in it. Much of what passes for "reality" is sifted through Consciousness I or II. Reich argues that a Consciousness III, which gives allegedly standard reality an essentially different shape, is now in the process of formation. Aldous Huxley[20] is merely one example of many observers who have held that what passes for "reality" is perceived oh so dimly, with great sloppiness and lack of interest and sensitivity.

Critics such as Reich and Huxley say that our quotidian way of perceiving has become blunted and ask that we clear the channels of seeing, hearing, and touching, open the doors of perception, and expand our consciousness to take in the riches that exist. The phenomenologists have argued for years that our conceptual apparatus has become so overgrown that we cannot properly perceive anymore. Their slogan: "Let's turn to the things themselves!"[21] was a clarion call meant to awaken us toward new openness to sounds and sights and feelings and things and situations, to respond to their appeal and to rediscover their richness. Linguists[22, 23] have pointed out how much of our contact with reality is determined by the words we happen to have available in our native tongue and the games that any language allows us to play: language is a grid that we place over the world, by means of which we chop up reality in discrete bits. Each language uses a different mesh for its grid, and the result is that patterns of reality bits are as numerous as the languages in the world. Students of culture warn us that reality is hardly available to us without cultural mediation—what we naïvely say is "reality" is largely a social construction which our culture imposes on us.

All these observations seem to indicate that our view of reality has become too stereotyped, too dull, too dim, too flat. We are no longer moved by our world and have lost the excitement of perceiving. The recommended alternative would be an intensification of perception, a less commanding and more sensitive attitude, and an increased knowledge of our biases. Travel might help, particularly between countries and even more particularly between East and West. Exposure to culture shock might have beneficial effects in the long run. Studying foreign

languages might be useful. Drugs, meditation, and other practices that alter or expand consciousness might give us a clearer
or more intense and moving view of reality.

Since the encounter between East and West is such a prominent feature of today's changing culture, it may be helpful to
know what the outstanding attitudinal differences are between
these two major parts of the world. From an essay by Fortmann,[24] *Eastern Renaissance*, which in turn relies on many
scholarly resources, I abstract the following main points (although, since they lack qualifications, they may come out too
starkly): (1) The ratio between activity and contemplation is
different in the East from what it is in the West. (2) Activity and
technique take an inward direction in the East and are turned
outward in the West. The East uses energy and methods to
produce sages and to unmask the substantive "I." The West
produces goods and engineers—it conquers the moon, as Fortmann says. (3) In the Eastern tradition, knowing and being
coalesce. Contemplation does not lead to *knowing* a truth but
being that truth. The West has greater respect for knowledge
which objectifies—that is, science. (4) Many Eastern cultures
have given a pivotal role to the body and its regulation as a royal
road to health, wisdom, and the deities. In comparison, Western
body culture seems underdeveloped. (5) *Being* and *having* are
differently valued in the East and the West. Buddhism teaches
that all suffering evolves from desire, including the desire to
live. Hinduism teaches that one should not find his thrill in the
results of his work but in the simple performance of duty. And
even Tantrism, which stimulates the enjoyment of everything,
nevertheless insists on guarding one's inner freedom and basic
detachment from things. (It sounds like a counterphobic variant
of the detachment philosophy.) Says Fortmann: The Hindu does
not aim at freedom *unto*, but freedom *from*.

To say that East is East and West is West no longer implies
that the twain shall never meet. Rather, it is now taken to mean
that refreshment, liberation from old perceptual habits, and a
renewal of reality views may be found precisely through East-
West encounters which modern travel and communication
make possible.

But if one can gain a more intense view of reality, a reality which is richer and more splendid, one still has to come to terms with the place and role of man in that reality. Here Murphy's[25-28] lifework adds an enormous contribution. How does man shape his world, and does he shape himself as a center of perception, cognition, and action in that world? Murphy's work first emphasized the large role that human needs play in perception.[25] All perception is motivated by needs: needs of the visceral tissues but also needs of perceptual organs and muscles, and the cerebral needs of curiosity and cognition. With Murphy's concept of canalization he painted a picture of man as a creature with highly diversified energy distributions resulting in great versatility and the capacity to approach reality in different perspectives at once. Reality also forces the individual to acknowledge that he must play many different roles at once and engage in many different situations, each with its particularity. Murphy's man seems always hungry for more—more of everything. This is no primitive oral lust, but the result of an increasing differentiation of needs when the person grows. The moment one need is satisfied, the individual is ready or set free to detect a more refined or cultured need, which he then seeks to satisfy. He is possessed by great curiosity and thus constantly adds new vistas to his cognitive repertoire and sees reality in ever increasing perspectives.

After having said that the notion of reality always contains some self-reference too, Murphy[26] became increasingly convinced that reality and self differentiate in proportion to each other and that a principle of isomorphism guides that double differentiation. Structures discovered outside become appropriated as structures inside, and vice versa. Outer reality is far more complex and fascinating than we have thought thus far, and so is internal reality. Consciousness becomes the pivotal point of life: it stands like a captain on the bridge of a ship, perpetually scanning the seas and horizons outside as well as the finely attuned mechanisms of the ship and its crew inside. It has a double vision, which through practice can grow in acumen and responsiveness. More and more, the world is seen as process, and so is the self. Whether we project the experience of ourselves as process on the world or introject the world's process character into ourselves, the result is that reality and self develop mutually. Hence, the world's élan vital, its creativity, is also our creativity, and vice versa. The renewal of our vision of the world becomes the renewal of ourselves, and the idea of potentiality[27] becomes central in life. Everything is in principle transcendable, and therefore today's reality view and self-perception are only way stations. They are always too simple, for tomorrow may bring new vistas. The unsolved problems of observation, such as the phenomena of parapsychology,[28] should not be shoved under the rug for comfort, but should stimulate us toward a deeper and wider view of things promoting comprehension.

This is no armchair philosophy. Murphy is an empiricist and an experimentalist, sufficiently instructed in philosophy to know the pitfalls of metaphysics. His ontology comes out at a reality of process, not because he disdains the sameness of things or considers appearances deceptive, but because he has minutely perceived how much of reality and the self is always in formation. The evidence of any particular picture of reality is not yet in, and there are enormous gaps in knowledge of world and self. All knowledge is only provisional, and that fact should make our attitudes playful and creative—as playful and creative as nature seems to be. We cannot allow ourselves pat answers to the question of what reality is.

This view of reality allows James's *more* to be in it rather than beyond it. In a way, the *more* is reality, and reality—if seen without blinders—is a *this* here and now as well as a *more*. Murphy's view also seems to imply the possibility that the categorical distinctions between the secular and the sacred are only provisional, like way stations of thought which man needed in the past. For the more we come to know about reality and ourselves, the more awesome and thrilling these become. The *mysterium tremendum et fascinosum* seems no longer bound to a place and a time and a particular perspective on things. It is everywhere, always, and it becomes a kind of master perspective on all things. And, if I fathom Murphy's temper accurately, that perspective of omnipresent *mysterium* stimulates enormous curiosity. Fascination becomes unimpeded by awe and may even get the edge over it.

The Integrative Power of the Transitional Sphere

We are back again, but with new sophistication, in Winnicott's transitional sphere of play. We are back at that intermediate view of things—detached from autism on one side and from mere objectivity on the other side—which keeps both autism and objectivity suspended (without denying them) and opts for an attitude of fun, zest, and venturesomeness, and yet with seriousness and utter dedication. What would reality be if it did not afford opportunities for play, and what would mind be if it never started playing?

We can now see that our words are tainted by an odd but persistent dualistic view that sees things in much too simple a fashion. This dualism places id and autism on the one side, world and reality testing on the other side. It posits a pleasure principle governing one series, which turns out to be too lusty; and a reality principle to govern the other series, which turns out to be too grim. And then the poor ego tries to synthesize both!

Far too little attention has been paid to the serious implications of the word "synthesis" when we speak of the synthesizing functions of the ego. Synthesis does not merely combine—it transforms the elements brought to it. Synthesis takes place in the transitional sphere, and into it the whimsicality of the inner world and the factualness of the outer world enter as contributions, while losing their specificity. Outer and inner are not as rigidly distinct as the ordinary view of reality would have it. In play, they interpenetrate: the private experience may be told as general human story, and the facts of history may be expressed as personal drama. Things may become impersonated, and people may be staged as things.

This "third world" of play is the matrix of growth and culture and the beginning of the human spirit. It overarches the encapsulation of the inner world and the sheer facticity of the outer world. In the dualistic view, science is dedication to factualness and objectivity. In the synthetic view, however, science is far more than mere enumeration and measurement—it becomes a serious (but not deadly serious) play with possibilities and "as if" views, a venturesome self-extension of man into the arena of things. Again, in the dualistic view, fantasy is seen as utterly whimsical and autistic. But in the synthetic view one discovers how communicable it is and how much it shares in the legends of mankind, the common tragedies and comedies of all ages.

Similarly, in the dualistic view, religious belief is pitted against scientific truth or rational pursuit. Gods become more or less "things" in the world or powerhouses which launched the world on its course. Or they become fanciful entities in the human heart serving as substitute parents, taskmasters, or bell ringers who issue periodic warnings in ominous times. In the synthetic view, however, one comes to the thought of a Ground of Being, or of a God behind the gods, or of the Holy which is no longer confined to burning bushes, altars, amulets, and fatherly caretakers. The Holy may now be seen in macroscopic as well as microscopic grandeur, in stars and cells, in evolution and in such beautiful conceptions as $E=MC^2$.

We seem to end up, then, with the paradoxical thought that coming to terms with reality (in its inner and outer aspects) requires coming to terms with playing. This is a strange thought to those whose outer world seems hard, fixed, factual, incontrovertible, and the source of all knowledge. It shakes their deepest belief. Those who would have their inner world soft, loose, whimsical, and full of contradictions, also find their highest value undermined by such a concept.

But could we know anything about the outer world or the inner world unless we bring the two together, in play—in culture? Culture softens the contours of the outer world and shapes the outlines of the inner world.

The thought that coming to terms with reality is to be mediated by coming to terms with play may be appealing to those who remember their childhood—their earnestness in building fortifications of sand on the beach, their intense identifications with animals at storytelling time, the privacy they practiced in their treehouses and the exhilaration they had while piloting a raft through a stream. They may remember that they wrote verse (awkwardly, perhaps, in retrospect) which brought out feelings and ideas whose presence they might not have realized otherwise. They played with words and made puns, discovering that some words have new meanings when spelled backwards, wondering what metaphysical connections made it so. In their teens they practiced other people's handwriting, periodically renewing themselves by adopting a new signature. They worked on small projects of helpfulness toward other people with the zeal that comes from a belief that one's contribution will alter the course of the world. In summers they roamed the land as paupers, leaving for a few weeks the safe shelter of their homes and the standards of their families, tinkering with new life styles. They left their old groups and clubs and churches for new ones, playfully sampling patterns of thought, feeling, and action, without lasting commitments. They read a lot, until late at night, thinking and feeling for a few hours that they were Huckleberry Finn, Captain Ahab, Siddhartha, or a hard-drinking Hemingway hero.

It will not do to say to the child on the beach: "Go, shovel!" For him, making a castle is not mere draining off of excess energy by carrying shovelfuls of sand. Nor will it do to say: "You better not make castles, for the tide will come." He knows that. His energetic motions must take form and shape by being attuned to a purpose, and his castle will have a definite, realistic structure—as long as it lasts. To the child, the sand cries for his shoveling and his muscles itch for the sand. His fantasies lust for the resistance of the grainy matter, and the beach demands to be molded by his hand. Child and beach present themselves to each other, beach appealing to child and child appealing to beach. It is not far-fetched to say that both engage in play. The child's work is not an imposed duty. If he obeyed the command "Go, shovel!" he could as well aimlessly carry sand around. But his act of building is spontaneous. While doing it, he is not in contract with his parents, but is engaged in a very special, temporary contract with the beach. And the beach yields temporarily the forms it has assumed in nature's routines. It now becomes a castle—until the tide comes. For a stretch of time, id and reality are synthesized into a creatively acting child and a creatively yielding nature. And the memory will linger.

The child who listens intently to *Winnie the Pooh* knows that he is not a bear. Nor is Pooh a child. But both are gloriously alive, eat and sleep with gusto, and play pranks by which they exercise their feelings and practice their fantasies. Children who hide in their treehouse do not think they are monkeys, squirrels, or owls: they are experimenting with new boundaries between privacy and publicness, between kinship and friendship, between separateness and intimacy.

Is make-believe then a ground of belief? Whoever has watched children at play and whoever has scrutinized himself on ceremonial occasions or in ritual acts must surely think so. Whoever abides by cultural mores, engages in civil amenities, or partakes in a game knows that these acts of make-believe legitimize his beliefs. Such acts are not merely imposed by a harsh reality that insists on their performance, nor are they merely demanded by the rules that have been incorporated into the superego. They can also be performed with an awareness of fittingness, a knowledge that going through motions is a natural correlate of having emotions, and the belief that a special contract has been negotiated between the id and the outer world that has softened the raw demands of either party.

Gifted as he was in the transitional sphere of creative play, Einstein could confess that he was "deeply religious," in his own way, inasmuch as he stood in awe of the mystery of a universe which yet yields some of its secrets to an utterly fascinated human mind. And he could describe himself in the same breath as an "unbeliever" when he considered the short view of reality so coded by the quotidian mind that it is fixed into doctrines which might pressure a man into conformity. For Einstein, religion was search, not find. To a searcher, finds are always old and disappoint quickly. To Einstein it was the not-yet-found that counted.

Goodenough had profound insight in the delicate combinations of belief and unbelief that we find in a mind such as Einstein's. He saw the modernity of the ambiguous stance. Pondering the inscriptions, old and new, on the curtain that shields man from the *tremendum*, he felt that modern man tends to be more accepting of the *tremendum* than his forebears were. This may be due to his discovery of the inner *tremendum* which follows him like a shadow. He cannot deny it, for it asserts itself time and again in his private life. He must learn to live with it and accept it with some degree of comfort. And he finds comfort by assuming a somewhat more pragmatic attitude than his forebears dared to manage. He is prone to inscribe his curtains with hypotheses instead of dogmas. And he tends to reinterpret some of the old dogmas as hypotheses.

Modern man is as interested in meaning as the people of old, but he has learned to run pragmatic tests of meaning. He makes plausible guesses and teases them out, knowing that these are his guesses and his tests—not the word of God. He raises questions, one after another. His provisional answers turn into new questions, in an open-ended series. Though he likes answers too, he is quick to discover that answers have limitations, for he is acutely aware of the gaps in knowledge. He does not mind assuming an agnostic stance, for he is less frightened by the hidden features of reality. He has tempered the animistic urge to personalize his ultimates, not because he has lost sensitivity to personhood and personal relations, but because the very idea of personhood has become more mysterious to him, more complex, more subtle. He cannot be pat about it. So he dwells on question after question, seeking an ever higher quality of questioning. He has new regard for openness—in a way, modern man is beginning to fear that closure may quickly deteriorate into fixity.

This new attitude need not be positivistic at all, despite the central role it gives to questioning and hypotheses. In fact, it is the modern way of keeping sacred things sacred: "Prayer for modern man is replaced by eager search, which is a form of prayer itself."[29]

CHAPTER X

Between Belief and Unbelief

The phrases "coming to terms with . . ." and "dealing with . . ." have figured heavily in the titles and subtitles of the preceding chapters. Involved have been major dimensions of the content of belief, issues and propositions that seem to have beset men's minds from time immemorial until today. Though the culture is full of towering edifices of abstraction about these issues, the issues themselves are clearly experiential. Before they are intellectualized, they are experienced. Each of us will eventually experience engagement or alienation, dependency or autonomy, humility or pride, mystery or clarity, drifting or choosing, benevolence or malevolence, turning to fantasy or turning to reality. Moreover, our experiences will precipitate pain or pleasure, endorsement or rebellion.

Many of our experiences tend to become quickly polarized in the accounts we give of them. Faced with a choice, we find ourselves arguing with others about the value, correctness, or merit in standing for one thing rather than the other. In such arguments we discover that what I stand for, you may stand against. Every belief thus becomes matched by a disbelief, even though, on closer inspection, such "opposites" are not necessarily irreconcilable.

More often than not, each of us argues with himself. Debates

about beliefs and disbeliefs are not necessarily interpersonal—
they can also be intrapsychic, in the bosom of one person. Whatever our belief, we may have doubt about it; whatever we
disbelieve, we may find ourselves in situations that lead us to
question our disbeliefs. This is not merely because life situations
change in the course of time, leading to periodic stocktaking
and reassessment, but because many beliefs are held with ambivalence. Seemingly opposite beliefs may be equally desirable,
each being the expression of a dear wish. Psychiatrists have
spoken for years of "passive-aggressive personalities" in whom
just such ambivalences prevail at levels of feeling, action, cognition, and values. Beliefs held consciously may be undermined
by deviant or contrary beliefs held unconsciously. This has been
amply demonstrated in studies of racial prejudice showing that
the belief that "all men are brothers" is effectively undone by
the same person's belief that certain classes of men are inferior
—an obvious instance of dissonance. A conscious disbelief such
as "there is no personal God" may only be a defense against a
strong unconscious wish for just such determinedly paternalistic guidance.

In a way, all *strong* beliefs are typically maintained in the face
of their alternatives, disbeliefs. Beliefs involve choice—they are
options—and as James remarked, they are momentous and not
trivial choices. Beliefs demand commitments, that is, a willingness to remain loyal to their truth and implications and channel
energies toward their upholding in word and deed. In Tillich's[1]
Dynamics of Faith, faith is described as a posture that requires
its seeming opposite, doubting, for its own possibility. Faith and
doubt, both conscious moreover, stand in dialectic relation to
each other, and that is precisely what makes faith dynamic: it
is a process given to fluctuations, an equilibration tenuously
achieved between diverse vectors of tension.

Relations between belief and disbelief are, however, not always as dialectic as Tillich describes the relation between faith
and doubt. Many beliefs and disbeliefs take their shape from
arguments between people. If I testify publicly to a belief in the
sacredness and inviolability of the individual, someone else will
soon pronounce his belief in the sacredness of the group, which

is to him of greater ultimate significance than individuals. One may thus maintain that every belief is socially matched by a disbelief. The other person remains incredulous toward my value affirmation, and I to his. Our arguments or debates are rarely exhaustive or conclusive—most of them occur in fragmentary snatches of conversation, sometimes heated, typically abortive or unfinished, and frequently in more or less pedagogical situations in which a parent wants to correct a child or a teacher seeks to influence a pupil. During political campaigns, beliefs of all sorts are blurted out with great vehemence, leading to assertions of disbelief and contrasting beliefs by the contenders, particularly in a two-party system in which "being against" may be more momentous than "being for."

One may discover that whole clusters of beliefs pattern by pattern rather than part by part, are contested. Not just each belief per se, but the way beliefs are organized into one whole, gives each partial belief a judicious weight and status in its pattern which may be subject to comparison and dispute. The patterned belief system may be a hierarchical organization of high-order and low-order beliefs all neatly ranked with a few very important beliefs at the top and many subordinate beliefs near the bottom of a triangle. Or it may be a different kind of whole, dominated and integrated by some regnant beliefs which attain the focus, with ancillary or derived or dependent beliefs located at the fuzzy edges.

It seems to me that religiosity is an attitude which holds religious beliefs to be regnant beliefs. People who describe themselves as "religious believers" are wont to discover, through the little tugs-of-war of everyday life, that the very pattern of their beliefs, particularly their regnant beliefs, meets with incredulity in other people with whom they may nevertheless share many specific lower-order beliefs. They may find themselves at odds with others in the way they have put their beliefs together. Finding their core beliefs unshared or challenged, they may view their seeming antagonists as "unbelievers," either in anger or in irritation (in which case they may use stronger language such as "heathen" or "infidel") or as an only mildly denigrating classification device (in the way ancient

Greeks called all other peoples *barbaroi*). While "unbelief" and "disbelief" may have the same dictionary meaning, the appellation "unbeliever" has acquired a somewhat more sweeping and judgmental meaning than the word "disbeliever." The Vatican has a Secretariat for Unbelievers which purports to deal not with faraway groups who have remained ignorant of Catholicism's gospel as in the erstwhile mission days, but with cultural equals who are stand-offs from Christian belief systems which are abundantly present in their immediate surroundings. Here, the word "unbelievers" implies a range of judgments from willful apostasy, stubborn rejection, or truculent opposition to secularization by drifting, sloth, lukewarmness, or emptiness. The word has imperialistic overtones the moment one takes religious belief as normative. It is hard to use "unbeliever" in a merely descriptive vein.

Belief, disbelief, and unbelief, then, are not only ways in which individuals in their solitude search for meaning in their lives, but also disputational judgments which emerge in social interactions. They are terms of approbation and disapprobation. They channel identifications and counteridentifications. They establish positive and negative identities, or affirm these. They are, psychologically and socially, "hot words."

Beliefs as Love Objects

During a recent speaking engagement, I was involved in a panel which at one point in its deliberations veered toward a discussion of the role of women in society. One of the panelists held forth on the virtues of the married state and the satisfactions of motherhood. Hers was a very traditional viewpoint, and she buttressed it by frequent citations of Bible verses and assertions that this traditional view was sacred, since it was ordained by God. When I pointed out that the Biblical God was rather masculine and could have been biased in favor of his gender and that her picture of the roles ordained for women and men was only a bit of Hellenistic culture in the New Testament, she focused the conversation on that old bugaboo: Whether I believed that the Bible was the Word of God (note the latter three capitalizations, all suggesting that here is something very special, sacred, and untouchable). As she emphasized the literal inerrancy of scripture and it dawned on her that I did not share any such belief, she felt like cutting off the conversation then and there: we obviously could never meet on the issues. To her "our Lord" had spoken once for all, and everything was perfectly clear. Belief in the inerrancy of scripture was apparently her key belief, and it seemed even higher a than belief in God —all other beliefs depended on it.

While such situations are not uncommon, I was struck by something special. My co-panelist obviously reaped lavish satisfaction from her regnant belief: it gave her much pleasure to know that God had spoken once for all in "His" book. She knew that through His book she was on a special wavelength with Him: her voice expressed adoration and boundless love when she spoke of "the Word of Our Lord." And her desire to cut off conversation with me had a noticeable element of panic in it: if we were to go on she would have to face possibilities that would give her pain or displeasure. In a way, she held to her belief as if she were holding on to a beloved person, for nurture, certainty, and approval on one hand, and to be safeguarded against pain, attack, intrusion, doubt, or uncertainty on the other hand. Her expressed belief had all the earmarks of clinging to a cathected person: it served as a love object. She held her belief *dear*, she *cherished* it, and she defended it against what she would feel to be maltreatment. She *clung* to it as a shy toddler clings to his father or mother.

A few weeks earlier as I sat in an airport, a young woman exchanged a brief greeting and then said emphatically to me: "Jesus loves you!" When I answered: "How do you know?" the emphatic pressure of her assertion grew even stronger. Her belief in a loving Jesus seemed to her quite natural and entirely self-validating—she showed it off like a young mother might proudly turn the attention of strangers to the antics of her baby, with an air of: Isn't he cute?

Such lover's games with beliefs are not rare. Much of the language of belief shows that beliefs and believing are at times highly eroticized. One *embraces* a faith and *cherishes* a belief, holds his beliefs *dear*, is *true* and *loyal* to his beliefs. One's own fidelity to his faith leads him to call others *infidels*, with considerable scorn. One tries to *woo* others to his beliefs by proselytizing, and converts are hailed as persons joining a new *family* of faith or belief. One *pledges* to be faithful to a belief system much as one pledges to be faithful to a spouse in marriage. In fact, one can speak of being *wedded* to a belief.

One can even eroticize the tokens or implements or symbols of any belief and adorn them as a lover bedecks his beloved. Scrolls are bedecked with silver crowns, and holy books are ornamented with jewels. Crosses, originally of pointedly religious significance, become pieces of jewelry, meant to make the self more beautiful and the crosses more personal. In the history of Christianity enormous energy and money have been spent on advocating a particular set of beliefs through the use of costly and colorful vestments.

The penchant for making belief itself a love object is of great psychological interest. It is clear enough that the *content* of some beliefs, particularly religious beliefs, is a love object: he is Allah, or God the Father, or she is Mother Mary. It is also clear that *behind* many beliefs stand memories of beloved persons who taught us these beliefs and who had a stake in our loyalty to them—loyalty both to these beliefs and to these persons. To stick to certain beliefs is a way of reciprocating the love of these persons; to depart from certain beliefs is to be disloyal to these persons. Third, in a more interiorized manner, the beliefs we have acquired from our beloved will eventually function as integral parts of our own personality through the differential development of the superego and ego ideal. By identification we become, in part, the people in whom we have invested ourselves, and they become parts of us. The superego and the ego ideal furnish us in this sense with psychically present internal lovers, teachers, and taskmasters who act with us even when the original persons are physically absent. When Luther stood before his enemies and said: "Here I stand" he was psychologically not standing alone; within him were the encouraging smiles and the consoling presence of just such benign internal lovers.

But beliefs themselves—can we invest our libidinal energies in them? Can we love them? Or, alternatively, can we hate them if they seem alien to our identity and contrary to our dearest precepts? Can we relate ourselves to beliefs as we do to external love and hate objects or internal imagos, quite apart from the divine persons to whom their content may refer or the human persons who transmitted them?

Though the particular form in which I put these questions is relatively new, the quest itself is old. Baldwin[2] struggled with it as early as 1893 when he investigated the kind and degree of certainty that adheres to beliefs. He felt that if the certainty is cognitively explicit and can be clearly verbalized, we are entitled to speak of "belief." But he recognized that many states of belief do not yield to verbal articulation and do not become cognitively explicit, even though one has a prevailing and strong feeling of their correctness and appropriateness. He used the term "reality feeling" to describe this quality of some beliefs. James Pratt[3] spoke later of the relation of belief and the object that will satisfy. Where does this quality come from? What is it that makes some beliefs so real without benefit of logical conclusiveness or rational proof?

Before these questions can be answered we must make a few more observations. People can choose to die for their beliefs. The history of mankind is filled with examples of martyrs who have gone all the way, clinging to their beliefs at the price of their lives. Telling examples of such martyrdom are available in the book *Dying We Live,*[4] which contains testimonials from victims of the Nazi holocaust. The beliefs for which these men and women died were by no means religious beliefs only— many of them were landmarks of heroic humanism, similar to the splendid determination of Sir Thomas More in the sixteenth century. Some martyrs for their belief have been canonized as saints (including Sir Thomas More), implying that their utter loyalty and fidelity are exemplary for the masses as guides for the courageous life. As saints or heroes of the spirit they are venerated as perfect demonstrations of the courage to be—in terms of their beliefs. All such persons, known or unknown in the annals of history, *defined themselves by their beliefs,* loving their convictions, unable and unwilling to part from them, until the bitter end. They refused to be dishonest to themselves. Their pedagogical appeal lies precisely in their honesty, courage, and fidelity, and in their great love for the tenets of their belief.

The dictionary defines "tenet" as principle, dogma, belief, or doctrine. The word, however, comes from the Latin verb *tenere*, "to hold." What basic feeling tones and experiential images do we bring to the word "holding"? The little monkey buries his head in his mother's hairy breast while she holds her little one with one strong, competent arm. All lovers hold each other, in any pairing, from the mother with her child to two adults in coitus. Much of human touching is only an abrogated holding. When language facility has been developed we can touch and hold each other through words. We can also hold to our beliefs, securing our *integrity* by standing up for our tenets and defining ourselves by our beliefs.

In studying members of diverse faith groups and denominations, Rokeach[5] found that each believer feels himself measurably close to or distant from other people who define themselves by *their* beliefs. The Baptist feels fairly close to the Methodist, not so close to the Presbyterian, rather distant from the Episcopalian, and very distant from the Roman Catholic; the atheist is in an entirely different world, separated by an unbridgeable gap. What Rokeach has captured in his closeness and distance scales are feelings of identity and integrity which determine with whom a person will at least symbolically hold hands, cling to, have intercourse with—all of these mediated by his feelings toward beliefs.

Beliefs have long defined the limits of marital choice. Apart from imperialistic desires of faith groups to maintain and protect themselves, any person who considers marriage to someone with strikingly different key beliefs will sooner or later perceive lurking difficulties. Interfaith marriage[6] is not easy, nor is an inter-ideology marriage in which the regnant beliefs of partners diverge widely.

Beliefs have also defined the quality and depth of filial relations. The Jewish parents whose son or daughter has recently become a "Jew for Jesus" are wont to be in agony. Their former closeness is threatened by an inability to reach the child who has redefined his beliefs. He has, they feel, rejected his love objects (no matter how much concern he may express over his parents); he is disloyal, unfaithful, rejecting—they have "lost their child."

Such tragic situations occur of course, only when beliefs on either side are strongly held. Shallow or lukewarm beliefs precipitate little conflict and will not lead to feelings of great closeness or distance. The "hot" beliefs count: they are what we cling to; they can produce martyrdom; they can give rise to serious conflict.

Beliefs also set strict limits to lateral relations in some groups. Noteworthy is the history of schisms within the community of Mennonites.[7] Peace-loving as these groups traditionally are, and aversive as they are to manifest aggression in any form, repressed aggression has periodically become symptomatic in them as a result of so-called deviancy from accepted "theological" formulations. Fierce verbal battles about belief have raged among the offspring of the Anabaptists. Deviant persons have been ostracized with a rather spectacular form of reinforcement: the faithful, under scriptural precept, have "shunned" or "banned" the deviant, keeping him at the greatest possible distance to effect his contrition. Because of differences in belief (in this case likely to be very slight anyway) different believers have had to remain miles apart in terms of actual human contacts. It is a good case of what Freud once called the *narcissism of small differences*:[8, 9] people who are basically very much alike seize at times with great vigor on minute differences among them to articulate their uniqueness. Freud's choice of terms for this observation also shows how much he was aware of the ego's involvement in such finicky discriminations, which he saw as cases of narcissistic object choice. Key beliefs tend to be invested with narcissistic libido—the theme running through all I have said.

Still another observation must be made. Conversions from one belief system to another are disruptive. Overseas missionaries have learned the hard way that "winning a soul" for a church has frequently meant uprooting a man or woman from family relations and cultural habits. Conversion in this sense can be the beginning of a prolonged and painful identity crisis. The convert, while redefining his beliefs, redefines his self, and consequently his object relations are altered.

Manipulation of object relations has been for centuries a key procedure in the lives of those who have sought a religious vocation. The prospective member of a religious order is symbolically or concretely stripped of his bonds with his family and friends: he has to seek distance from them, if not relinquish them entirely, in order to embrace the new community of the monastic house, the brothers, the devoted servants of God. He assumes a new name—a most telling symbol of taking on a new identity.

All these observations suggest that strong beliefs function as definers of personality and personal identity. Beliefs play a role in giving content to the superego and ego ideal, but beliefs also have a quasi-interpersonal character. The ego is consciously engaged in beliefs, maintaining a love relationship with them much as it engages itself in other persons; it invests itself in beliefs, clings to them, respects and cares for them, and in so doing obtains from them reciprocal satisfactions. A person's love for his beliefs makes him lovable to and beloved by these beliefs, precipitating a constant flow of nutrient energy. Beliefs, like persons, command attention, care, protection, and loyalty. One lives with them tenderly or passionately, as the situation demands. When they are attacked one will rise to their defense, with the feeling that one is really defending one's self.

And so one can stand arm in arm with his beliefs, as it were, defiantly before his ideological opponents. Those who love their beliefs and find them seriously threatened claim for themselves the right to resist. While the alienated from society may feel *ressentiment*, firm believers join the Resistance. They let their voices be heard in existential affirmation, prepared to die if there are no alternatives. Seaman Kim Malthe-Bruun, captured by the Nazis in 1944, wrote the following lines to his family soon after his arrest:

Now listen, in case you should find yourself some day in the hands of traitors or of the Gestapo, look them—and yourself—straight in the eye. The only change that has actually taken place consists of the fact that they are now physically your masters. Otherwise they are still the same dregs of humanity they were before you were captured.[4, p.78]

Tortured and condemned to death, he wrote in a final letter to his girlfriend: "Remember that I am in you a reason for being; and if I leave you, that means merely that this reason lives on by itself."[4, p. 82] This is the voice of a young man to his lover. But is not it also the internal voice of a believer in dialogue with his belief? To his mother he wrote:

I am an insignificant thing, and my person will soon be forgotten, but the thought, the life, the inspiration that filled me will live on. ... I have never evaded the dictate of my heart, and now things seem to fall into place. I am not old, I should not be dying, yet it seems so natural to me, so simple. It is only the abrupt manner of it that frightens us at first. The time is short, I cannot properly explain it, but my soul is perfectly at rest. . . .[4, p. 84]

And so this young political victim, martyr for his beliefs, wrote what he himself called his *testament* in this last letter. To use a word of Gordon Allport, his beliefs were his *proprium* and he bequeathed it to the rest of mankind.

In one of his prayers for his fellow prisoners, Dietrich Bonhoeffer wrote:

Award me freedom once again
And then let me so live
That in thy sight and that of man
I can answer for my acts. . . .[4, pp. 216–217]

Answering for his acts, accounting for the use of his freedom—these are the things that make a man fully human. But how can one answer for his acts except by showing that he is wedded to his beliefs?

Beliefs as Hate Objects

In recent years, a good many studies have grappled with the observation that persons or groups who firmly underwrite certain key beliefs may simultaneously espouse incongruent beliefs —one belief contradicts the other in the same person. For instance, a person may identify himself as a humanist and espouse liberal causes, working for the abolition of capital punishment and prison reform, but after the latest skyjacking he is full of vengeance and demands the death sentence for such culprits. A celebrated instance of incongruence in the research literature is the correlation, repeatedly found, between religiosity and racial prejudice.[10] Many such studies can be criticized on methodological grounds and for pairing too glibly immensely complex and global notions which need to be broken down into specific categories. Nevertheless, some incongruences cannot be denied: the self-confessed Christian may also be anti-Semitic, and some corporation managers loudly advocate a participatory management ethic but continue to make highly authoritarian decisions. One adolescent girl, taken to task by her parents for her tendency to moralize, promptly said: "If people would only be better, I would not have to be such a moralist!"

Such cases indicate "cognitive dissonance."[11] Beliefs of opposite tenor and with contrary implications are held within one bosom and defended with ad hoc argumentation, typically without painful awareness of conflict by the person himself. Students of such phenomena may stress the *cognitive* incompatibility of a person's belief and devise strategies for bringing it to the person's awareness in the hope of correcting dissonance. Psychodynamic reasoning would stress the *emotional* dissonance which underlies such incompatible beliefs and describe them as cases of marked ambivalence: a conscious belief is held in apposition with an unconscious contrary belief, and both are invested with considerable energy derived from attitudes of love and hate. The hated belief is also cherished, and the loved belief is also despised, in varying mixtures of conscious and unconscious reasoning. Behind the consciously held belief may stand the image of a beloved parent against whom one also felt the urge to aggress; behind the unconsciously professed belief may lie parental imagos toward which one may harbor many discordant feelings, not yet sorted out or synthesized.

In addition to dissonance and ambivalence, the whole notion of belief per se has come under criticism. An old German poem, probably stemming from the Enlightenment era and to the best of my knowledge never translated into English, has the assertive title "My Belief." A kind of spiritual testament of a person who believes that the world is governed by some lofty and wise spirit whom one should revere, it is strongly skeptical that this spirit is interested in formulations of belief that would make differences between Jews, Muslims, and Christians. The poem goes on to say that we may hope in some resurrection of our own spirit after death, when we shall have to account for the two great gifts with which we have been endowed: our Heart and our Reason. The author, concluding that our deeds and our attitudes will be decisive, ends up with the emphatic lines:

> At last, when I shall rise from death's deep grave
> To stand before the World Judge, face to face,
> He will judge all my deeds without reprieve,
> But my Belief—
>   No, that I won't believe![12]

Here is an almost belligerent attitude toward belief, made possible by splitting acts and attitudes from creedal formulations. The popular conviction is that the head counts, not the heart. Our German poet was averse to doctrines and dogmas, but scores of people find any formulation of belief thoroughly suspect. Even within organized religion, whole denominations and sects claim to find their cohesiveness in a style of life or in a tradition rather than in articles of belief. On closer inspection, however, one does find specific beliefs in these groups: for instance, the divine inspiration or the inerrancy of scripture is assumed, or the conviction that believers are in close touch with the form and spirit of the early Christian church. Such attitudes may be reinforced by the somewhat bumbling statement of the late President Eisenhower that religion is good for people—and that any religion will do! In this adhortation the cognitive component of belief and the cohesiveness of beliefs have been completely deflated. It is all a matter of meaning well, and the very vagueness of belief is held to be ennobling, if not a test of sincerity.

Much fiercer, of course, is the hatred which one set of beliefs may receive from people upholding another set. Organized anti-Semitism, the Spanish Inquisition, the St. Bartholomew's Day massacre in France, and the religious wars of Europe are primary examples of such hatred as a mass phenomenon. One could add witch hunts and should add the methodical torture and extermination of political prisoners who are considered "enemies of the people" or "enemies of the regime" in such countries as Russia, Greece, and Brazil today, to name only a few of the crassest examples.

What I wish to emphasize, however, is the *individual* penchant toward intolerance with which most of us grow up as persons. For each belief we are taught to love, we are taught to hate or despise several alternative beliefs. Positive identity formation accompanies negative identity formation. The boy or girl who grows up to be an Episcopalian will sooner or later say denigrating things about Baptists, and vice versa, or join in in-group conversations which ridicule some out-group. To reinforce this tendency, vulgar swearwords are amply available: Jews have their "goys" and Christians their "kikes." With the circulation of the large assortment of distorting legends about other fellows' alleged beliefs and practices, it takes considerable fortitude and acumen to avoid exposure to such influences or to overcome their effects after inculcation. Not so long ago our newspapers used to describe Russians as Reds or "Commies," while *Pravda* described Americans as capitalists. Men and boys learn to describe women and girls in denigrating terms, with the result that they come to believe firmly that women are an inferior species.

A distinction must be made, then, between the common process of identity formation in which negative identity is subsidiary to positive identity and the special process in which the force of negative identity outweighs the positive one. Inasmuch as identity is defining oneself through his beliefs, to be fiercely against the beliefs of others, coupled with paucity of thought about the beliefs one is for, leaves a person with a shaky identity. It must be sadly conceded that persons with such a shaky identity are numerous today, and that the modern phenomenon described by Bellah as civil religion[13] is attractive to just such people. Their positive identity consists of an easy feeling of comfort in pairing God and country, a vague feeling of correctness about invocations and prayers on public occasions, and the cherished notion that the American presidency and Wall Street are divinely inspired. The negative identity, referring to the hated alternative beliefs, is asserted with great vigor and articulateness. Atheists are regarded as veritable ogres; theological critics of civil religion are suspected of being Communists, and such groups as the National (let alone World) Council of Churches, the American Civil Liberties Union, and the Sex Information and Education Council of the United States are felt as huge, poisonous thorns in the side. Such pointedly negative beliefs lead to hate campaigns conducted in the frantic conviction that the world will fall apart if such pinpointed evils are not promptly warded off or, better, abolished once for all. The underlying attitude is one of intolerance, albeit some deference for the Constitution (which is, in this view, a divine ordinance) may restrain most ardent civil religionists from totalitarian ambitions. This restraint is, however, the outcome of a double bind: if God and country are fused, there must at least be a semblance of upholding the sacred constitution with its guarantees of freedom, while at the same time one must manifest that basic decency becoming to the pious religionist who advocates that everyone regularly visit the church of his choice!

We are here teetering on the brink between tolerance and intolerance; a bit more anxiety, a bit more provocation, a bit more hatred, a louder scream for law and order, and the intolerant society will be at hand. There have already been reports that judges have sentenced juvenile delinquents to forced attendance at Sunday schools.

Two additional instances of beliefs as hate objects are conspicuous today. One is the disdain for and suspicion of beliefs of "the establishment" felt by a large assortment of individuals and groups, including restless innovators, radical revisionists, people gripped by the charismatic movement, and various alienated or anomic segments. The other is the opposition, among those who locate themselves in the center of the establishment, to any and all "radicals," as they are wont to call them. In both cases, since very little accurate and digested knowledge of the opposed beliefs may be present, the judgments are largely based on clichés and have an air of flippancy. Mutual derogation is the order of the day, true dialogue is rare, and concentration on the precise tenets of one's own beliefs tends to be poor. The case of a young psychiatric patient I have known illustrates both sides of the coin.

Cecil was admitted to a state hospital by court order at the age of seventeen. He came from a lower-middle-class family which had nominal ties to a mainline Protestant church, and he had attended church school in his early youth, without much interest or reinforcement from his parents. He had drifted away from this church several years earlier, not so much in conflict as from a feeling of irrelevance. Prior to admission to this hospital, his schoolwork had begun to decline, and he had dabbled with drugs, stayed away from home for several nights, and committed some minor offenses. While his court case was pending, he more or less accidentally discovered a local chapter of The Way, where he found peers concerned with his lot who were trying to mend their own lives and were glad to help Cecil also. They read the Bible, prayed with one another, and led each other to quiet confessions of sin. Some of the older group members spoke in tongues, and it was a great day for Cecil when he was persuaded, with much group support, to engage in glossolalia himself. As he babbled that night,[14] he felt he had come to a turning point in his life.

His parents, however, nominal Protestant mainliners that they were, felt that this bit of behavior was the clincher. It convinced them that their son was ill and elicited their cooperation in getting him to the hospital. As I talked with Cecil several times during his hospitalization, I found him thoroughly inarticulate about almost everything. He felt that speaking in tongues had been a breakthrough for him, but he had never repeated the one-time experience and felt no desire for it anymore. But he did praise the peer group who had made that experience possible, and he indicated that this had been about the only time in his life that people had taken him seriously: "They listened to me when I was speaking in tongues!" And he had been able to "say something"—in tongues to be sure—as he had never done before. The "establishment" of his family and his church of origin had not lent him their ear, but these quasi-wayward boys and girls had, and could do so only because they had felt the same alienation from their "establishments." The distraught parents, meanwhile, had felt that Cecil had never made a move to confide in them.

Cecil never was a convinced advocate of any charismatic movement. He did not know what to believe, and he never pitted his "gift of the spirit" against the psychiatric treatment he received. He realized that he needed treatment, made good use of it, and thus was shortly discharged. One thing he had now to contend with, over and beyond his court-ordered hospitalization, was a certain reserve and disapprobation from his family and former friends over his "weird religiosity" which was considered rampant in the "radical group" with which he had been briefly associated. The case is a tragicomedy of errors, abounding in clichés and full of negative belief fragments.

Cecil's situation can also be seen as a stepping stone to the more radical disengagement from positive beliefs which earmarks the cynic. If the cynic has any belief at all, it is a belief in the absurdity of everything. This should logically include the absurdity of his own existence, and therefore, if the cynic insists on staying alive, there is probably more in him than cynicism alone—maybe a deep longing for regaining other beliefs once held, or a wish to be contradicted in his assertions of the absurdity of things. As Cecil's brushes with the law and glossolalia were a cry for help, so may be the cynic's insistence on absurdity. But that cry is so bungling and its sound seems so self-assured that it may be unheeded—for who dares come with gifts of belief to a person who seems to dismiss them all?

Toleration of Beliefs, and Belief in Tolerance

If beliefs are indeed the love and hate objects I have made them out to be, it is small wonder that the practice of toleration, which took so long to be recognized by the body politic, remains beset with many difficulties. We may live in an age of acknowledged religious pluralism, but the pressure to be religious at any rate is still on. It is far from clear that the principle of pluralism is applied with conviction to the quiet or outspoken atheist or even to the religious eccentric who happens to locate himself outside the framework of civil religion and tries to evade its insidious pressures. Ethical beliefs, moreover, are not only bitterly fought about in verbal battles, but enacted by law with the result that one group of believers imposes its will on all citizens. Antiabortion laws, state regulations against the open saloon, and statutes against pornography are only a few examples of the process whereby one group of devotees prescribes its beliefs to the community as a whole, complete with legal sanctions. And in the sphere of political beliefs, the term "subversive" and the watchful eye of the House Un-American Activities Committee denote a large margin of intolerance in our otherwise allegedly pluralistic society.

If toleration of divergent beliefs is still such a precarious flower, although it has been planted and is alive, one might well ask what arguments and convictions have traditionally been marshaled in its favor. Why should any one person or any one group tolerate beliefs that are different from or opposed to his own? On what grounds is toleration to be fostered, given the fact that the very word "toleration" implies an attitude of disapproval, dislike, or condemnation of the things one is asked to put up with under its banner? Indeed, how *can* toleration be fostered if all of us treat our own beliefs as love objects and the divergent beliefs of others as objects of hate? Why should anyone show patient forbearance to something he despises?

Barring an attitude of radical indifference, in which case neither belief nor toleration would have any relevance, one could hold, as some of the Greeks of the classical period did, that intelligence has a necessary element of breadth and therefore demands a cultural largess leading to a realistic acceptance of divergence. Scope and breadth of thinking do not imply moral approval of everything, but they do mean openness to the complexity of reality, particularly the complexity of the human mind. Such thought also implies the precept "know thyself," which, if practiced, takes part of the blame off the others and puts it on the self, which has enough foibles of its own to worry about.

Historically,[15, 16] toleration has also been advocated on syncretistic grounds: in the Hellenistic period, gnosticism strove to present itself as a kind of superreligion built up, like a mosaic, from pieces of very diverse belief systems then prevailing in the Mediterranean and Near Eastern world. It is in the nature of syncretism to embrace everything, as it is in the nature of gnosticism to offer itself as a special kind of deep knowledge which recognizes nuggets of truth in the most diverse convictions and beliefs.

Toleration may be advocated on strategic grounds also. When one is caught, as the early Christians were, in patterns of persecution and oppression, and discovers that today's victors may be tomorrow's victims and vice versa, one may become weary of the shifting patterns of oppression and their attending uncertainty. Toleration may then be advocated for stability's sake, even when one's penchant is to win the whole world for one's own belief system.

Somewhat nobler, of course, is toleration pursued from a desire to be conciliatory. The belief system itself may give a central role to loving one's neighbor, even when he is the ideological or religious enemy, and such conciliatory feelings may spread to include the wayward and the deviant of any kind. This theme has been shared by Stoics and Christians alike, though it has been tainted in Stoicism with an element of resignation which is foreign to the zealous spirit of many Christians and Jews.

Strategic grounds for toleration can also be discovered in the arguments of seventeenth-century rationalists such as Locke, who reflected that attempts by the state or organized religion to suppress divergent beliefs simply do not work. The price of suppression is too high, in civic feelings of well-being, in good will toward the state, or in economic dislocation, and its long-range effect is negligible. The blood of the martyrs has proven too often to be the seed of the church or some other popular movement. Such practical realism can very well accompany the preservation of islands of suppression: Locke's advocacy of toleration did not allow room for atheists, for Locke felt that they could not take any valid oaths, which he considered essential to the engagement in social relations in the state.

An attitude of philosophical skepticism can give impetus to toleration. If one holds that there are no ultimate certainties, nobody has a valid claim to truth, and therefore no system of belief has the right to impose its ideas on others. Toleration is then the necessary outcome of our poor state of certitude, or at least is the only decent posture to assume if one is to avoid dogmatism of any sort.

Toleration of divergent beliefs can also flow from an attitude of good sportsmanship and fair play. Whoever wants to have a fair hearing for his beliefs must grant that wish to others too. In fact, a good part of the more recent history of the principle of toleration which was to eventuate in the modern phenomenon of pluralism goes back to feelings of fair play for all induced by the Enlightenment with its enthronement of Reason. It took, however, the acumen of a John Stuart Mill[17] to see the difference between legal protection against crass impositions of particular beliefs and the insidious pressure of mores and public morality which persists after edicts of toleration have been passed and constitutional guarantees of freedom have been given. Mill saw the oppressiveness of what we now call civil religion, as he saw the insidious pressure of male chauvinism on curbing the liberties of women, and he argued for widening the sphere of freedom from all such pressures.

Many other motives for toleration of divergent beliefs can be examined. Aversion to the cruelty of oppression witnessed at close range in time or space may shock people into advocating a tolerant attitude. The Crusades may have ended out of sheer satiation with cruelty. One could promote toleration out of a deep respect for others in a civil sense, or one could promote it, as St. Francis did, out of a deep feeling of oneness with all creation under the fatherhood of God. Most of these motives, however, continue to keep toleration in the sphere of "second thoughts": the impulse to dislike, disapprove, or condemn certain beliefs is taken for granted as belonging to the natural man, to which is then added the adhortation that the civilized or pious man should step on the brakes, restrain himself, "put up" with what he despises, and practice patient forbearance.

Noble as patient forbearance may be, it falls short of espousing tolerance as a positive value in its own right. I sense a difference between toleration and tolerance: the former is "putting up with something despicable," and the latter is "letting be with respect for the nature of divergent states of being." What would be the psychological or existential grounds for the latter attitude? What is the source of the reverence toward otherness that is implied in "letting be"?

We noted earlier that the function of any concept of the infinite is to teach man that he is not *it*, that he is not God. Man is only finite. An ontological gulf separates him from the ultimate. That function of the concept of the infinite is very pedagogical, for man has an uncanny penchant for asserting himself as if he were infinite and ultimate. He likes to play god and lord it over his fellowman. He assumes omnipotence for himself and is prone to boundless grandiosity. And as Freud pointed out, even when he is religious he does not quite go far enough in ceding his omnipotence to his gods: he keeps a portion for himself in order to influence these gods in his favor. He is not likely ever to see the extent of his narcissism unless he be confronted with a radical alternative: the ultimate power of the cosmos, of God, of fate, or, in abstract terms, the noncontingent. Tolerance can be born only from some such confrontation in which the person gains insight into the extent of his self-inflation, the tenacity of his omnipotent strivings, and his penchant for one-upmanship over his fellowman—and grants other people with other beliefs the respect they deserve.

Freud insisted on a humility by which a person will know and accept his small scope vis-à-vis the large universe. The humility that Freud has in mind stems from reality testing: it is the realization that unchecked indulgence in wishing and giving free reign to one's impulses lead to delusion. All gratifications must be tempered and apportioned by the reality principle, which alone can becalm the turbulent seas of instinctual strivings. Reality is not to be acknowledged grudgingly, and with all kinds of private hedgings, but roundly. Reality, because of its superiority of power, demands assent. Such an affirmation of reality, with the humility and renunciations it entails, is an important condition for the practice of tolerance taken in the positive sense as willingness to let be—for some things simply *must* be, such as an enormous diversity of belief systems.

Another chapter brought us face to face with the existence of mystery. Mysteries are not problems that can be solved, but challenging presences that force us to an encounter in which we take off our hats, fall into silence, or mumble something to the effect that we cannot quite grasp what's there. Mystery requires respect and reverence. So did Schweitzer see all life, even that of mosquitoes. Reverence for life taught him the virtue of self-abnegation. In human intercourse, reverence for life means first of all being reverent toward the mystery of someone else's being—with his beliefs, disbeliefs, and unbeliefs. Openness to mystery is a condition that may move a person from an attitude of mere toleration of divergent beliefs to the active practice of tolerance as a virtue. Tolerance is not merely a nice gesture to the alien. Like all virtues, it enriches and enlarges the mind of its practitioner.

We have also seen that believing and disbelieving entail what James called the *Will* to believe, that they entail choosing and risk taking, and that we tend to believe only what is momentous for us and to disbelieve the things for which we have no use. This makes belief and disbelief situational: much depends on where we are in life, what we are experiencing, where we feel we are going, and what we feel we need at this moment. Each of us goes through many different situations, both as compared to others and in terms of the succession of events in our own life. Therefore, if my beliefs speak to my needs of the moment, the beliefs of others presumably speak to their needs of the moment. Beliefs have an inevitable relativity. How then can I impose my beliefs on others? What right have I to deny someone else's right to believe in his fashion, in his situation, for his existential purposes? Reflections on my own processes of choosing between momentous options, on my own need to revise my beliefs periodically and to reevaluate my prior beliefs with some degree of humor, may induce me to practice tolerance: the same kind of tolerance to the beliefs of others that I practice to the beliefs of myself. We are all involved in growth processes, and growth means change. Our beliefs need to grow with us, and we must grow with our growing beliefs. Tolerance for divergent beliefs is thus also a tolerance for growth—loyalty to a universe that is changing, to a reality that is not fixed but in process, as Whitehead saw.

In our discussion of the nature of caring, we found that caring has a double benefit: if caring becomes a way of life one actualizes himself as he helps others to actualize themselves. Caring gives a person a place in reality and a delicately poised certainty, both of which are satisfying in themselves. Caring is always personalistic, and thus the person who adopts a caring life style will approach divergent beliefs with an awareness of the person who holds these beliefs, the love he has for his beliefs, the ambivalence he may have toward some of his own stated tenets, and the hate he may feel toward beliefs contrary to his own. Such an attitude of caring prepares the soil for tolerance: tolerance that lets the other fellow be as he defines himself through his beliefs. Such tolerance can also promote in the cared-for person the desire to care for himself, to examine his beliefs and disbeliefs, and to revise them according to the light he will gain as he cares for himself.

We also caught a glimpse of hope in the chapter on caring. Hope is standing on one leg in experienced tragedy while one holds the other leg on untrodden ground: the vast tracts of unexplored reality where novelty may be found and discoveries made that will revise our limited picture of the whole. We found in hoping a belief in benevolence also, an apperception of the *more* as having a friendly, sustaining, and caring disposition. And thus it is that we can approach our own beliefs with

268 BETWEEN BELIEF AND UNBELIEF

a dose of humor, in awareness of their limitations determined by our past and present, but before which the future stretches out with realities yet unknown. It behooves us to have some modesty, to practice tolerance for other people's beliefs and disbeliefs from an awareness that our own beliefs and disbeliefs cannot yet be finalized.

Another chapter examined the power of fantasy, with its uses and misuses. It neither dethroned nor extolled the fantasy—it only asked that we come to terms with its peculiar reality in order to keep life appropriately rich and our minds maximally attuned to what is going on. It alerted us to the possibility that myths may lie behind our greatest certitudes and rituals may lurk behind our most advanced skills. Many of our own beliefs and practices could benefit from being placed in the crucible of a demythologizer, after which they may turn out pale as the moon and thin as air. Again, such scrutiny of our own beliefs should make us tolerant of the beliefs and disbeliefs of others.

In the preceding chapter we found two *tremendums,* an outer and an inner one, with curtains of repression hanging before each. We took a look at those curtains with their graffiti from many ages and many civilizations and found them indescribably dense and chaotic. So many "truths" have been written down, so many beliefs advocated, so many dogmas asserted, that modern man, standing before these curtains, throws up his hands in despair of ever settling for one or the other great claim that the ages have written down. Man is only becoming more curious, willing to form some new hypotheses but not to declare himself in possession of truth. He lives open-endedly, no longer insisting on premature closure. Such an attitude toward ultimate reality is of course a powerful inducement for the active practice of tolerance, very different from the attitude of toleration which may flow from skepticism.

Two more motives for tolerance remain to be discerned. Throughout this book and pointedly in its title there has been an emphasis on the ambiguity of choice and the ambivalent feelings with which many choices are made. To the extent that some ambivalence seems an irreducible fact of life, it attaches to our beliefs and disbeliefs—and thus also attaches to the beliefs and disbeliefs of others which we praise or blame. It is always possible that our conscious opposition to other people's beliefs is tainted by some unconscious attraction on our part to just those beliefs we despise in others. It is also possible that we cherish certain beliefs of others because we have doubts about their validity or veracity for ourselves. We may have some secret envy of the beliefs of others we say we hate, just as we may secretly despise the beliefs of our own to which we verbally testify. The more we know of our own ambivalences toward any belief or disbelief, the more we should—and can—practice tolerance toward the divergent beliefs of our fellowman.

Lastly, we must have a final rendezvous with the late D. W. Winnicott, who has made some very important contributions to this book. The transitional sphere and the transitional object are in my view, and I think in Winnicott's, the first testing ground of belief. Belief stems neither from the isolated id nor from an isolated external world. It arises when the id and the outer world are brought judiciously together by the contrivance of play in which the old and the young, the serious and the lighthearted, the dependent and the autonomous, the braggers and the timorous, the fantasts and the realists, come together to practice that greatest of all gifts: to play and to make beliefs. Such mutual engagements in play require a social contract in which tolerance is the highest virtue.

Bibliographical Notes

To avoid repetitiousness, all entries of the works of S. Freud refer to *The Standard Edition of the Complete Psychological Works of Sigmund Freud*, edited by J. Strachey, published in London by the Hogarth Press at various dates for different volumes, as listed. For certain classical works, the date in parentheses immediately following the name of the work refers to the original publication date, and is followed by the full reference to the currently more available edition.

I. Sacred and Secular Contexts of Beliefs

1. G. Holton, "On Trying to Understand Scientific Genius," *The American Scholar*, XLI (1971–72), 95–110. Upon my inquiry, Professor Holton was kind enough to trace the quote to a book by Carl Seelig, *Helle Zeit-Dunkle Zeit* (Zurich: Europa Verlag, 1956), which traces it in turn to a letter by Einstein to Hans Muehsam of April 5, 1954: " . . . man wird zum tief religiösen Ungläubigen."

2. A. Toffler, *Future Shock* (New York: Random House, 1970).

3. L. C. Eiseley, *The Immense Journey* (New York: Random House, 1957).

4. L. C. Eiseley, *The Firmament of Time* (New York: Atheneum, 1960).

5. L. C. Eiseley, *The Invisible Pyramid* (New York: Charles Scribner's Sons, 1970).

271

6. Since literature on this subject is too abundant to make specific references here, I recommend for an overview: N. Birnbaum and G. Lenzer, eds., *Sociology and Religion, A Book of Readings* (Englewood Cliffs, N.J.: Prentice-Hall, 1969), especially Part I.

7. L. Lévy-Brühl, *Le surnaturel et la nature dans la mentalité primitive* (Paris: F. Alcan, 1931).

8. C. Lévi-Strauss, *Structural Anthropology*, trans. by C. Jacobson and B. Grundfest Schoepf (New York: Basic Books, 1963; Garden City, N.Y.: Doubleday Anchor Books, 1967).

9. R. N. Bellah, "Civil Religion in America," *Daedalus*, XCVI (Winter 1967), 1–21.

10. S. Kierkegaard, *Attack upon Christendom*, (1854–55) trans. by W. Lowrie (Princeton, N.J.: Princeton University Press, 1944; Boston: Beacon Press, 1956).

11. K. Barth, *The Epistle to the Romans* (1921), trans. by E. C. Hoskyns (London: Geoffrey Cumberlege, Oxford University Press, 1933).

12. L. Feuerbach, *The Essence of Christianity* (1841), trans. by G. Eliot (New York: Harper & Bros., 1957).

13. K. Marx, "Contribution to the Critique of Hegel's Philosophy of Right (1884)," in *Karl Marx and Friedrich Engels: On Religion* (Moscow: 1957).

14. M. Weber, *The Protestant Ethic and the Spirit of Capitalism* (1904–05), trans. by T. Parsons (New York: Charles Scribner's Sons, 1958).

15. M. Weber, *Wirtschaft und Gesellschaft* (1922). Portions of this book have been translated in *From Max Weber: Essays in Sociology*, trans. and ed. by H. H. Gerth and C. Wright Mills (New York: Oxford University Press, 1946), and in M. Weber, *The Sociology of Religion* (1922), trans. by E. Fischoff (Boston: Beacon Press, 1963).

16. E. Shills, "The Intellectuals and the Powers: Some Perspectives for Comparative Analysis," in *Comparative Studies in Society and History*, Vol. I, No. 1 (Cambridge: Cambridge University Press, 1958), and *On Intellectuals*, ed. by P. Rieff (Garden City, New York: Doubleday & Co., 1969; Anchor Books, 1970, p. 33).

17. E. Durkheim, *The Elementary Forms of the Religious Life* (1912), (London: George Allen & Unwin, 1915).

18. T. Luckmann, "Belief, Unbelief and Religion," in *The Culture of Unbelief*, ed. by R. Caporale and A. Grumelli (Berkeley: University of California Press, 1971), p. 24.

19. P. Tillich, *The Religious Situation*, trans. by H. R. Niebuhr (New York: Henry Holt & Co., 1932; Meridian Books, 1956).

20. P. Tillich, *Systematic Theology*, I (Chicago: University of Chicago Press, 1959), 217–218.

21. D. Bonhoeffer, *Prisoner for God* (New York: Macmillan, 1959).

22. H. Cox, *The Secular City* (New York: Macmillan, 1968).
23. J. Daniélou, "Variations in Perspective on Secularization and Unbelief," discussion by H. Cox, J. Daniélou, and M. Machovec, chaired by P. Berger, in *The Culture of Unbelief*, ed. by R. Caporale and A. Grumelli (Berkeley: University of California Press, 1971), pp. 91–105.
24. R. N. Bellah, "Between Religion and Social Science," *ibid.*, p. 271.
25. T. Parsons, "Introduction to Max Weber," in *The Sociology of Religion*, trans. by E. Fischoff (Boston, Beacon Press, 1963), pp. lxii–lxiii.
26. T. Parsons, "Belief, Unbelief and Disbelief," in *The Culture of Unbelief*, pp. 215–216 and ff.
27. E. Durkheim as quoted in T. Parsons, "Belief, Unbelief and Disbelief," in *The Culture of Unbelief*, p. 209.
28. R. Otto, *The Idea of the Holy* (1917), trans. by J. W. Harvey (London: Humphrey Milford-Oxford University Press, 1928).
29. J. Whithe, "The Highest State of Consciousness," *Journal for the Study of Consciousness*, IV (1971), 13–22.
30. T. C. Oden, "Inconsistencies and Miscalculations of the Encounter Culture," *The Christian Century*, LXXXIX (Jan. 26, 1972), 85–88, and his book *The Intensive Group Experience: The New Pietism* (Philadelphia: Westminster Press, 1972).
31. N. O. Brown, *Life Against Death: The Psychoanalytic Meaning of History* (Middletown, Conn.: Wesleyan University Press, 1959).
32. N. O. Brown, *Love's Body* (New York: Random House, Vintage Books, 1966).
33. M. E. Marty, "Sects and Cults" (1960), in *Sociology and Religion: A Book of Readings*, ed. by N. Birnbaum and G. Lenzer (Englewood Cliffs, N.J.: Prentice-Hall, 1969).

II. Religious Beliefs and Alienation

1. G. Petrovic, "Alienation," in P. Edwards, ed., *Encyclopedia of Philosophy*, I (New York: Macmillan and Free Press, 1967), 76–81.
2. R. Aron, *Progress and Disillusion—The Dialectics of Modern Society* (New York: New American Library, Mentor Book, 1969).
3. K. Marx, "Capital," trans. by S. Moore and E. Aveling in R. M. Hutchins, ed., *Great Books of the Western World*, L, (Chicago: Encyclopaedia Britannica, 1952), 111–146.
4. E. R. Goodenough, *The Psychology of Religious Experiences* (New York: Basic Books, 1965), p. 2.
5. M. Weber, *The Sociology of Religion* (1922), trans. by E. Fischoff (Boston: Beacon Press, 1963).
6. M. Weber, *The Protestant Ethic and the Spirit of Capitalism*

(1904–05), trans. by T. Parsons (New York: Charles Scribner's Sons, 1958).

7. Weber, *The Sociology of Religion*, p. 166.

8. T. Parsons, "Introduction," *ibid.*

9. T. Parsons, *The Structure of Social Action* (New York: The Free Press, 1949).

10. R. K. Merton, *Social Theory and Social Structure*, rev. and enl. ed. (New York: The Free Press, 1957). Merton's elaborate discussion of anomie has been helpful to me in clarifying my thoughts on alienation.

11. A. H. Maslow, *Motivation and Personality* (New York: Harper, 1954).

12. F. Pfeiffer, *Meister Eckhart*, trans. by C. de B. Evans (London: John M. Watkins, 1924), p. 246.

13. M. W. Harder, J. T. Richardson, and R. B. Simmonds, "Jesus People," *Psychology Today*, VI (1972), 45–50, 110–113.

14. E. H. Erikson, *Young Man Luther: A Study in Psychoanalysis and History* (New York: W. W. Norton & Co., 1958), pp. 49–97.

15. K. Keniston, *The Uncommitted: Alienated Youth in American Society* (New York: Harcourt, Brace & World, 1960).

16. K. Keniston, *Young Radicals: Notes on Committed Youth* (New York: Harcourt, Brace & World, 1968).

17. *Ibid.*, p. 329.

18. R. J. Lifton, "Protean Man," *Archives of General Psychiatry*, XXIV (1971), 298–304, and *Partisan Review*, XXXV (1968), 13–27.

19. T. Roszak, *The Making of a Counterculture: Reflections on the Technocratic Society and Its Youthful Opposition* (Garden City, N.Y.: Doubleday & Co., 1969), p. 1.

20. S. Freud, "Civilization and Its Discontents" (1930), Vol. XXI (1961).

III. A Psychological Perspective on Unbelief

1. S. Freud, "Civilization and Its Discontents" (1930), Vol. XXI (1961).

2. S. Freud, "Three Essays on the Theory of Sexuality" (1905), Vol. VII (1953).

3. K. Menninger, M. Mayman, and P. W. Pruyser, *A Manual for Psychiatric Case Study*, 2d ed. (New York: Grune & Stratton, 1962), pp. 46–84.

4. M. Klein, P. Heiman, S. Isaacs, and J. Riviere, *Developments in Psycho-Analysis* (London: Hogarth Press, 1952).

5. M. Klein, *Contributions to Psycho-Analysis, 1921–1945* (London: Hogarth Press, 1968).

6. W. R. D. Fairbairn, *Psychoanalytic Studies of the Personality* (London: Tavistock, 1952).

7. W. R. D. Fairbairn, "Synopsis of an Object Relations Theory of the Personality," *International Journal of Psychoanalysis,* XLIV (1963), 224–225.

8. W. R. D. Fairbairn, "Observations in Defence of the Object-Relations Theory of the Personality," *British Journal of Medical Psychology,* XXVIII (1955), 144–156.

9. H. Guntrip, *Personality Structure and Human Interaction* (New York: International Universities Press, 1961).

10. E. Jacobson, *The Self and the Object World* (New York: International Universities Press, 1964).

11. M. Balint, "Criticism of Fairbairn's Generalization about Object-Relations," *British Journal of Philosophical Science,* VII (1957), 323.

12. A. H. Modell, *Object Love and Reality* (New York: International Universities Press, 1968).

13. P. W. Pruyser, *A Dynamic Psychology of Religion* (New York: Harper & Row, 1968), pp. 286–328.

14. K. Menninger, M. Mayman, and P. W. Pruyser, *The Vital Balance* (New York: Viking Press, 1963).

15. F. Bacon, "Essay 17, of Superstition," in *The Essays or Counsels, Civil and Moral, of Francis Lord Verulam* (Mt. Vernon, N.Y.: Peter Pauper Press, n.d.), p. 69.

16. W. James, "The Will to Believe" (1896), in *The Will to Believe and Other Essays in Popular Philosophy* (New York: Longmans, Green & Co., 1897).

17. Bacon, *Essays,* p. 71.

18. R. Browning, "Bishop Blougram's Apology," in *The Complete Poetic and Dramatic Works of Robert Browning,* ed. by H. E. Scudder (Boston: Houghton Mifflin, 1895), p. 351.

19. F. E. D. Schleiermacher, *Über die Religion: Reden an die Gebildeten unter ihren Verächtern* (1799) (Berlin: Deutsche Bibliothek Verlag Gesellschaft, n.d.); *On Religion,* trans. by J. Oman (New York: Frederick Ungar Publishing Co., 1955).

20. R. Otto, *Das Heilige* (1917), 23–25 Auflage (München: C. H. Beck'sche Verlags Buchhandlung, 1936); *The Idea of the Holy,* trans. by J. W. Harvey (New York: Oxford University Press, 1928).

21. W. James, *The Varieties of Religious Experience* (New York: Longmans, Green & Co., 1902).

22. P. Rieff, *The Triumph of the Therapeutic* (New York: Harper & Row, 1966).

23. E. Jones, "Psycho-analysis and the Christian Religion," in *Essays in Applied Psycho-analysis,* 2 vols. (London: Hogarth Press, 1951), II, 203.

24. S. Freud, "Totem and Taboo" (1913), Vol. XIII (1955).

25. S. Freud, "Psychoanalysis and Religious Origins" (1919), Vol. XVII (1955).

26. S. Freud, "The Future of an Illusion" (1927), Vol. XXI (1961).
27. S. Freud, "Civilization and Its Discontents" (1930), Vol. XXI (1961).
28. S. Freud, "Moses and Monotheism" (1939), Vol. XXIII (1964).
29. S. Freud, "Obsessive Actions and Religious Practices" (1907), Vol. IX (1959).
30. S. Freud, "Notes upon a Case of Obsessional Neurosis" (1909), Vol. X (1955).
31. S. Freud, "Psychoanalytic Notes on an Autobiographical Account of a Case of Paranoia (Dementia Paranoides)" (1911), Vol. XII (1958).
32. S. Freud, "From the History of an Infantile Neurosis" (1918), Vol. XVII (1955).
33. S. Freud, "A Seventeenth-Century Demonological Neurosis" (1923), Vol. XIX (1961).
34. S. Freud, "A Religious Experience" (1928), Vol. XXI (1961).
35. E. R. Goodenough, *The Psychology of Religious Experiences* (New York: Basic Books, 1965), p. 181.

IV. Dealing with Dependency and Autonomy

1. T. S. Eliot, "Choruses from 'The Rock,' " in *Collected Poems 1909-1962* (New York; Harcourt, Brace & Co., 1963).
2. F. E. D. Schleiermacher, *Über die Religion: Reden an die Gebildeten unter ihren Verächtern* (1799) (Berlin: Deutsche Bibliothek Verlag Gesellschaft, n.d.); *On Religion*, trans. by J. Oman (New York: Frederick Ungar Publishing Co., 1955).
3. T. Paine, *The Age of Reason* (1794) (New York: The Thomas Paine Foundation, n.d.).
4. S. E. Mead, "In Quest of America's Religion," *The Christian Century*, LXXXVII (June 17, 1970), 752–756.
5. W. James, *The Varieties of Religious Experience* (New York: Longmans, Green & Co., 1902), p. 41.
6. S. Freud, "The Future of an Illusion" (1927), XXI (1961), 32–33.
7. James, *Varieties*, p. 51–52.
8. Spinoza, *Ethics*, III, prop. 6 ff.
9. E. H. Erikson, "Identity and the Life Cycle," *Psychological Issues*, Vol. I, No. 1 (New York: International Universities Press, 1959).
10. E. H. Erikson, *Childhood and Society*, 2d ed. (New York: W. W. Norton & Co., 1963), p. 266.
11. W. Kähler, *Angelus Silesius* (Munich: Georg Müller, 1929), p. 27. Kähler himself pairs Silesius's line with Rilke's.
12. D. Macleod, "Excerpta et Commentaria," *Princeton Seminary Bulletin*, LXIV (Dec. 1971), 8. "Does God know we don't believe in him?" attributed to W. Strickler, guest editorial in the *New Jersey Lutheran*, November 1971.

13. E. H. Erikson, *Young Man Luther: A Study in Psychoanalysis and History* (New York: W. W. Norton & Co., 1958), pp. 21–22.

14. Erikson, *Childhood and Society*, p. 250.

15. A. Mitscherlich, *Society without the Father*, trans. by E. Mosbacher. (New York: Harcourt, Brace & World, 1969).

16. *Letters of James Agee to Father Flye* (New York: George Braziller, 1962; Bantam Books, 1963), p. 94.

17. E. A. Ticho, "Termination of Psychoanalysis: Treatment Goals, Life Goals," *Psychoanalytic Quarterly*, XLI (1972), 315–333.

v. Coming to Terms with Mystery

1. T. Roszak, *The Making of a Counterculture: Reflections on the Technocratic Society and Its Youthful Opposition* (Garden City, N.Y.: Doubleday & Co., Anchor Books, 1969), p. 41.

2. C. A. Reich, *The Greening of America* (New York: Random House, 1970).

3. H. Marcuse, *One-Dimensional Man* (Boston: Beacon Press, 1964).

4. M. Esslin, *The Theater of the Absurd* (Garden City, N.Y.: Doubleday & Co., Anchor Books, 1961).

5. S. Beckett, *Waiting for Godot* (New York: Grove Press, 1954).

6. M. Novak, *Belief and Unbelief: A Philosophy of Self-Knowledge* (New York: Macmillan, 1965).

7. R. J. Lifton, "Protean Man," *Archives of General Psychiatry*, XXIV (1971), 298–304, and *Partisan Review*, XXXV (1968), 13–27.

8. E. H. Erikson, *Gandhi's Truth* (New York: W. W. Norton & Co., 1969), p. 98.

9. M. Buber, *Between Man and Man*, trans. by R. G. Smith (Boston: Beacon Press, 1955). See especially chap. 5, "What Is Man?"; the realm of the "between."

10. M. Buber, *Writings*, selected, ed., and introduced by W. Herberg (New York: Meridian Books, 1956).

11. M. Buber, *A Believing Humanism: Gleanings by M. Buber*, trans. by M. Friedman (New York: Simon & Schuster, 1967).

12. M. A. Diamond, *Martin Buber: Jewish Existentialist* (New York: Oxford University Press, 1960).

13. G. Marcel, *Etre et avoir* (Paris: Aubier, 1935), pp. 248 ff.

14. G. Marcel, *Journal métaphysique* (Paris: Gallimard, 1935), pp. 160 ff.

15. F. Kafka, *The Castle* (New York: Modern Library, 1969).

16. F. Kafka, *The Trial* (New York: Random House, 1969).

17. M. Marty, *Varieties of Unbelief* (New York: Holt, Rinehart & Winston, 1964; Doubleday & Co., Anchor Books, 1966). See especially chap. 4, "The Originality of Modern Unbelief," pp. 35–68.

18. R. Otto, *The Idea of the Holy* (1917), trans. by J. W. Harvey (New

York: Oxford University Press, 1928).

19. R. Otto, *Das Heilige* (1917), 23–25 Auflage (München, C. H. Beck'sche Verlags Buchhandlung, 1936).

20. D. W. Winnicott, *Playing and Reality* (New York: Basic Books, 1971).

21. D. W. Winnicott, "Transitional Objects and Transitional Phenomena," in his *Collected Papers* (London: Tavistock Publications, 1958), pp. 229–242.

22. E. H. Erikson, "Ontogeny of Ritualization," in *Psychoanalysis— A General Psychology: Essays in Honor of Heinz Hartmann,* ed. by R. M. Loewenstein, L. M. Newman, M. Schur, and A. J. Solnit (New York: International Universities Press, 1966).

23. E. H. Erikson, *Young Man Luther: A Study in Psychoanalysis and History* (New York: W. W. Norton & Co., 1958), pp. 21–22.

24. D. P. Schreber, *Memoirs of My Nervous Illness* (1903), trans. by I. Macalpine and R. A. Hunter (London: W. Dawson, 1955).

25. A. Boisen, *Out of the Depths* (New York: Harper & Bros., 1960), pp. 88–89.

26. E. Swedenborg, *Angelic Wisdom Concerning the Divine Love and the Divine Wisdom* (New York: American Swedenborg Printing and Publishing Society, 1885).

27. M. Rokeach, *The Open and Closed Mind* (New York: Basic Books, 1960).

28. M. Rokeach, *Beliefs, Attitudes and Values: A Theory of Organization and Change* (San Francisco: Jossey-Bass, 1968).

29. J. Huizinga, *Homo Ludens: A Study of the Play-Element in Culture* (1938) (Boston: Beacon Press, 1955).

30. K. Keniston, *Young Radicals: Notes on Committed Youth* (New York: Harcourt, Brace & World, 1968), p. 336.

31. Interview with J. Ehrenwald: "Myth Deprivation Held a Cause of Wide Appeal of the Occult," *Frontiers of Psychiatry (Roche Report),* II (June 1, 1972), 1–2, 8.

32. A. H. Maslow, *The Farther Reaches of Human Nature* (New York: Viking Press, 1971) contains in chap. 21 a rare, and very useful, list of various meanings of the idea of transcendence.

33. P. A. Bertocci, "Psychological Interpretations of Religious Experience," in *Research on Religious Development,* ed. by M. P. Strommen (New York: Hawthorn Publishers, 1971). See especially pp. 23–26.

VI. Coming to Terms with Options

1. W. James, *The Principles of Psychology,* 2 vols. (New York: Henry Holt & Co.; London: Macmillan & Company, 1890), I, 496.

2. W. James, *Psychology: Briefer Course* (New York: Henry Holt & Co.; London: Macmillan & Co., 1892), p. 29.

3. W. James, *The Will to Believe, and Other Essays in Popular*

Philosophy (New York: Longmans, Green & Co., 1897).

4. R. J. Lifton, "Protean Man," *Archives of General Psychiatry*, XXIV (1971), 298–304, and *Partisan Review*, XXXV (1968), 13–27.

5. R. M. Enroth, E. E. Ericson, Jr., and C. B. Peters, *The Jesus People —Old-Time Religion in the Age of Aquarius* (Grand Rapids, Mich.: W. B. Eerdmans Publishing Co., 1972).

6. P. Marin, "Children of Yearning," *Saturday Review*, LV (May 6, 1972), 58–63.

7. "The New Rebel Cry: Jesus Is Coming!" *Time*, XCVII (June 21, 1971), 56–63.

8. W. James, *The Varieties of Religious Experience* (New York: Longmans, Green & Co., 1902).

9. R. N. Bellah, "Civil Religion in America," *Daedalus*, XCVI (Winter 1967), 1–21.

10. K. R. Eissler, *Goethe: A Psychoanalytic Study* (Detroit: Wayne State University Press, 1963).

11. Goethe, "Faust," Part I, Study, trans. by G. M. Priest in R. M. Hutchins, ed., *Great Books of the Western World*, XLVII (Chicago: Encyclopaedia Britannica, 1952), 33.

12. D. M. Kelley, *Why Conservative Churches Are Growing: A Study in Sociology of Religion* (New York: Harper & Row, 1972).

13. S. Freud, "The Future of an Illusion" (1927), XXI (1961), 37.

14. S. Freud, "Dostoevsky and Parricide" (1928), XXI (1961), 177.

15. B. D. Lewin, "Some Observations on Knowledge, Belief, and the Impulse to Know," *International Journal of Psycho-analysis*, XX (1939), 426–431.

16. R. D. Laing, *The Divided Self* (London: Tavistock Publications, 1959; Penguin Books, 1965).

17. A. Camus, *The Stranger*, trans. by S. Gilbert (New York: Random House, 1946).

18. F. Dostoevsky, *The Brothers Karamazov*, trans. by C. Garnett (New York: Modern Library, Random House, 1943), bk. 5, chap. 5.

19. *Letters of James Agee to Father Flye* (New York: George Braziller, 1962; Bantam Books, 1963), pp. 156–157.

20. G. W. Allen, *William James: A Biography* (New York: Viking Press, 1967), p. 431.

21. K. Jaspers, *Psychologie der Weltanschauungen* (Berlin: Springer, 1919).

22. W. R. Looft, "The Psychology of More," *American Psychologist*, XXVI (1971), 561–565.

VII. Coming to Terms with Providence

1. E. Jones, "The Psychology of Religion," in *Essays in Applied PsychoAnalysis*, II (London: Hogarth Press, 1951), 195.

2. E. Jones, "Psycho-analysis and the Christian Religion," in *Essays*

in Applied Psycho-Analysis, II (London: Hogarth Press, 1951), 201, 203.

3. S. Hiltner, *Theological Dynamics* (Nashville: Abingdon Press, 1972), pp. 55–80.

4. The Westminster Confession of Faith, chap. 5, "On Providence," in *Book of Confessions* (Philadelphia: Office of the General Assembly of the United Presbyterian Church in the United States of America, 1967).

5. A. C. Outler, *Who Trusts in God: Musings on the Meaning of Providence* (New York: Oxford University Press, 1968).

6. A. Mitscherlich, *Society without the Father*, trans. by E. Mosbacher (New York: Harcourt, Brace & World, 1969).

7. P. Rieff, *Freud: The Mind of the Moralist* (New York: Viking Press, 1959).

8. E. Jones, "The God Complex," in *Essays in Applied Psycho-Analysis*, II (London: Hogarth Press, 1951), 244–265.

9. S. Freud, "A Seventeenth Century Demonological Neurosis" 91923), Vol. XIX (1961).

10. K. Boulding, "Nor to Revenge Any Wrong," in *There Is a Spirit: The Naylor Sonnets* (New York: Fellowship Publications, 1945).

11. S. Freud, "The Ego and the Id" (1923), Vol. XIX (1961).

12. K. Menninger, *Love against Hate* (New York: Harcourt, Brace & Co., 1942).

13. C. G. Jung, *The Development of Personality*, trans. by R. F. C. Hull (Bollingen Series XX, Vol. XVII [New York: Pantheon Books, 1954]), pp. 167–186, and regarding transformation symbolism in the Mass, see C. G. Jung, *Psychology and Religion: West and East*, trans. by R. F. C. Hull (Bollingen Series XX, Vol. XI [New York: Pantheon Books, 1958]), p. 263.

14. N. Berdjajew, "Het Booze en de Verlossing," in *Vrijheid en Geest*, trans. by H. Buys (Den Haag: Servire, n.d.), pp. 181–213.

15. J. H. Sims and D. D. Baumann, "The Tornado Threat: Coping Styles of the North and South," *Science*, 176 (1972), 1386–1392.

16. A. Camus, *Resistance, Rebellion and Death*, trans. by J. O'Brien (New York: Knopf, 1961), pp. 70 ff.

17. M. Mayeroff, *On Caring* (New York: Harper & Row, 1971).

18. W. James, *The Varieties of Religious Experience* (London: Longmans, Green & Co., 1902), p. 508.

19. G. Marcel, *Homo Viator: Introduction to a Metaphysic of Hope*, trans. by E. Crawford (Chicago: Regnery, 1951).

20. P. W. Pruyser, "Phenomenology and Dynamics of Hoping," *Journal for the Scientific Study of Religion*, III (1963), 86–96.

21. W. C. M. Scott, "Depression, Confusion and Multivalence," *International Journal of Psychoanalysis*, XLI (1960), 497–503.

22. H. J. Schlesinger, "Contributions to a Theory of Promising,"

Transactions of the Topeka Psychoanalytic Society, *Bulletin of the Menninger Clinic*, XXXIII (1969), 129–132.
23. H. J. Schlesinger, "Promises, Promises: Making Them Sets Up a Tension System," *Roche Report, Frontiers of Clinical Psychiatry*, VI (July 1, 1969), 5–6.
24. P. W. Pruyser, "A Psychological Commentary on D. E. Miller's 'Salvation and Man's Life' " (paper delivered at National Colloquium on Salvation and Life, Fourth National Faith and Order Colloquium, National Council of Churches, St. Louis, Mo., June 8–12, 1969).

VIII. Coming to Terms with Fantasy

1. P. W. Pruyser, "Sigmund Freud and His Legacy: Psychoanalytic Psychology of Religion," in *Beyond the Classics in the Scientific Study of Religion*, ed. by C. Y. Glock and P. E. Hammond (New York: Harper & Row 1973). pp. 243–290
2. S. Freud, "The Interpretation of Dreams" (1900), Vols. IV–V (1953).
3. S. Freud, "Civilization and Its Discontents" (1930), Vol. XXI (1961).
4. H. Meng and E. L. Freud, *Psychoanalysis and Faith: The Letters of Sigmund Freud and Oskar Pfister*, trans. by E. Mosbacher (New York: Basic Books, 1963).
5. S. Freud, "Charcot" (1893), III (1962), 22.
6. S. Freud, "Moses and Monotheism" (1939), XXIII (1964), 123.
7. R. Waelder, "The Psychoanalytic Theory of Play," *Psychoanalytic Quarterly*, II (1932), 208–224.
8. P. McKellar, *Imagination and Thinking—A Psychological Analysis* (New York: Basic Books, 1957).
9. E. Bleuler, *Dementia Praecox; or the Group of Schizophrenias*, trans. by J. Zinkin (New York: International Universities Press, 1950).
10. R. R. Holt, "The Development of the Primary Process: A Structural View," in *Motives and Thought, Psychoanalytic Essays in Honor of David Rapaport*, ed. by R. R. Holt (New York: International Universities Press, 1967).
11. K. Jaspers and R. Bultmann, *Die Frage der Entmythologisierung* (Munich: R. Piper & Co., Verlag, 1954).
12. R. Schafer, "Ideals, the Ego Ideal and the Ideal Self," in *Motives and Thought, Psychoanalytic Essays in Honor of David Rapaport*, ed. by R. R. Holt (New York: International Universities Press, 1967), p. 160.
13. E. Jacobson, *The Self and the Object World* (New York: International Universities Press, 1964), p. 39.
14. H. Guntrip, *Psychoanalytic Theory, Therapy, and the Self* (New York: Basic Books, 1971), pp. 53–54.
15. J. Piaget, *The Construction of Reality in the Child* (1937), trans.

by M. Cook (New York: Basic Books, 1954).

16. E. Kris, *Psychoanalytic Explorations in Art* (New York: International Universities Press, 1952).

17. E. H. Gombrich, *Art and Illusion: A Study in the Psychology of Pictorial Presentation*, 2d ed. (Princeton, N.J.: Princeton University Press, 1961).

18. E. H. Gombrich, "Meditations on a Hobby Horse or the Roots of Artistic Form," in *Aspects of Form*, ed. by L. L. Whyte (Bloomington: Indiana University Press, 1961), pp. 209–224.

19. E. H. Erikson, *Young Man Luther: A Study in Psychoanalysis and History* (New York: W. W. Norton & Co., 1958).

20. E. H. Erikson, *Gandhi's Truth* (New York: W. W. Norton & Co., 1969).

21. L. Levy-Brühl, *La mentalité primitive* (Paris: 1922).

22. C. Lévi-Strauss, "The Structural Study of Myth," in *Structural Anthropology*, trans. by C. Jacobson and B. G. Schoepf (New York: Basic Books, 1963), p. 206–231.

23. C. Lévi-Strauss, *The Raw and the Cooked: Introduction to a Science of Mythology: I*, trans. by J. and D. Weightman (New York: Harper & Row, 1969).

24. T. C. Oden, *The Intensive Group Experience: The New Pietism* (Philadelphia: Westminster Press, 1972). Also see "Inconsistencies and Miscalculations of the Encounter Culture," *The Christian Century*, LXXXIX (Jan. 26, 1972), 85–88.

25. S. Freud, "The Future of an Illusion" (1927), Vol. XXI (1961), p. 53

26. D. W. Winnicott, "Transitional Objects and Transitional Phenomena," in his *Collected Papers* (New York: Basic Books, 1958), p. 242.

27. R. Schafer, "Ideals, the Ego Ideal, and the Ideal Self," in *Motives and Thought, Psychoanalytic Essays in Honor of David Rapaport* ed. by R. R. Holt (New York: International Universities Press, 1967), p. 160.

28. Freud, "The Future of an Illusion," pp. 30–31

29. D. P. Schreber, *Memoirs of My Nervous Illness*, trans. by I. Macalpine and R. A. Hunter (London: W. Dawson, 1955).

30. A. T. Boisen, *Out of the Depths* (New York: Harper & Bros., 1960).

31. A. T. Boisen, *The Exploration of the Inner World: A Study of Mental Disorder and Religious Experience* (1936) (New York: Harper & Bros., 1962).

32. R. Pannikkar, "Simyata and Pleroma: The Buddhist and Christian Response to the Human Predicament," in *Religion and the Humanizing of Man*, ed. by J. M. Robinson (Council on the Study of Religion, 1972), pp. 67–86.

33. H. Jonas, "Technology and Responsibility: Reflections on the

New Tasks of Ethics," *ibid.* pp. 1–19
34. T. Reik, *Ritual: Psycho-analytic Studies,* trans. by D. Bryan (New York: W. W. Norton, 1931).
35. S. Freud, "Obsessive Actions and Religious Practices" (1907), Vol. IX (1959).
36. E. H. Erikson, "Ontogeny of Ritualization," in *Psychoanalysis— A General Psychology: Essays in Honor of Heinz Hartmann,* ed. by R. M. Loewenstein, L. M. Newman, M. Schur, and A. J. Solnit (New York: International Universities Press, 1966), pp. 614, 601–621.
37. I. Illich, *De-Schooling Society* (New York: Harper & Row, 1971).
38. M. Eliade, *Myth and Reality,* trans. by W. R. Trask (New York: Harper & Row, 1963), pp. 5–6.
39. W. F. Zuurdeeg, *An Analytical Philosophy of Religion* (Nashville: Abingdon Press, 1958).
40. *The Koran,* trans. by G. Sale (London: Frederick Warne & Co., n.d.), "Chapter LIV of the Moon," p. 510, including footnote commentary.
41. N. Chomsky, *Language and Mind,* enl. ed. (New York: Harcourt-Brace Jovanovich, 1972). For a discussion of Chomsky's theories, see also J. Searles, "Chomsky's Revolution in Linguistics," *New York Review of Books,* XVIII (June 29, 1972), 16–24.

IX. Coming to Terms with Reality

1. F. Dostoevsky, *The Brothers Karamazov,* trans. by C. Garnett (New York: Random House Modern Library, 1943), p. 289.
2. *Ibid.,* bk. 5, chaps. 4 and 5.
3. G. Murphy and H. E. Spohn, *Encounter with Reality* (Boston: Houghton Mifflin, 1968).
4. K. Jaspers, *Psychologie der Weltanschauungen* (Berlin: Springer, 1919).
5. K. Jaspers, *Existenzphilosophie* (Berlin-Leipzig: W. de Gruyter & Co., 1938).
6. B. Pascal, *Pensées,* sect. 3, no. 206.
7. M. Heidegger, *Being and Time* (1927) (New York: Harper & Row, 1962).
8. P. W. Pruyser, "Sigmund Freud and his Legacy: Psychoanalytic Psychology of Religion," in *Beyond the Classics in the Scientific Study of Religion,* ed. by C. Y. Glock and P. E. Hammond (New York: Harper & Row 1973), pp. 243–290
9. S. Freud, "Civilization and Its Discontents" (1930), Vol. XXI (1961).
10. S. Freud, "From the History of an Infantile Neurosis" (1918), Vol. XVII (1955).
11. S. Freud, "The Future of an Illusion" (1927), Vol. XXI (1961).

12. T. Parsons, "Belief, Unbelief, and Disbelief" in *The Culture of Unbelief* ed. by R. Caporale and A. Grumelli (Berkeley: University of California Press, 1971), p. 216.

13. A. Einstein, *Out of My Later Years* (New York: Philosophical Library, 1950), pp. 28, 29.

14. E. R. Goodenough, *The Psychology of Religious Experiences* (New York: Basic Books, 1965).

15. For a splendid history of the concept, see H. F. Ellenberger, *The Discovery of the Unconscious: The History and Evolution of Dynamic Psychiatry* (New York: Basic Books, 1970).

16. G. W. Groddeck, *The Book of the It* (1923), trans. by V. M. E. Collins (New York: Funk & Wagnalls, 1950).

17. W. James, *The Varieties of Religious Experience* (London: Longmans, Green & Co., 1902), p. 58.

18. L. Binswanger, *Grundformen und Erkenntnis menschlichen Daseins* (Zurich: Max Niehaus, 1942).

19. C. Reich, *The Greening of America* (New York: Random House, 1970).

20. A. L. Huxley, *The Doors of Perception* (New York: Harper & Brothers, 1954).

21. E. Husserl, *The Idea of Phenomenology,* trans. by W. P. Alston and G. Nakhnikina (The Hague: Nijhoff, 1964).

22. B. L. Whorf, *Collected Papers on Metalinguistics* (Washington, D.C.: Department of State, Foreign Service Institute, 1952).

23. E. Sapir, *Selected Writings in Language, Culture and Personality,* ed. by D. G. Mandelbaum (Berkeley: University of California Press, 1949).

24. H. Fortman, *Oosterse Renaissance* (Bilthoven: Uitgeverij Ambo, 1970), pp. 19–30.

25. G. Murphy, *Personality: A Biosocial Approach to Origins and Structure* (New York: Harper & Brothers, 1947).

26. Murphy and Spohn, *Encounter with Reality.*

27. G. Murphy, *Human Potentialities* (New York: Basic Books, 1958).

28. G. Murphy, *Challenge of Psychical Research,* World Perspectives, Vol. XXVI (New York: Harper & Bros., 1961).

29. Goodenough, *The Psychology of Religious Experiences,* p. 181.

x. Between Belief and Unbelief

1. P. Tillich, *Dynamics of Faith* (New York: Harper & Brothers, 1957).

2. J. M. Baldwin, *Feeling and Will* (New York: Henry Holt & Co., 1893).

3. J. B. Pratt, *The Psychology of Religious Belief* (New York: Macmillan, 1907), p. 43.

4. H. Gollwitzer, K. Kuhn, and R. Schneider, eds., *Dying We Live*, trans. by R. C. Kuhn (New York: Pantheon Books, 1956).
5. M. Rokeach, *The Open and Closed Mind* (New York: Basic Books, 1960).
6. A. Walters and R. Bradley, "Motivation and Religious Behavior," in *Research on Religious Development*, ed. by M. P. Strommen (New York: Hawthorn Books, 1971), pp. 618–619.
7. J. M. Grasse, Jr., "Peculiar Ways in Which Mennonites Handle Aggression" (unpublished graduation paper, Menninger School of Psychiatry, Topeka, Kansas, 1972).
8. S. Freud, "Civilization and Its Discontents" (1930), XXI (1961), 114.
9. S. Freud, "Group Psychology and the Analysis of the Ego" (1921), XVIII (1955), 101.
10. B. Spilka, "Research on Religious Beliefs: A Critical Review," in *Research on Religious Development*, ed. by M. P. Strommen (New York: Hawthorn Books, 1971), pp. 485–520.
11. L. Festinger, *A Theory of Cognitive Dissonance* (Evanston, Ill.: Row, 1957).
12. "My Belief." I have never been able to trace the author of this poem. Since its anticreedal tenor is so strong, readers of German may enjoy reading the whole text of "Mein Glaube," which I have in a typewritten copy only:

Ich glaube dass die schöne Welt regiere
ein hoher, weiser, nie begriffener Geist.
Ich glaube dass Anbetung ihm gebühre;
doch weiss ich nicht, wie man ihn würdig preist.
Nicht glaub' ich dass der Dogmen blinder Glaube
dem Hohen würdige Verehrung sei;
er bildet uns ja, das Geschöpf vom Staube,
von Irrtum nicht und nicht von Fehlern frei.
Drum glaub' ich nicht dass vor dem Geist der Welten
des Talmud und des Alkoran
Bekenner weniger als Christen gelten;
verschieden zwar, doch alle beten an.
Ich glaube nicht, wenn wir von Kanzeln hören,
der Christenglaube mache nur allein
uns selig; wenn die Unduldsamen lehren:
"verdammt muss jeder Andersdenker sein."
Das hat der Meister, der einst seine Lehre
mit seinem Blut besiegelt, nie gelehrt;
das hat fürwahr—dem Herrlichen sei Ehre—
kein Jünger je aus seinem Mund gehört!
Er lehrte Schonung, lehrte Duldung üben,

Verfolgung war der hohen Lehre fern;
er lehrt' ohn' Unterschied die Menschen lieben,
verzieh dem Schwachen, jedem Feinde gern.
Ich glaube an des Geistes Auferstehen,
dass, wenn im Tod das matte Auge bricht,
geläuterter wir uns dort wiedersehen,
Ich glaub' und hoff' es—doch ich weiss es nicht.
Dort glaub' ich, werde sich die Sehnsucht stillen,
die hier das Herz oft foltert und verzehrt,
die Wahrheit, glaub' ich, wird sich klar enthüllen,
dem Blicke dort, dem hier ein Schleier wehrt.
Ich glaube dass fur dieses Erdenleben,
glaub's zuversichtlich, trotz der Deutlerzunft,
zwei schöne Güter mir der Herr gegeben:
das eine Herz, das andere heisst Vernunft.
Das letzt're lehrt mich prüfen und entscheiden,
was ich für Pflicht und Recht erkennen soll.
Laut schlägt das erste bei des Bruders Freuden,
nicht minder, wenn er leidet, warm und voll.
So will ich denn mit regem Eifer üben,
was ich als Recht, was ich als Pflicht erkannt.
Will brüderlich die Menschen alle lieben,
am Belt, am Hudson und am Gangesstrand.
Ihr Leid zu mildern und ihr Wohl zu mehren
sei stets mein heiligster Beruf.
Durch Taten glaub' ich würdig zu verehren
den Geist, der mich wie sie erschuf.
Und tret' ich einst dann aus des Grabes Tiefen
hin vor des Weltenrichters Angesicht,
so wird er meine Taten strenge prüfen,
doch meinen Glauben—
nein, das glaub' ich nicht!

13. R. Bellah, "Civil Religion in America," *Daedalus*, XCVI (Winter 1967), 1–21.

14. J. P. Kildahl, *The Psychology of Speaking in Tongues* (New York: Harper & Row, 1972).

15. W. F. Adeney, "Toleration," in *Encyclopaedia of Religion and Ethics*, ed. by J. Hastings, XII (New York: Charles Scribner's Sons, 1955), 360–365.

16. M. Cranston, "Toleration," in *The Encyclopedia of Philosophy*, ed. by P. Edwards, VIII (New York: Macmillan Company, 1967), 143–146.

17. J. S. Mill, "On Liberty" (1859), in *Great Books of the Western World*, ed. by R. M. Hutchins, XLIII (Chicago: Encyclopedia Britannica, 1952), 312–323.

Index

Abstinence, 76, 77, 79, 165–166, 207
Absurd
absurdity, 261
Theater of the, 41, 96, 105
Action, theory of, 23, 28 ff.
Adaptation to reality, 234–235
Adeney, W. F., 286
Agee, J., 93, 151, 277, 279
Aggression, 102, 165, 174–175, 190, 253, 257
Agnosticism, 54, 60, 63, 139, 155–156, 244
Alienation, xv, 21–43, 67, 72, 96, 122, 136, 146, 196, 204, 245, 254, 260 ff.
as defiance, 91
definitions of, by
Feuerbach, 23
Hegel, 22–23
Marx, 23–24
factional, 37
institution—specific, 37
of intellectuals, 10
of the oppressed, 25–26
religious, 26–38
as state of consciousness, 24
various meanings of, 30 ff.
Allen, G. W., 279
Allport, G. W., 255

Ambivalence, 61, 171, 245–246, 256, 267, 269
American Civil Liberties Union, 259
Anangke, 77, 219
Angelus Silesius, 82, 276
Animism, animistic stage, 4, 61, 185, 225
Anthropology, 3–5, 196, 217
Anti-Semitism, 190
Anxiety, 18, 120, 206–207, 259
Apocalypse, 182–187
Apollonian type, 136
Apologetics, 7
Apostasy, 248
Arcane, pursuit of, 104, 197
Archaeology, 3, 215
Aristotle, 192
Aron, R., 273
Art, 55, 58, 67, 69, 100, 112–114, 117, 131, 158, 166, 190, 194, 195, 198, 202, 219, 226, 228, 229
Articles of faith, 7
Asceticism, as form of radical salvation, 26 ff., 135
Astrology, 18, 55, 100, 197
Atheism, atheist, 54, 139, 151, 155, 169, 252, 259, 262, 264
Atonement, 33, 142–143, 206–208
Augustine, Saint, 107

Augustine's *Confessions*, 145
Authenticity, 2, 147n
Authority, 2, 34
  See also Obedience
Authoritarianism, 12, 70, 119, 197
Autistic thinking, 116, 192, 195, 198,
  200, 203, 217–218, 235, 240
Autonomy, 66–94, 130, 149, 164
  of Superego, ego ideal, drives, 93
Avicenna, 21
Awe, 58, 100, 105–107, 116, 239, 243
Aztec, cruel rituals of, 204

Bacon, F., 53, 54, 60, 275
Baldwin, J. A., 251, 284
Balint, M., 275
Barnes, M., 147
Barth, K., 8, 16, 272
Baumann, D. D., 176, 280
Beckett, S., 96, 277
Being-cognition, 120–122
  See also Maslow, A.
Belief(s)
  ambiguity of, 96–97, 137, 245–261
  in benevolence, 173–187
  as choosing between options, 59 ff.,
    123–156
  as collective representations, 11
  in creatureliness, 56 ff., 67 ff., 80–90,
    105 ff.
  defensive, 133 ff., 147, 159 ff., 171,
    186
  in evil, 101–103
  and humility, 73–80
  derived from ideals, 199
  and identity, 251 ff.
  as ideology, 11
  as function of institutional domains,
    11, 12
  in a More, 153–156
  in mystery, 95–122
  mythical forms of, 213–220
  in numinosity, 57 ff., 230–234
  embedded in object relations, 87 ff.,
    117, 125, 137–148, 180–181
  as objects of love and hate, 248–261
  as partial omniscience, 144
  over-beliefs, 153–156, 181, 216,
    223
  philosophical, 83–84

originating in play, 241–244
  as projects, 125 ff.
  in Providence, 157–187
  derived from ritual, 205–213
  in sacred social order, 90–94
  in self-sufficiency, 67 ff.
  in someone else's belief, 125
  and symbols, 200 ff., 233–234
  and talent for numinosity, 107–114
  and thought control, 62
  in tolerance, 262–269
  originating in transitional sphere,
    108–114, 201–202, 206–207, 217,
    240 ff., 269
  in truth, 126 ff.,
  in the Unseen, 59 ff.
Bellah, R. N., 14, 134, 259, 272, 279,
  286
Benevolence, 84, 162–187, 267
Berdjajew, N., 175, 280
Berke, J., 147
Bertocci, P. A., 121, 278
Binswanger, L., 284
Birnbaum, N., 272, 273
Blaspheming, 61
Bleuler, E., 192, 281
Bliss, 58, 77, 105 ff.
Boisen, A. T., 115, 203, 278, 282
Bonhoeffer, D., 13, 255, 272, 273
Boulding, K., 280
Bradley, R., 285
Brecht, B., 167
Brotherhood, 118, 208
Brown, N. O., 19, 273
Browning, R., 54, 275
Bryan, K., xiv
Buber, M., 98, 116, 120–122, 124, 207,
  277
  See also Mystery of being
Buddhism, 135, 237
Bultmann, R., 193, 219, 281
  See also Myth, Demythologizing

Cabala, 55, 197
Calvin, J., 36, 81
Camus, A., 147, 176, 279, 280
Caring, 177–187, 267
Carlyle, T., 74
Case illustrations, vignettes, and cita-
tions

Augustine's experience of the divided self, 145
Anton Boisen's religious fantasies, 115, 203
Cecil: glossolalia in an alienated and inarticulate youth, 260–261
Albert Einstein's paradox, 1, 114, 220, 229, 243
Charles Haitzman; Freud's study of demoniac possession, 170
Job's persistent trust, 202
Martin Luther King; the author's fantasy about him, 217–218
R. D. Laing's description of two patients arguing, 148
K. Malthe-Bruun's martyrdom, 254–255
Judge Schreber's cosmic fantasies, 115, 203
The Wolf-Man's (Freud's case) sublimation, 226
Obsessions of restitution in a case of involutional melancholia, 142–143
A patient who felt "close to God," 188, 190, 198–200, 212, 220
A woman with profound ambivalence toward human and divine family figures, who held herself refractory to grace, 157–158, 164, 168
A bibliolatrous woman's belief in divinely ordained gender roles, 248–249
Hypnotically induced pleasurable memories in a burn victim, 191
Catechetics, 7
Cathexis, 76, 87
  See also Object relations
Catholics, Catholicism, 16, 36, 128, 138, 248, 252
  neo-Pentecostal, 20
Celebration, 118, 120, 205–213
Charismatic movements, 260 ff.
Charity, 118, 135
Choice, 123–156, 267, 268
Chomsky, N., 216, 283
Christianity, Christians, 28, 40, 43, 44, 53, 119, 135, 138, 143, 147, 152, 156, 158, 159, 176, 177, 197, 204, 206, 215, 248, 250, 256, 257, 258, 263
Christian Scientists, 133, 134, 137
Churchill, W., 98
Chutzpah, 70
Civil disobedience, 93
Civil religion, 8, 44, 134, 259, 262, 264
Civil rights movement, 19, 217
Cognitive dissonance, 256
Commitment, 246
  See also Choice, Options
Communes, 17, 33
Compartmentalization, 131, 132
Competence, 70, 95, 172
Compulsions, 206
  See also Ritual
Comte, A., 3, 14, 131
Confessions, 7, 141, 260
Confessions, Augustine, 145
  See also Augustine's *Confessions*
Confucius, 9
Conscience, 33, 50 ff., 78, 91–93, 127, 139–144, 165
  See also Superego, Ego ideal
Consciousness
  alienation as state of, 24
  cosmic, 195
  expansion of, 17, 118, 153, 236
  as piloting a ship, 238
Consciousness-raising, 72
Contemplation, 118, 237
  See also Meditation
Conversion, 6, 7, 59, 62, 97, 119, 121, 132, 135, 138–139, 153–154, 209, 250, 253–254
Convictions, 144–145
  convictional language, 215
Cox, H., 13, 273
Cranston, M., 286
Creativity, 70, 154, 195, 198, 202, 205, 211, 219, 226, 239, 242–243
Creatureliness, 58, 67, 80, 105–106
Creed, credo, 7, 55, 62, 67, 72, 83, 197, 205, 223, 257
Cromwell's Parliament of the Saints, 27
Cruelty, 172, 222, 264
Crusades
  campus, 197

for Christ, 43
against Islam, 53, 215, 264
Cult, 67, 77, 83, 197, 205
  See also Ritual
Culture, cultural
  defined by beliefs, 11
  factors in unbelief, 69–71, 74, 139
  and sublimation, 226, 229–230
  as practiced in the transitional
    sphere, 17, 166, 198 ff., 217, 240–
    244
  transmission of beliefs, 68, 117,
    160–161, 170, 211, 216 ff., 233 ff.
Curiosity, 70–71, 226–227, 238–239,
  268
Cynicism, 261

Damnation, 168, 208–209
Daniélou, J., 13, 273
Darwin, C. R., 123
De-alienation, 23–25, 120–122
Death, 102, 105, 172, 174, 187, 215n,
  251, 255
Death instinct, 102, 175
Deciding, decisions, 8, 123–156
Defense mechanisms,
  See Denial, Displacement, Identifi-
    cation with the aggressor, Intel-
    lectualization, Introjection, Pro-
    jection, Reaction formation, Re-
    pression, Suppression, Splitting
Defiance, 90–92
Deism, 83
Delusion, 111–112, 115, 120, 166,
  170–171, 180, 200, 203, 266
Demandingness, 165
  See also Humility, Narcissism
Democratization, 15, 163
Demonic
  See Malevolence, Mystery of evil,
    Tremendum
Demonology, 18, 115
  See also Satanism, Witchcraft
Demythologizing of beliefs, 21, 79,
  120, 193, 218, 268
Denial, 126, 171, 207
Denomination
  See Faith group
Dependency, 56, 58, 66–94, 106, 149,
  158, 164, 168, 184

Depersonalization, 223
Derealization, 223
Development of children, 45–52, 75,
  82–86, 108–111, 140–142, 180,
  192–195, 201–202, 210–211, 241–
  243
  See also Object relations, Transi-
    tional sphere
Developmental principle, 3, 61–62
Devil, 61, 91, 119, 170, 174, 202–
  203
  See also Demonic, Demonology,
    Evil, Satanism
Diamond, M. A., 277
Differentiation
  of ego functions, 48, 193
  of social institutions and functions,
    5, 6
  of needs, 238
  of satisfactions, 45–52
Dionysian type, 136
Directionality of ideals and beliefs,
  201
Disbelief
  definition, xv
  in reality of evil, 101–103
  in magic, 116
  in mystery and tremendum, 57–58,
    92–122
  in providence, 60 ff., 164–173
  in propositions for which we have
    no use, 126
Displacement
  from human to divine objects, 76,
    157–187
  of numinous objects, 66
  as feature of the primary process,
    192
Distrust, 60, 128, 167
"Divided self," 78, 132–148
Doctrine, 63, 162–163, 168, 173, 177,
  234, 243, 252, 257
Dogma, dogmatism, 63, 123, 127, 200,
  244, 252, 257, 264, 268
Domains, 5
Don't Worry movement, 133
Dostoyevski, F., 34, 144, 148, 176,
  221, 279, 283
Doubt, 54, 61, 86, 107, 246, 249
Drama, dramatic, dramatization

as aspect of ritualization, 210–212
See also Myth, Ritual
Dreams, 114–115, 120, 154, 189, 191, 195, 197
Drifting
in secularization, 12–16, 44, 227
Drives
parameters of, 45–46
See also Primary process, Sublimation
Durkheim, E., 11, 14, 17, 272, 273

Eastern Renaissance, East-West differences, 237
Eckhart, Meister, 30, 274
Ego
autonomy of, 94
ego-id conflict, 136–137
ego psychology, 193
ego relation with internal object, 180, 254
ego-superego conflict, 139–144, 206
functions of, 48–52
satisfactions of, 78–80
synthetic functions of, 131, 195, 240–244
Ego ideal, 50–52, 78, 86, 94, 127, 138–139, 165, 194, 250, 254
Ehrenwald, J., 120, 278
Einstein, A., 1, 2, 5, 44, 114, 116, 220, 229, 243, 271, 284
Eiseley, L., 3, 271
Eisenhower, D. D., 258
Eissler, K. R., 136, 279
Eliade, M., 214, 283
See also Myth
Elijah, 215
Eliot, T. S., 66–67, 276
Ellenberger, H. F., 284
Emancipation, 13–14, 61–62, 71, 139, 193, 225–230
Encounter movement, 18, 197, 220
Enlightenment, 56, 69, 71, 213, 219, 257, 264
Enroth, R. M., 279
Episcopalian, 10, 147, 209, 241
Epistemology, 121
Erasmus, 9
Ericson, E. E., Jr., 279
Erikson, E. H., xvi, 41, 82–86, 88, 90,

98, 113–114, 165, 196, 201, 210–211, 213, 274, 276, 277, 278, 282, 283
Eros, 195, 219, 231
Eroticization of beliefs, 248–261
Escapism, 133–134
Eschatology, 182–187
Esslin, M., 277
Estrangement, xv
from religion, 21–23, 43
within religion, 29–38, 43, 72
See also Alienation
Ethics, 31 ff., 81, 141, 166, 196, 204, 209–210, 224, 226, 227–228, 231, 262
Eucharist, 208
Evangelism, evangelists, 7, 19, 148, 197, 208–209, 253–254
Evil, 78, 80, 85, 91, 101–103, 105, 107, 119, 133, 134, 139, 170, 173–176, 222, 233, 259
See also Malevolence
Excellence, 201
Existentialism, 15, 39, 96, 98–99, 118, 124, 132, 134, 136, 146, 220
existential theologians, 16, 152
Exorcism, 170

Fabulation, 213–214
Facilitating environment, 206 ff.
Fairbairn, W. R. D., 274, 275
Faith, 53, 60, 67, 84, 107, 124–125, 129, 137, 166, 202, 225, 246, 249
Faith group, 7, 30, 37, 212, 252, 257, 260
Faith healing, 20
Families, theme of the two, 60, 159–161, 173, 179
Fanaticism, 190
Fantasy, 75, 85, 100, 114, 120, 146–147, 161, 169, 182, 188–220, 226, 241, 242, 245, 268, 269
See also Imagination, Myth, Play
Fascinans, fascinosum, 103–107, 230
See also Mysterium Tremendum
Fate, 77, 176, 182, 222, 265
Father
fatherhood of God, *see* Providence, 173

fatherless society, 91–92, 163
Faust, 139, 279
Fear, 18, 107, 151, 180
  See also Awe
Feminism, issues of gender, 19, 89–90, 248–49, 264
Festinger, L., 285
Fetish, 112, 207
Feuerbach, L., 8, 23, 24, 25, 122, 272
Fidelity, 252
Fischoff, E., 27n
Fixation, 225
Flye, Father, 93, 151, 277, 279
  See also James Agee
Forgiveness, 141–144, 148, 158, 185, 206
  See also Grace
Formal
  as aspect of ritualization, 211
Fortmann, H., 237, 284
Francis of Assisi, Saint, 34, 265
Free thinking, 71 ff., 81
Freedom, 35, 178, 182, 237, 255, 259, 264
Freud, E. L., 281
Freud, S., 42, 43, 45, 60–62, 74–77, 81, 88–89, 102, 114, 143–144, 161, 165, 170, 175, 189–190, 192–194, 196–198, 200, 206, 212–213, 215, 219, 225–229, 230–232, 253, 266, 271, 274, 275, 276, 279, 280, 281, 282, 283, 285
Fuller, M., 73
Fundamentalism, fundamentalists, 13, 119, 137–138, 143
Fusion of drives and affects, 175

Gandhi, M., 210, 282
Gantry, Elmer, 148
Gardner, E. A., 215n
Generational, as aspect of ritualization, 211
Generation gap, 41–42, 97
Geneva theocracy, 36
Glossolalia, 20, 197, 260–261
Gnosticism, 147, 263
God(s)
  in civil religion, 259
  Creator, Ground of Being, 66–94, 152–153, 241, 265

existence of, 125, 222
Hebrew epistemology of, 121
mystery, numinous, 95–122
personalistic relations with, 83, 174–175, 188, 198–200, 212, 220, 246, 249
process conception, 152
providence, 60–61, 71, 143–144, 151, 157–187, 226, 229
  See also Mystery, Numinous, Transcendent
God complex, 169–170
God-is-dead, 62, 100, 196, 222
Godin, A., xii
Goethe, J. W. von, 136, 139, 279
  Faust, 139, 279
  psychoanalytic study of, by Eissler, 139
Gollwitzer, H., 285
Gombrich, E. H., 196, 282
Good, goodness, 133–134, 142, 170, 173–174, 210, 222, 233
  See also Benevolence
Goodenough, E. R., 26, 55, 62–64, 231, 233, 243, 273, 276, 284
Gospel of Relaxation, 133
Grace, 80, 144, 149, 151, 158, 163, 207, 209, 212
Grand Inquisitor, 148, 222
Grandiosity, 57, 169–170
Grasse, J. M., Jr., 285
Gratification, 75, 79, 109, 138, 165, 191, 226, 266
  See also Satisfaction
Greek, 5
  mystery cults, 98
  myths, 215–216
  thought, 13, 263
Groddeck, G. W., 232, 284
Ground of Being, 67–68, 108, 152–154, 241
  See also God, More
Group dynamics, group therapy, 18
Growth, 225, 267
  See also Development
Guiltfeelings, 50, 107, 120, 140, 142 ff., 206, 209
Guntrip, H., 194, 275, 281

Haitzmann, C., 170
Hallucination, 109, 111–112, 115, 166, 184, 200, 203
Happiness, 45 ff., 73, 78, 133, 148–153, 164–166, 182
Harder, M. W., 32n, 274
Hate, 76, 91, 102, 141, 171, 174, 175, 251
  beliefs as hate objects, 256–261
Healthy-minded, 133 ff.
Hebrew
  epistemology, 121
  world view, 13
Hegel, G. W., 22, 23, 122
Heidegger, M., 219, 224, 283
Heiman, P., 274
Heteronomy, 68–69
Hindu, Hinduism, 128, 150, 237
"Hippie" groups, 17
Hirschberg, J. C., xiii
History
  of ideas, 9 ff.
  of mystery cults, 115
  of myth, 214
  of philosophy, 115
  of religion, 3–16, 115–116, 206
Hiltner, S., 280
Hitler, A., 88
Holiness sects, 19
Holt, R. R., 281
Holton, G., 271
Holy, the, 57–58, 103–120, 230–234, 241
  See also Mysterium Tremendum
Honesty, 39, 42
Hope, 151, 159, 167, 181–187, 203, 267
Hopelessness, 33
House Un-American Activities Committee, 262
Hubris, 70
  See also Humility
Hugo, V., 167
Huizinga, J., 118, 169, 210, 278
Humanism, 165, 201, 204, 256
Human potential movement, 18, 197
Humility, 56–57, 68–77, 81, 88–89, 116, 205, 229, 245, 265
Husserl, E., 284
Huxley, A., 236, 284

Hypnosis, 191
Hypotheses, 63, 244
Hysterical personality, 127

I Ching, 197
I-Thou relations, 99, 125, 130, 150
Id
  concept of id in ego-psychology, 193
  ego-id conflicts, 136–137
  experienced as Tremendum, 230–234
Ideals, idealism
  idealistic thought, 134
  philosophical idealism, 153, 224
  belong to play sphere, 199
  production of ideal images in wishing, 104, 199 ff.
Identification with the aggressor, 207
Identification, mechanism of, 89–90, 92, 93, 97, 125, 140, 169, 170, 194, 248, 250
Identity, identity formation, 48, 88–89, 94, 97, 118, 125, 130, 181, 210–213, 248–261
Ideological, as aspect of ritualization, 211
Ideology, 3 ff., 149, 153, 204, 263
Idolatry, 13, 53, 156
Illich, I., 211, 283
Illusion, 196–205
  religious ideas as illusion, 189–190, 200
  illusion practiced in the transitional sphere, 111–114, 165–166, 198–204
Imagery in modern religious movements, 43, 63, 203, 231–234
Imagination, 59, 82, 115, 161, 180, 188–220
Immortality, 57, 76, 186
  See also Humility, Narcissism, Omnipotence
Independence
  See Autonomy
Indifference, 126, 262
Individuation, 175
Infanticide, 137
Infidels, 53, 247, 250
Infinite, concept of, 73, 169, 265

Inquisition, 190, 258
Institutionalization of religion, 5
  of religious values, 16–17, 29–38
Instrumental theory of evil, 173
Integration
  function of the ego, 48 ff.
  of good and bad objects, 174–176
  in the transitional sphere, 240–244
  See also Ego, Synthetic Functions
Integrity, 252
Intellectualization, 207
Intellectuals, 9–11, 21, 67, 69–70
Intimacy, cult of, 197
Intolerance, 258–259, 262
Introjection, 49 ff., 83, 108–109
Irreligious
  Freud's definition, 74–75
Islam, 7, 28, 44, 53, 135, 150
Isomorphism, 125, 152, 238
Isaacs, S., 274

Jacobson, E., 194, 275, 281
James, W., 32, 53, 55, 58, 59, 77, 78, 81, 83, 88, 121, 123–136, 148–151, 153–154, 166, 176, 181, 202, 216, 220, 223, 232, 239, 246, 266, 275, 276, 278, 279, 280, 284
Jaspers, K., 152, 193, 224, 279, 281, 283
Jesus, 115, 138, 148, 169, 215, 218, 235, 249
Jesus "freaks," groups, movements, 20, 32, 43, 132, 138, 253
Job, 151, 202
Jonas, H., 204, 282–283
Jones, E., 60, 159–161, 164, 169, 177, 187, 275, 279, 280
Judaism, Jew, Jewish, Judeo-Christian, 16, 28, 36, 44, 70, 119, 121, 128, 135, 138, 152, 156, 190, 197, 204, 206, 209, 215, 252–253, 257–258, 263
Judicial as aspect of ritualization, 210
Jung, C. G., Jungian, 175, 197, 216, 280
Justification of faith by James, 124

Kafka, F., 99, 147, 277
Kähler, W., 276

Kant, I., 103, 224
Kekulé, F. A., 154
Kelley, D. M., 279
Keniston, K., 39, 40, 119, 274, 278
Kerygma, 16, 219
Kierkegaard, S., 8, 39, 40, 53, 54, 62, 136n, 147, 272
Kildahl, J. P., 286
King, M. L., 217–218
Klein, M., 194, 274
Koinonia, 16
Kovel, J., 147n
Kris, E., 195, 196, 282
Kuhn, K., 285

Labor
  as alienated class, 23
Language
  belief, 249–250
    affecting belief, 69, 152, 258
  convictional, 215
  God-talk, 188–190
  of James, 117
  mythological, 220
  primary process, 195
  transitional sphere, 113, 202
Leap of faith, 53
Laing, R. D., 32, 146, 148
Leibnitz, G. W., 83
Lenzer, G., 272, 273
Lévi-Strauss, C., 5, 196, 216, 272, 282
Lévy-Brühl, L., 5, 196, 272, 282
Lewin, B. D., 144–145, 279
Lifestyle, 131, 136, 138, 242, 257, 267
  See also Types
Lifton, R. J., 41, 97, 131, 274, 277, 279
Linguistics, 216, 236
Locke, J., 264
Logical thought, 132, 192, 232
  See also Reality principle
Loneliness and megalomania, 169
Looft, W. R., 153, 279
Love, 105, 107, 109, 128, 140, 142, 149, 151, 159, 164, 171, 175, 181, 195, 206, 207
Love object, 46, 47, 50, 90, 171
  Beliefs as, 248–255
  See also Object relations
Loyalty, 34, 128, 250, 251–252, 254

Luckmann, T., 11, 272
Luther, M., 7, 34, 90, 91, 107, 196,
    250, 274, 278, 282

Magic, magical thought, 109, 115–
    116, 145, 154, 169–171, 185, 225
Make-believe, 243
Malevolence, 84, 101–103, 166–176,
    245
Mana, Polynesian, 4
Marathons, weekend, 18, 197
Macleod, D., 276
Marcel, G., 98–99, 101, 120, 121, 182,
    184, 277, 280
Marcuse, H., 95, 277
Marin, P., 279
Marty, M. E., 100, 273, 277
Martyrdom, 19, 251, 253, 255, 263
Marx, K., 8, 11, 14, 23, 24, 25, 28, 39,
    122, 196, 272, 273
Marxism, Marxist, 25, 167
    Theory of action, 24
Mary, Mariology, 136–137, 169, 250
Maslow, A. H., 29, 120–122, 274,
    278
Maturity
    treatment goals in psychoanalysis,
    94
Mayeroff, M., 178, 280
    See also Caring
Mayman, M., 274, 275
McKellar, P., 192, 281
Mead, S. E., 73–74, 169, 276
Meaning, search for, 179, 244, 248
Meditation, 17, 62, 134, 197, 220,
    237
Megalomania, 170–171
    See also Demonology, Hubris, Nar-
    cissism
Meng, H., 281
Menninger, K., 175, 274, 275, 280
Mennonite schisms, 253
Mephistopheles, 139, 174
Merton, R. K., 274
Mill, J. S., 264, 286
Mind cure movements, 133
Mitchell, K. R., xiv
Mitscherlich, A., 91–92, 163, 173, 277,
    280
Modell, A. H., 275

Moral, as aspect of ritualization, 210–
    211
Morality, moral beliefs, 103, 128–129,
    139–144, 148, 165, 195, 263, 264
Moral Rearmament, 134
More, James's concept of the, 123,
    153–156, 181, 184, 185, 202, 220,
    239, 267
More, Sir T., 251
Moses, 107
Mourning in alienation, 38
Movements
    charismatic, 29
    modern civil rights, 17
    prophetic, 29
    See also Feminism
Muhammad, Muslims, 107, 128, 215,
    233, 257
Murphy, G., 222, 238–239, 283, 284
Mutuality
    as aspect of dependency, 82 ff.
    as aspect of ritualization, 210–211
Mysterium Tremendum, 18, 57–58,
    62–64, 103–107, 116, 118, 122,
    230–234, 239, 243, 268
Mystery, 83, 95–122, 164, 171, 243,
    245, 266
    cultural recognition of, 117
    and de-alienation, 120–122
    definitions of, 98–100, 104–105
    of evil, 101–103, 222
    origins of, in the transitional sphere,
    111–114
    talent for experiencing, 107–114
    See also *Mysterium Tremendum*
Mystery cults, 98, 115, 197
Mystical participation, 4
Mysticism, 55, 59, 63, 82, 135, 143,
    154
    as force of radical salvation, 26 ff.
Myth, 43, 60, 63, 152, 193–196, 213–
    220, 233, 240, 268
Mythopoesis, 194, 215–217, 228
Myth deprivation, 120

Narration, in thought organization,
    213 ff.
    See also Myth
Narcissism, 56, 58, 74–77, 94, 165,
    168–169, 265

of small differences, 253
National Council of Churches, 259
Nationalism, chauvinistic, 55
Nay-sayers, 127
Nazi, Nazi victims, 174, 251, 254–255
Neoplatonism, 147, 158
Newman, F., 133
Newton, I., 162
Nietzsche, F., 41, 80, 88, 136, 150, 152, 169
Nihilism, 96
Novak, M., 96, 277
Novelty
  in hoping, 182–187, 267
  See also Play, Transitional sphere
Numerology, 203
Numinous, numinosity, 57–58, 66, 103–114, 207, 210–211, 214, 231–232
  definition, 104
  talent for numinous experience, 107–114

Obedience, 34, 90–94, 140, 159 ff.
Object, Object relations, xvi
  mutuality in object relations, 82–83
  narcissistic object choice, 253
  theory of object relations, 45–52, 108–120, 191, 194–195
  transference from human to cosmic objects, 125, 150–152, 160–161
  transitional objects, 110–114, 202, 206–207
Obsessions, 206
  obsessional neurosis, 61
Obsessive-compulsive personality or symptoms, 32, 127, 206, 209, 210
Occult, preoccupation with, 104, 118–119, 171
Oden, T. C., 273, 282
Oedipal, Oedipus, 76, 119, 136, 140, 215, 219
Omnipotence of thought, feelings of, 60, 61, 75, 112, 115, 144, 146, 170, 225, 227, 265
Omniscience, 144
Once-born, 133–134
Ontogeny, 61

Ontological options, 223–230
Ontology, 152, 223, 232, 239
Optimism, 133, 173, 184
Options, 59, 123–156
Other, "wholly other," conceptions of, 120–122
Otto, R., 57, 58, 62, 103–107, 116, 120, 122, 124, 230–231, 273, 275, 277, 278
Outler, A. C., 280
Outreach, 7
Over-beliefs, 123, 154–156, 181, 216, 220, 223

Pain, 143, 174, 191
Paine, T., 71–73, 276
Palm reading, 120
Pannikar, R., 204, 282
Pansexualism, 19
Parapsychology, 239
Parricide, 137
Parsons, T., 16, 27, 28, 35, 228, 273, 274, 284
Pascal, B., 59, 125, 224, 283
Passive-aggressive personalities, 246
Patriarchal patterns, decline of, 92
Paul, Saint, 18, 136, 183
Peak experience, 29
Penance, 141, 143
Pentecostal groups, Neo-Pentecostalism, 19, 20
Perception, 234–238
  renewal of, 239
Personalistic relations, personalization, 60, 68, 83, 129, 130, 150–151, 178–181, 244
Pessimism, 184, 224
Peters, C. B., 279
Petrovic, G., 273
Pfeiffer, F., 274
Pfister, O., 62, 190, 281
Phenomenology, 222, 236
Phylogeny, 61
Philosophical beliefs, 83, 115, 149–150, 152, 184, 223–224
  See also Ontology
Philosophy
  religion "maturing" into philosophy, 62, 227
Piaget, J., 195, 281–282

Pico della Mirandola, G., 9
Pietism, secular, 197
Placation, 141–143
Plato, 21, 152, 224, 233
Platonism, 147
Play, 112–114, 117–118, 191, 198–199, 202, 207, 210, 213, 217, 219, 229, 239–243, 269
Pleasure, 31, 71, 78–79, 109, 149, 191, 219, 245
    See also Gratification, Happiness, Satisfaction
Pleasure principle, 45–52, 75, 110, 112, 116, 144, 149, 189, 191, 228–229, 240
Pluralism
    philosophical, 123
    religious, 5, 8, 12, 42, 44, 92, 97, 119, 161, 262
Pope
    John XXIII, 197
    Paul VI, 197
Positivism, 59, 61, 118, 124, 131, 190
Pratt, J., 251, 284
Prayer, 63, 72, 197, 221, 244, 259
Preconscious in myth, 216
Predestination, 32, 33, 163
Pre-established harmony, 83
Prejudice, racial, 246, 256
    See also Intolerance
Pride in abstinence, 77
Priests
    priestly imagination, 190
    power of, 229
    priestly vs. prophetic, 26, 36
    priestly work, 205
Primary process, 189
    See also Autistic thinking, Fantasy, Imagination, Myth
Primitive man, 3–5
Principles of Psychology, 123, 278
    See also James, W.
Privacy as value, 1
    Privatization of religion, 16
Problem
    problem vs. mystery, 98 ff.
    religion as problem-solving, 227–230
Process philosopphy, 152, 184, 239

Projection, 23, 60, 63, 91, 110, 115, 137, 168, 179, 233, 238
Promise, 185–187, 226
Prophets, 8, 13, 154, 158
    prophetic vs. priestly, 26, 36
Proselytizing, 250
    See also Conversion, Evangelism
Protean Man personality, 41, 97, 131
Protestant, Protestantism, 16, 28, 33, 36, 128, 138, 212
Providence, 60–61, 157–187
    as deus ex machina, 172
Prudence, 165
Pruyser, P. W., xii, xiii, 274, 275, 280, 281, 283
Psychoanalysis
    attitude of faith in, 60
    genre of psychoanalytic writings on religion, 53–54, 161, 163, 179, 195–196, 206
    treatment goals in, 76, 94
Psychodynamic theory, 45–52
Psychology of religion, strategic views in, 26, 56–64, 123, 159–160, 179
Puritanism, 28, 35, 36, 135, 144

Quakers and ritual, 209
Quaker state of Pennsylvania, 27

Racism, 215, 256
Rationality, rationalism, 25, 68, 69, 79, 171, 189, 193, 196, 204, 213, 217, 220, 241, 263
Real, feeling of being, 145–147
Reality
    coming to terms with, 221–244
    commonsense, 189, 234–239
    of evil, 174
    forced choice between and fantasy, 191
    in hoping, 183–185, 267–268
    endowed with features of human object relations, 150–153, 180–181
    tinkering with (denial, distortion, etc.), 76, 115, 116, 133–134, 144, 226
    intermediate reality of the transitional sphere, 112–114, 198–204,

214, 216–217, 240–244, 269
  ultimate, 80, 149–150, 166, 267
  untidiness of, 54–55
Reality of the Unseen (James), 59
  See also More
Reality principle, 46–47, 51, 75, 110,
  112, 149, 183, 185, 189, 191, 195,
  225, 228–229, 235, 240, 266
Reality testing, 51, 75, 109–113, 115,
  118, 127, 137, 184, 189, 191, 194,
  198, 202, 235, 240, 266
Rebirth, 134–135
  See also Conversion
Reductionism, 123, 159
Reformation, 7, 34, 208
Regression, 135, 139, 194, 225
Reich, C. A., 95, 236, 277, 284
Reik, T., 206, 283
Religion
  bureaucratic, 34–35
  as social control, 9, 25 ff.
  as controlling force in human ac-
    tion, 16
  critiques of, 28 ff., 42, 53, 70, 188–
    189
  definitions of, 26, 52–65, 55, 58,
    60 ff., 78, 83–84, 103–107, 129,
    148–153, 159–160, 200, 226–
    227
  as force in social change, 26–38
  high-demand, 141
  as social integrator, 22
  in intellectuals, 9, 10, 21, 22
  embedded in object relations, 150–
    151
  psychopathology of, 115–116, 203
  as recognition of the holy, 57 ff.
  as remedy, rescue, 75–76, 134
  as seriousness of life, 17
  in undifferentiated societies, 3–6
  and the state, 5–12
    See also Civil religion, Pluralism
  rooted in transitional sphere, 198–
    199
    See also Belief, Disbelief, Numi-
      nous, Sacred, Unbelief
Remorse, 151, 175
Renaissance, 219–220
  Eastern, 237
  myth, 219–220

Renunciation, 75–77, 165–166, 193,
  226, 266
  See also Abstinence, Asceticism
Repression, 63, 94, 96, 132, 216, 231–
  232, 253, 268
Ressentiment, 254
Restitution, 141–143
Resurrection of the body, 186
Revelation, 53, 182
Revenge, in apocalyptic writings, 182
Reverence, 57, 67, 69–70, 76, 116, 266
Richardson, J. T., 32n, 274
Richness, 32, 123, 127, 166, 219, 224,
  230, 236, 238, 266, 268
Rieff, P., 60, 165, 275, 280
Righteousness, as motif in alienation,
  29–38
Rilke, R. M., 82, 276
Ritual, 137, 138, 157, 171, 201, 204,
  205–213, 231, 235, 268
  compulsive vs. playful, 206–207
  in identity formation, 210–211
  practiced in the transitional sphere,
    111–113, 120, 201, 206–207
Riviere, J., 274
Robinson, J. A., 196
Rokeach, M., 117–118, 252, 278, 285
Role-playing
  See Drama
Rosenberg, A., 88, 215
Roszak, T., 41, 95, 274, 277
Rousseau, J. J., 21, 22, 173, 215

Sacred, 45, 103–107, 111–112, 150,
  172, 199, 207, 210–211, 214, 239,
  244, 249
  cosmos, sacred, 12, 44
Saintliness, 135
Salvation, 134, 137, 212, 220
  radical, 26 ff.
Sapir, E., 284
Satanism, 18, 55, 100, 103, 116, 170
Satisfaction, 70, 82, 184, 191
  of caring, 267
  through fantasy, 75, 109
  polyvalence of, 51–52
  of project-orientation, 79
  as psychological principle, 47 ff.
  pursuit of, 45–52
  of religion, 76, 128, 226, 249

of superego, 78, 90–91
in sublimation, 225–226, 229–230, 238
in transitional objects, symbols, 166, 200 ff.
of unbelief, 70–71
See also Gratification
See also Beliefs as love/hate objects, 248–261
Schafer, R., 194, 199, 281, 282
Schelling, F. W., 56, 136
Schleiermacher, F. E., 55, 57, 58, 67–71, 73–75, 80–81, 88–89, 106, 275, 276
Schlesinger, H. J., 186, 280, 281
See also Promise
Schizoid personality, 146, 148
Schneider, R., 285
Schopenhauer, A., 224, 232
Schreber, D. P., 115, 203, 278, 282
Schweitzer, A., 266
Science, scientific ideal, 162–163, 172, 220, 225–227, 229, 237, 240–241
Scientism, 196
Scientology, 134
Scott, W. C. M., 184–185, 280
Searles, J., 283
Secondary process, 191–195, 198–199, 217–218
Sects, 7, 19, 20
See also Faith group
Secular, 4, 5, 197, 239
Secularization, 10, 12–20, 25–26, 44, 196–197, 227–228, 248
definitions, 13–15
kinds of
by drift, 16, 44
by theological purpose, 248
Self
actualization, 120
as carer and object of care, 180
divided
See "Divided self"
esteem, 69, 71, 86, 140, 142–143, 150n
hatred, 141
ideal, 194–195, 200–201
inflation
See Narcissism

object of satisfaction, 45–52
psychological person, 45–52
sufficiency, 168–169, 171–172
See also Autonomy
-view consistent with world view, 179, 239
Sensitivity training, 18
Sex Information and Education Council of the United States, 259
Shame, 50, 86, 120, 139, 210
Shills, E. A., 10, 272
Sick soul, 134 ff.
Simmel, G., 14
Simmonds, R. B., 274
Sims, J. H., 176, 280
Sin, 80, 126, 142–144, 183, 185
Skepticism, 54, 127–128, 130, 264, 268
Smith, S. R., xiii
Socialists, romantic, and evil, 173
Society for the Scientific Study of Religion, xii
Society-without-the-father,   91–92, 163
Sociology
of knowledge, 8, 9
intertwined with religion, 14
of religion, 9
Socrates, 9
Solitude, 151, 180, 248
Specialization, 5, 6, 11
Sophocles, 120, 215, 219
Spells, casting, 171
Spencer, H., 124
Spinoza, 21, 56, 81, 152, 224, 276
Spilka, B., 285
Splitting, 146, 147, 170–171
Spohn, H. E., 222, 283, 284
Spontaneity, 94, 149, 151, 163
Stirner, Max, 80
Stoicism, 62, 76–77, 149, 263
Stories, true and false, 214, 217
See also Myth, Narration
Strommen, M. P., 285
Sturm und Drang, 136
Structuralism, 216
Sublimation, 225–230
Suffering
See Evil, Malevolence, Pain
Superego, 50–52, 78–80, 86, 93, 127,

139–143, 156, 165, 206, 243, 250, 254

Supernaturalism, 13, 115, 121, 201

Superstition, 54, 70, 116, 204

Suppression, 126

Surrender, 77–78, 81, 85, 88, 133

Swearing as vestige of belief, 151

Swedenborg, E., 115, 278

Symbols, symbolic acts, 10, 19, 22, 42–43, 57, 63, 66, 69, 87, 92, 111, 137, 143, 150, 154, 158, 161, 190, 192–194, 198–201, 203–204, 207, 212, 216

  symbols arise from the transitional sphere, 198–202

  transitional object as symbol, 111

Syncretism, 5, 263

Taboos, 62, 70, 137, 173, 207

Tantrism, 237

Tarot cards, 120, 197

Technology, technocracy, 95–97, 172, 204

Teilhard de Chardin, P., 3, 154

Temptation, resistance to, 144

Tenet, 252, 260, 267

  See also Belief, Doctrine, Dogma

Tertullian, 53

Thanatos, 195, 219, 231

Theism, 155

Theodicy, 174

Theology, 57, 161–162, 163, 168, 182, 196, 205–206

Theophanies, 57, 107

Thomas Aquinas, 152

Thought control, 61, 190

Ticho, E. A., 94, 277

Tillich, P., 13, 16, 152, 246, 272, 284

Time experience in hoping, 184

Toffler, A., 2, 271

Tolerance, xvi, 94, 262–269

Tornadoes, 176

Transcendence, transcendent jargon, 197

  "other," 121–122

  as projection, 115–116

  reluctance to deal with, 100

  search for transcendent experience, 17–18, 44, 100–101, 118

talent for experiencing, 107–114

of the transitional object, 111 ff.

in the transitional sphere, 108–111, 217

in the two-families model, 160

vagueness of the term, 99n

  See also More, Mystery, Tremendum

Transference, attitudinal in, religion, 151–152

Transformation of beliefs, 62, 227

Transitional object, 111–114, 166, 198–199, 201, 206–207, 269

Transitional sphere, 111–114, 116–118, 120, 198, 201–203, 205, 210, 217, 219, 240–244, 269

Transmission of ideas and beliefs, 117 ff., 160–161, 166, 223, 233–234, 264

Tremendum; See Mysterium Tremendum

Trivialization of options, 131–132

Trust, 60, 85, 107, 128, 145, 147, 151, 165–168, 176, 201–202

Truth, 126–130, 133, 134, 144, 149–150, 153, 154, 190, 205, 215, 216, 229, 237, 241, 246, 263, 268

Twice-born people, 133–135

Two-families

  See Families

Types, Typology

  See Apollonian/Dionysian, 136

  See divided self, 78, 132–148

  See James, 133–135

  See once-born/twice-born, 133–135

  See sick soul, 78, 134–135

  See Weber-Parsons, 28 ff.

Unconscious, 87, 154, 189, 192–193, 216, 232

Underground churches, 55

Unidentified flying objects, 100, 115, 230

Unification of self, 135, 144, 145, 147, 153

Unitarians, 209

Unity School of Christianity, 19–20, 134

Universe, 68, 73, 75, 105, 123–124, 130–131, 133–135, 148–153, 164,

173, 179, 185, 224, 243, 264, 267
  feelings about, 225
  See also More
Unbelief(s)
  effects of alienation, 26–38, 38 ff.
  ambiguity of, 96–97, 137, 245–
    261
  from autonomy strivings, 80–90
  as blunting of feelings, 58
  as lack of commitment, 59–60
  from feeling of competence, 171–
    173
  definitions of, 52–65, 70 ff.
  as denial of utter dependency, 56 ff.
  as distrust, 60, 166–167
  from fear of dupery, 127–128, 130
  as objection to fantasy, 188–220
  and humility, 73–80
  and identity, 252–254
  as functions of institutional do-
    mains, 11–12
  from megalomanic feelings, 168–
    171
  as rejection of numinosity, 58, 107–
    114
  as objection to myth, 213–220
  as love/hate objects, 248–261
  embedded in object relations, 87 ff.,
    117, 137–148, 180
  from positivism, 59
  as protest against tradition, 79
  from rationalism, 79, 139
  religion as, 8, 53
  "religious unbeliever"
    See Einstein, 1
  as objection to ritual, 205–213
  as reluctance to transcendence, 100
  varieties of, 56–65
  See also Disbelief

Values, 10, 16, 22, 47, 50, 66, 79, 99,
    117, 179, 201, 211, 265
  appreciation of modern, 118–119
  critiques of modern, 66, 95–97,
    119–120, 235–236

  See also Morality
Vatican Secretariat for Unbelievers,
    248
Vedantism, 151–152n
Virtue
  of humility, 205
  of obedience, 90–91
  of tolerance, 269
Vocation, religious, 254
  life as, 35, 38
Voltaire, 9
Voluntarism, 124–125

Waelder, R., 191, 281
Walters, A., 285
Wars, 7, 53, 174, 190, 197, 258
Weber, M., 9, 14, 16, 26, 27, 28, 33, 35,
    39, 45, 272, 273, 274
Weber-Parsons typology of radical sal-
    vation, 28 ff.
Whitehead, A. N., 152, 184, 203, 267
Whithe, J., 273
Whorf, B. L., 284
Will to believe, 59, 81, 144 ff., 156, 266
  See also Options
Winnicott, D. W., 108–112, 115, 117,
    119, 166, 180, 198–199, 201–203,
    206, 210, 213, 217, 228, 240, 269,
    278, 282
Wisdom, 195, 217, 233, 237
Witches, witchcraft, 18, 55, 100, 103,
    116, 170, 190, 197, 203, 258
Withdrawal, 30 ff.
World view
  of caring, 179–180
  philosophical, 149–150, 152, 224
  positivistic, 59
  religious, 130
  social, 25
Worship, 7, 67, 77, 120, 205–213

Yahweh, 150

Zen, 201
Zuurdeeg, W. F., 215, 283